A. N. SHANBHAG is a
widely syndicated colun
taxation.

SANDEEP SHANBHAG, a chartered accountant by training, has practised as a tax and investment adviser for over 15 years. He writes regular columns on investment and tax planning for financial websites such as moneycontrol.com and rediff.com, and newspapers including *DNA*, *Financial Express*, etc. He also features regularly on All India Radio and Television channels such as CNBC, CNN-IBN, ZEE Business, Doordarshan, etc. to comment on current tax and investment issues. Sandeep Shanbhag has addressed a number of seminars and lectures arranged by corporates and other organizations.

No government has the right, in the process of extracting tax, to cause misery and harassment to the taxpayer and the gnawing feeling that he is made a victim of palpable injustice.

— Nani Palkhivala

IN THE WONDERLAND OF INVESTMENT FOR NRIs

FINANCIAL YEAR 2015-2016

A N SHANBHAG
SANDEEP SHANBHAG

VISION
BOOKS

www.visionbooksindia.com

www.vision**books**india.com

Sixteenth Edition, 2015

ISBN 10: 81-7094-958-0
ISBN 13: 978-81-7094-958-9

Published by
Vision Books Pvt. Ltd.
(Incorporating Orient Paperbacks & CARING imprints)
24 Feroze Gandhi Road, Lajpat Nagar 3
New Delhi 110024, India.
Phone: (+91-11) 2984 0821 / 22
e-mail: visionbooks@gmail.com

Printed at
Anand Sons
C 88 Ganesh Nagar, Pandav Nagar Complex
Delhi 110092, India.

Contents

Preface

Amongst the non-residents across the globe, Indians shine bright because of their inherent multi-professional and multi-technological expertise. This is coupled with the Indian cultural and traditional attitude towards result-oriented application to the job on hand. Therefore, the NRIs are the most respected and sought after resource for foreign entrepreneurs. As a corollary, they have become an affluent group which can influence the world economy. The combined wealth of NRIs is estimated to be close to the current GDP of India of more than $350 billion! Tens of thousands of such Indians are now offering their professional and entrepreneurial skills to boost the economy of the country they serve. If such Indians sow some seeds of foreign remittances **In the Wonderland of Investment** that India is, they are bound to reap a rich harvest which can be enjoyed by them and their family members at their chosen 'El Dorado'.

Incidentally, this is the title of our first book which, fortunately happens to be a best-seller and is currently in its 34th edition. It deals with the various investment avenues available for an individual and the related Indian tax implications. We have also written **Taxpayer to Taxsaver** that deals with many strategies an individual can adopt taking advantage of the current tax provisions to obtain the maximum mileage from his investible funds and also addresses *Kinks in Tax*. This book is in its 23rd edition.

Both these books contained a large portion dealing with NRIs. This portion was becoming larger and larger, edition by edition, purely because of the demand. We have therefore, taken out the relevant portion from both the books and added the long overdue meat and flavour, which we could not do because this would be unkind to the residents who were not interested in the material dealing with NRIs.

Thus was born **In the Wonderland of Investment for NRIs**.

As is the wont with all dedicated professionals, their preoccupation with work leaves very little time on hand for a heavy-duty exercise on their investible funds. A little objectivity will make them realise that they would be doing themselves, their families as well as their motherland a great favour if they use their reservoir of funds optimally to make it richer over the passage of time. It is a known fact that India, especially after its new liberated economy, provides the greenest pastures for them to graze on.

Unfortunately, some prophets of doom and gloom have emerged advising the NRIs to adopt the policy of sitting on the fence, waiting and watching the Indian scenario with indifference. Instead of brooding over imaginary negative features which have little relevance for the Indian economy, it would be prudent to inspect hard-core facts.

Important amongst these opportunities are availability of cheap skilled and unskilled labour, abundance of untapped resources and most important, the sops offered by government in terms of subsidies and tax concessions, with repatriation facilities. NRIs planning to return to their motherland in the foreseeable future for good, will do well to look at non-repatriable avenues, where the returns are significantly higher.

A. N. Shanbhag
Sandeep Shanbhag

1st June 2015.

Glossary of Abbreviations

AAR	Authority Advance Rulings
AD	Authorised Dealer/Bank
ADR	American Depository Receipt
AY	Assessment Year
BSE	Bombay Stock Exchange
BTQ	Business Travel Quota
CCP	Customs Clearance Permit
CD	Convertible Debenture
CGAS	Capital Gains Accounts Scheme, 1988
CII	Cost Inflation Index
CIT	Commissioner of Income Tax
Co-FDs	Fixed Deposits of Public Limited Company
DDT	Dividend Distribution Tax
DP	Depository Participant
ECB	External Commercial Borrowing
ECS	Electronic Clearing System
EEFC	Exchange Earner's Foreign Currency Account
ELSS	Equity-Linked Saving Scheme
EMI	Equated Monthly Installments
ESOP	Employees Stock Option Plan
F&O	Futures & Options
FA11	Finance Act, 2011
FCCB	Foreign Currency Convertible Bond
FCNR	Foreign Currency Non-Resident Account
FCRA	Foreign Contribution (Regulation) Act, 1976
FDI	Foreign Direct Investment
FE	Foreign Exchange
FEA	Foreign Exchange Asset
FEMA	Foreign Exchange Management Act, 1999
FEMR	Foreign Exchange Management Rules, 1999
FERA	Foreign Exchange Regulation Act, 1973
FI	Financial Institution
FII	Foreign Institutional Investor

FMV	Fair Market Value
FY	Financial Year (1st April to 31st March)
GDR	Global Depository Receipt
HNI	High Networth Individual
HUF	Hindu Undivided Family
ICC	International Credit Card
IDC	International Debit Cards
IDR	Indian Depository Receipt
IPO	Initial Public Offer of Shares
IRDA	Insurance Regulatory & Development Authority
ITA	Income Tax Act, 1961
ITO	Income Tax Officer (= AO, Assessing Officer)
JV	Joint Venture
KYC	Know Your Customer
LIC	Life Insurance Corporation
LLP	Limited Liability Partnership
LT	Long-Term
LTA	Leave Travel Assistance
LTCG	Long-Term Capital Gains
MFs	Mutual Funds
MoF	Ministry of Finance
NAV	Net Asset Value
NBFC	Non-Banking Financial Company
NCD	Non-Convertible Debenture
NHB	National Housing Bank
NOC	No Objection Certificate
NPA	Non-Performing Asset
NRE	Non-Resident External Rupee Account
NRI	Non-Resident Indian
NRO	Non-Resident Ordinary Account
NSE	National Stock Exchange
OCB	Overseas Corporate Body
PIO	Person of Indian Origin, not a citizen of India.
PMS	Portfolio Management Scheme
PoA	Power of Attorney

PODs	Pure-growth Open-ended Debt-based Schemes
PPF	Public Provident Fund, 1969
RBI	Reserve Bank of India
RD	Recurring Deposit
RFC	Resident Foreign Currency Account
RNOR	Resident but Not Ordinarily Resident
ROI	Resident Outside India
ROR	Resident and Ordinarily Resident
SCRA	Securities Contracts (Regulation) Act, 1956
SBI	State Bank of India
SCSS	Senior Citizens Savings Scheme
SEBI	Securities and Exchange Board of India
Sec.	Section
SPV	Special Purpose Vehicle
ST	Short-Term
STCG	Short-Term Capital Gain
STT	Security Transaction Tax
SWP	Systematic Withdrawal Plan
TDS	Tax Deduction at Source = Withholding Tax
TR	Transfer of Residence
u/s	under section
ULIP	Unit Linked Insurance Plan
w.e.f.	with effect from
w.r.e.f.	with retrospective effect from

Taxes are the lifeblood of any government, but it cannot be overlooked that the blood is taken from the arteries of the taxpayer and therefore the transfusion is not accomplished on dictate of political expediency but in accordance with the principles of justice and good conscience
— Nani Palkhiwala

Nothing Big and No Bang Budget

One and all have been praising Shri Arun Jaitley's Budget 2015. The Economic Survey 14-15 states that Indian economy appears to have now gone past the economic slowdown, persistent inflation, elevated fiscal deficit, slackening domestic demand, external account imbalances and oscillating value of the rupee. It projects the growth at market prices for FY 15-16 between 8.1% to 8.5% provided a clear political mandate for reforms is laid down. Yes, a number of reforms have already been undertaken and more that are being planned for. The Survey enlists various reform measures like deregulation of diesel price, taxing energy products, replacing cooking gas subsidy by direct transfer on national scale, reform the coal sector *via* auctions, increasing the FDI caps in defense, etc.

Thanks to these and several other measures taken, now India has perhaps become an attractive investment destination for most other countries, particularly, the Indian diaspora. The expected high growth rate in the coming years gives an opportunity to the increasingly young, middle-class and inspirational India to realise its full potential. The future of India is dependent upon the Big Bang reforms that the Budget is likely to take.

Unfortunately we sincerely feel that there was nothing Big nor there was any Bang in the Budget.

Let us go through various NRI-related provisions, one by one. Note that all the changes become effective from the very first date of the fiscal, i.e., 1.4.2015, unless specified otherwise.

Basic Rates Unchanged but Surcharge Raised

There is no change in the existing basic rates of income tax and the 3% cess with just one exception — the surcharge on income tax which was slapped by FA13 for super-rich persons has been raised from 10% to 12%. In the case of domestic companies, those with a total income between ₹ 1 crore and ₹ 10 crore, it has been raised from 5% to 7% and those with income of over ₹ 10 crore, from 10% to 12%. In the case of foreign companies, the corresponding rates of surcharge were lower at 2% and 5% respectively and there is no change therein, possibly because such companies are normally charged to tax at the higher rate of 40% (50% in some rare cases).

The marginal relief according to which the total income over the threshold of ₹ 1 crore (or ₹ 10 crore) shall not exceed the tax payable, stands continued.

This increase in surcharge takes the maximum marginal tax rate at 33.99% to 34.608%, higher by 0.618%. It is this maximum marginal tax rate which is applicable on —

Sec. 115-O   : Distributed profits of domestic companies
Sec. 115-QA : Buy-back of shares by domestic companies
Sec. 115-R   : Distributed income to Unit holders, and
Sec. 115-TA : Distributed income by securitization trusts.

Consequently, the exchequer is slated to get more revenue from the poor you and me than the super rich. This extra revenue is slated to balance the loss incurred due to the abolishment of wealth tax. The overall tax burden on India Inc will be higher @34.608% in place of 33.99%.

Most countries have low tax rates, with exception of the US where it is 35%. UK is slated to reduce the corporate tax rate from 21% to 20% this year. The rate in China, Israel and Indonesia is 25% whereas it is much lower in Mauritius and Singapore at 15% and 17% respectively. High tax rates invite generation of black money.

Wealth Tax Abolished
This 2% extra surcharge is being justified by simultaneously abolishing wealth tax. At present, wealth tax is levied on an individual or HUF or company, if the value of some specified assets owned by the person exceeds ₹ 30 lakh.

Yes, wealth tax is abolished but the Income Tax Returns Forms will be suitably modified to capture the information relating to the relevant assets. Consequently, we will have to declare such assets owned by us even when their total value is less than ₹ 30 lakh. And God forbid! If it is found that value was over ₹ 30 lakh....

Limit on Deductions u/s 80D Enhanced — Mediclaim
The ceiling on deduction on health insurance premia paid, and also on expenses incurred on preventive health check-up, by an individual for himself and his family members has been raised. For Details refer Chapter *Income Tax*.

Relaxing Requirement of Obtaining TAN
U/s 203A, every person deducting or collecting tax is required to obtain Tax Deduction and Collection Account Number (TAN). To reduce the compliance burden, for sale of immovable property (other than rural agricultural land) an NRI can quote his PAN.

Effective from 1.6.15.

100% Deduction u/s 80G
Since the following brand new funds are of national importance, Sec. 80G has been amended to provide 100% deduction in respect of donations made to —

(a) National Fund for Control of Drug Abuse.
(b) Swachh Bharat Kosh, and
(c) Clean Ganga Fund.

However, any sum spent in pursuance of Corporate Social Responsibility (CSR) will not be eligible for the deduction.

Tax Neutrality on Merger of MF Schemes
A new Sec. 47(viii) has been inserted to provide tax neutrality when two or more schemes of equity oriented funds or of other than equity oriented funds get merged or consolidated. Refer Chapter *Mutual Funds* for details.

Merger/Demerger of Foreign and Indian Companies
It has been clarified that transfer of shares by a foreign company to another foreign company where the transferred shares have underneath assets in India (during mergers and demergers), would be tax-free transactions (subject to some specified conditions. For details refer Chapter *Capital Gains*.

Indirect Transfer of Shares of an Indian Company

Sec. 9(1i) states that any share or interest in a company or entity registered or incorporated outside India shall be deemed to be situated in India if the share or interest derives, directly or indirectly, its value substantially from the assets located in India. The meaning of 'substantial value' was neither explained nor could be inferred from the statute book. The issue is now corrected. For details refer Chapter *Capital Gains.*

Foreign Tax Credits where there is No DTAA

Sec. 295(2) is amended to provide that CBDT makes rules to provide the procedure for granting such reliefs.

Effective from 1.6.15.

Cash Used During Transfer of Real Estate

Sec. 269SS and Sec. 269T have been amended to mandate that any amount of loan, deposit or specified advance given for transfer of real estate should not be ₹ 20,000 or more. For details refer Chapter *Immovable Property.*

Effective from 1.6.15.

Black Money Bill

The Undisclosed Foreign Income and Assets (Imposition of Tax) Bill (Black Money Bill) is slated to be made effective from 1.4.16.

For the past 2 years, income tax returns required declaration of foreign income alone. Now, it will require a disclosure of foreign income as well as assets. The Bill defines undisclosed assets as those held by taxpayers and beneficial owners or nominees of these.

In the case of nondisclosure, there is a penalty of 90% of the undisclosed income and value of the assets and also imprisonment of up to 10 years. The Bill provides a one-time amnesty window to taxpayers to disclose foreign assets and accounts. However, they have to give 60% of the value of those assets (30% tax + 30% penalty). This window is not available to accounts and entities against which the Department has already launched prosecution or probes.

Residential Status of a Foreign Private Equity Fund
To remove several hurdles, in deciding residential status of an offshore fund, the concept of 'Permanent Establishment in India' has been replaced with 'a Place of Effective Management in India.' For details refer Chapter *Residential Status.*

Interest Paid by Indian PE to its HO
It has now been clarified that payment of interest by a Permanent Establishment in India to a foreign bank or its head office abroad is taxable in India. For details refer Chapter *Tedious TDS.*

Minimum Alternate Tax (MAT)
It has now been clarified that capital gains from transfer of securities, interest, royalty and technical service fees accruing or arising even to a foreign company has been excluded from chargeability of MAT if tax payable on such income is less than 18.5%. Unfortunately this clarification is not applicable retrospectively and all old cases where the tax authorities had taken a stand that MAT is applicable in such cases will be decided by the judiciary. For details, refer Chapter *Shares and Securities.*

194LD — Extension of Concessional Tax Period
The limitation date for TDS at the lower level of 5% in the case of interest payable by FIIs and QFIs on external commercial borrowings has been extended for 2 years at 30. 6.17. For details refer Chapter *Tedious TDS.*

Royalty and Fees for Technical Services
The tax on such income has been reduced to 10% from 25%. For details refer Chapter *Income Tax.*

Resident Status of Crew Members on a Ship
The uncertainty of residential status of crew members who are Indian citizens of foreign bound ships where the destination of the voyage is outside India has been addressed by amending Sec. 6 to provide that in such cases the period of stay in India shall be notified by CBDT in due course. For details refer Chapter *Residential Status.*

Global Depository Receipts (GDRs)
The current scope for DRs has been vastly expanded, and some tax issues related with cost of acquisitions and period of holding has been clarified. For details refer Chapter *Shares and Securities*.

Gold
To curb the menace of smuggling and also to divert investment in gold to productive assets the government plans to —

1. Introduce a Gold Monetisation Scheme.
2. Develop an alternate financial asset, a Sovereign Gold Bond.
3. Develop an Indian Gold Coin.

To assess whether this 3-pronged attack will work or not, refer Chapter *Gold Does not Glitter*.

Service Tax
FA94 brought in this brand new tax with 3 services under its net — Telephone, Stockbroker and General Insurance. The rate was 5%. Next year 3 more services were promulgated — advertising agencies, Courier agencies and radio pager services. At that stage we had observed that this tax will eventually engulf anything and everything which can be even remotely termed as service. True to our fears, 1998 witnessed 9 more services, 2001 witnessed 21 services — and then there was no looking back. The list became so big that in 2014 the legislation brought in each and every service into its net and prepared a negative list as exempt services. Now this year, the tax base has been further broadened by reviewing the negative list with one exception — service tax exemption has been extended to Varishtha Bima Yojana.

The impact of this withdrawal of exemption from some key services can be understood by just one example — Service tax exemption to construction, erection, commissioning or installation of original works pertaining to an airport or port was withdrawn. This has resulted in the cost of the ₹ 14,000 crore Navi Mumbai Airport going up by ₹ 560 crore! We wonder whether this project will get completely stalled now because of this escalation in the cost. Are we really walking towards progress? The country needs infrastructure badly and we are taxing infrastructure!!

The Service Tax rate has been increased from the current level of 12.36% to 14%. Additionally, an enabling provision is being made to empower the Central Government to impose a Swachh Bharat Cess on all or any of the taxable services @2% of the value of such taxable services. If and when this is introduced, the effective rate will be 14.28%.

Both the new Service Tax rate and the Swachh Bharat Cess shall come into effect from a date to be notified by the Central Government.

We are afraid that in near future, service rendered by an employee to his employer will be brought under the service tax.

MISCELLANEOUS

* Most provisions of the proposed Direct Taxes Code have already been included in the ITA. There is no merit in going ahead any more. We wonder how much effort and money has gone into creating and amending the drafts. If this is the attitude, we would still be having the 1922 ITA.
* The target date of implementation of GAAR has been shifted by 2 years to FY 17-18. Investment made up to 31.3.2017 shall be outside the purview of GAAR. We sincerely hope that in FY 17-18, GAAR gets postponed by another 2 years.
* GST will see daylight within one year. This has been the dream of all the finance ministers for the past around 5 years.
* To permit tax-free infrastructure bonds for the projects in the rail, road and irrigation sectors.
* Launched the e-Biz Portal which integrates 14 regulatory permissions at one source.
* To enter into Monetary Policy Framework Agreement with RBI, to keep inflation below 6%.
* Visas on arrival to be increased to 150 countries in stages.

* GDP growth in 2015-16 is projected to be between 8 to 8.5%.
* The fiscal deficit targets have been revised at 3.9%, 3.5% and 3.0% for FY 2015-16, 2016-17 & 2017-18 respectively.
* To set up 5 new Ultra Mega Power Projects, each of 4,000 MWs in the plug-and-play mode. All clearances and linkages will be in place before the project is awarded by a transparent auction system. This should unlock investments to the extent of ₹ 1 lakh crore. The Government would also consider similar plug-and-play projects in other infrastructure projects such as roads, ports, rail lines, airports, etc.
* The second unit of Kudankulam Nuclear Power Station will be commissioned in 2015-16.
* To create a Task Force to establish a sector-neutral Financial Redressal Agency that will address grievances against all financial service providers.
* Renewable energy capacity to be increased to 1,75,000 mw, comprising of 1,00,000 mw solar, 60,000 mw wind, 10,000 mw biomass and 5,000 mw small hydro.
* To make India, the manufacturing hub of the world through Skill India and the Make in India Programmes.

Our Comments

The 'Modi Wave' has taken a strong nose-dive downwards, as is evident from the recent Delhi elections and share market reactions since it is felt that the government is strong on rhetoric but weak on action. Most importantly, the 'Make in India' is a very good concept but not at the cost of neglecting the various work in progress projects which are stalled for various reasons, including a look of clearances from a multitude of windows. The one-window clearance is nowhere in sight.

The Indian voters want to see their dreams getting converted into reality.

1

General Provisions

FEMA has Replaced FERA

The Foreign Exchange Regulation Act (FERA) was enacted way back in 1973. A myriad amendments and clarifications were issued in the name of liberalisation reaching a situation where it became difficult to differentiate between the wood and trees.

Therefore, FEMA replaced FERA with effect from 1.6.2000.

The same situation is encountered by the Income Tax Act, 1961 and it was slated to be replaced by Direct Tax Code. The FM has declared in his Budget-15 speech that DTC has been shifted to cold storage, because (he feels that) the ITA has already incorporated within itself all such simplifications and streamlining.

FEMA is a civil law, whereas the FERA was a criminal law. Contravention under FEMA are dealt with through civil procedures resulting in no prosecution, arrest and imprisonment. It has also curtailed the powers of Directorate of Enforcement. Most importantly, it has provided for compounding of penalty. The burden of proof will be on the enforcement agency and not on the implicated person. FEMA describes an elaborate redressing machinery for total justice and fairness while deciding on the question of contravention. It has also narrowed down RBI's role only to supervision and control by giving all executive powers to Authorised Dealers (ADs) within the framework of FEMA.

An AD Category-I is a bank specifically authorised by the RBI to deal in forex and foreign securities. For providing greater reach, the RBI grants licences to certain entities by authorising them as AD Category-II or Category-III or Full Fledged Money Changers to undertake a range of non-trade current account transactions.

List of activities handled by different categories is available on www.fedai.org.in.

BASIC CONDITIONS

With a view to avoid repetition, the following is a list of general conditions applicable to all the areas. You are requested to keep these in mind while reading the rest of the book.

Prohibited Transactions

An ROI shall not make investment in India, in any form directly or through any entity, whether incorporated or not, which is engaged or proposed to be engaged in —

(a) Chit fund or Nidhi Company.

(b) Agriculture or plantation activities. These exclude — Floriculture, Horticulture, Development of seeds, Animal husbandry, Pisciculture, Cultivation of vegetables, mushrooms etc., under controlled conditions and Services related to agro and allied sectors and Plantations (other than tea plantations).

(c) Housing and real estate business or construction of farm houses. This shall not include development in townships, construction of residential and commercial premises, roads or bridges, educational institutions, recreational facilities, city and regional level infrastructure, townships.

(d) Trading in Transferable Development Rights (TDRs). This is a certificate issued in respect of land acquired for public purpose by government for surrender of land by the owner without monetary compensation. These are transferable in part or whole.

(e) Lottery, gambling and betting in casinos or otherwise, including government, private or on-line lotteries.

(f) Partnership firms and proprietorship concerns having investments as per FEMA are not allowed to be engaged in print media sector.

(g) Retail Trading except single brand product retailing.

(h) Atomic Energy.

(i) Manufacturing of cigars, cheroots, cigarillos and cigarettes, of tobacco or of tobacco substitutes.

The same restrictions are applicable to a Resident in respect of the amount borrowed, if any.

Prohibited Remittances

Prohibited remittances out of India by any person or entity are —

1. Income from lottery winnings, racing, riding, or any other hobby.

2. For purchase of lottery tickets, banned or proscribed magazines, football pools, sweepstakes, etc.

3. Payment of commission on exports of equity investment in Joint ventures or wholly owned subsidiaries abroad of Indian companies or on exports under Rupee State Credit Route except commission up to 10% of invoice value of tea and tobacco.

4. Dividend by any company to which the requirement of dividend balancing is applicable.

5. Payment related to 'Call Back Services' of telephones.

6. Drawal of exchange for travel to Nepal or Bhutan and also transactions with a person resident therein, unless specifically exempted by the RBI by general or special order.

However, remittance of prize money or sponsorship of sports activity abroad by a person other than international, national or state level sports bodies, if the amount involved exceeds US$ 1,00,000 requires permission from Ministry of Human Resources Development, Department of Youth Affairs and Sports.

ROI, PIO and NRI

The Act uses these nomenclatures rather loosely. The confusion caused by such an use has been dealt with in Chapter, *Residential Status*. For the sake of clarity, throughout this book we shall stick to the following nomenclature —

* 'ROI' is a person Resident Outside India. Obviously, such a person may be a rank foreigner, PIO or NRI.

* 'NRI' is an Indian citizen who is not Resident in India.

* 'PIO' is a foreign citizen of Indian origin.

Since all the rules, regulations, provisions, etc., are common for both NRIs and PIOs, for the purpose of this book, NRI would include PIO, unless otherwise separately mentioned.

Close Relative

ITA has defined 'close relative' in Sec. 56 (Refer Chapter *Gift Tax has Come Back*). FEMA refers to Sec. 6 of Companies Act. This results in confusion.

For FEMA, a person shall be deemed to be a 'relative' of another if, and only if —

(a) they are members of Hindu undivided family; or
(b) they are husband and wife; or
(c) relative as defined by Schedule-IA which is as follows :

Father.	Son's daughter.
Mother.	Son's daughter's husband.
Son.	Daughter's husband.
Son's wife.	Daughter's son.
Daughter.	Daughter's son's wife.
Father's father.	Daughter's daughter.
Father's mother.	Daughter's daughter's husband.
Mother's mother.	Brother.
Mother's father.	Brother's wife.
Son's son.	Sister.
Son's son's wife.	Sister's husband.

Note : Mother, son, daughter, brother and sister include step entities also.

Know Your Customer (KYC) Compliance

Investments of all the ROIs related with banks, Depository Participants for shares, units for MFs, life and general cover for insurers, etc. , should be compliant with 'KYC' and also Anti Money Laundering guidelines. It is also mandatory to possess a PAN.

Clubbing of NRE & FCNR

NRE and FCNR accounts are forex in nature and all rules are common for both. Therefore, reference to FCNR is dropped in all such cases. However, take note of the fact that since FCNR is a term deposit, withdrawals, though legal, are virtually impossible.

Repatriation v Remittance

Repatriation is sending money abroad which was originally remitted from abroad. Such an amount received from abroad can be credited to NRE account and is repatriable. This amount along with income generated therefrom can be sent outside India without any restrictions. It is mandatory for all the receipts and dispatches to be made through normal banking channels.

Funds on non-repatriable basis cannot be remitted abroad. The income from such funds or the maturity proceeds should be credited only to the NRO accounts. Depositor transferring funds from NRE to NRO loses repatriability.

Nepal & Bhutan

Release of forex is not admissible for travel to and transaction with Residents of Nepal and Bhutan. Investments in Nepal are permitted only in Indian Rupees. Investments in Bhutan are permitted in Indian Rupees as well as in freely convertible currencies. All dues receivable on investments made in freely convertible currencies, as well as their sale or winding up proceeds are required to be repatriated to India in freely convertible currencies only. Use of International Credit Cards for payment in forex in Nepal and Bhutan is not permitted.

Vide Notification FEMA 17/2000-RB dt. 3.5.00 (a) citizen of India, Nepal or Bhutan, resident in Nepal or Bhutan, (b) a branch in Nepal or Bhutan of a company or corporation in India or Nepal or Bhutan and (c) a branch in Nepal or Bhutan of a partnership firm or otherwise of citizens of India, Nepal or Bhutan are permitted to deal in INR freely. Such persons can invest in shares and convertible debentures of Indian companies under FDI Scheme on repatriable basis, subject to the condition that the amount of consideration for such investments shall be paid only by way of inward remittance in forex.

Indian currency notes above ₹ 100 denomination were banned for over a decade. Now, Notification FEMA 331/2014-RB dt. 16.12.14 allows an individual travelling from India to Nepal or Bhutan to carry notes of denomination ₹ 500 and/or ₹ 1,000 up to a limit of ₹ 25,000.

Payments Subject to Tax Compliance

Sec. 195 mandates application of TDS (= withholding tax) from payments made or credit given to NRIs at the rates in force. RBI also requires that except in cases of specifically exempted personal remittances, no remittance shall be allowed to an NRI unless he has obtained a no objection certificate from the Department.

Such a certificate is not required if the NRI submits a letter of undertaking along with an accountant's certificate.

To monitor and track transactions in a timely manner, Circular 04/2009 dt. 29.6.09 has laid down the revised procedure as follows:

* Remitter obtains certificate of Accountant (Form-15CB).
* Remitter accesses www.tin-nsdl.com.
* Takes printout of the undertaking (Form-15CA), fills the remittance details, signs it electronically and uploads it.
* Takes printout of filled Form-15CA with system generated acknowledgement number.
* Submits both the forms to the RBI/AD in duplicate.
* If the remitter has obtained a certificate from AO for applying tax at lower or nil rate, this certificate is required to be submitted in place of Form-15CB.
* RBI/AD remits the amount.

In the case of NRIs who do not maintain NRO account and have no taxable income in India, ADs can allow remittances after obtaining a simple declaration from them.

International Credit & Debit Cards

The restrictions contained in Rule 5 of the FEMR (Current Account Transactions) will not be applicable for use of International Credit Cards (ICCs) by Residents for making payment towards expenses, while on a visit outside India.

Residents can use ICCs on internet for any purpose for which exchange can be purchased from an AD e.g., for import of books, purchase of downloadable software or import of any other item permissible under EXIM Policy.

There is no aggregate monetary ceiling separately prescribed for use of ICCs through internet.

NRIs can pay credit card dues, in respect of ICCs issued by banks in India, even from the balances in NRO account if the payments satisfy the conditions laid down for use of ICCs by Residents.

Resident individuals maintaining foreign currency accounts with an AD or a bank abroad, as permissible under extant Foreign Exchange Regulations, are free to obtain ICCs issued by overseas banks and other reputed agencies. The charges incurred against the card either in India or abroad, can be met out of funds held in such forex accounts of the card holder or through remittances from India only through a bank where the card-holder has a current or savings account. The remittance should be made directly to the card-issuing agency abroad, and not to a third party.

The applicable credit limit will be the limit fixed by the card issuing banks. There is no monetary ceiling fixed by the RBI for remittances, if any, under this facility.

AD banks are also issuing International Debit Cards (IDCs) which can be used by a Resident for drawing cash or making payment to a merchant establishment overseas during his visit abroad.

Certain AD banks are also issuing Store Value Card, Charge Card or Smart Card to Residents travelling on private or business visit abroad. These are used for making payments at overseas merchant establishments and also for drawing cash from ATM terminals. Such cards can be used only for permissible current account transactions and the item-wise limits as mentioned in the Rules are equally applicable to payments made through use of these cards.

Drawal of foreign exchange includes use of ICC, IDC, ATM cards, etc. "Currency", *inter alia*, includes such cards. Accordingly, all Rules, Regulations made and Directions issued under the Act apply to the use of these cards. Use of these cards for payment in forex in Nepal and Bhutan requires RBI Permission.

It appears that the RBI has excluded spends on ICCs from BTQ for private and business travel, or for drawing cash from ATM effectively increasing the annual foreign exchange limit for overseas travellers. Consequently an individual with two international credit cards in 'gold' category with a credit limit of ₹ 3 lakh each can effectively increase his BTQ by ₹ 6 lakh, payable from his NRO account.

Its use is limited to permissible current account transactions. Resident Indians who purchase their travel cards, are permitted refund of the unutilised forex balance only after ten days from the date of last transaction. Since International Debit Cards/Store Value Cards/Charge Cards/Smart Cards issued to Resident Indians while on a visit outside India act as substitutes for cash or travellers cheques, the facilities available to the user will have to be similar.

Therefore, AP (DIR) Circular 102 dt. 2.4.12 mandates all Authorised Persons to redeem the unutilised balance outstanding in the cards immediately upon request by holders of such cards subject to retention of —

(a) The amounts that are authorised and remain unclaimed or not settled by the acquirer as of the date of redemption till completion of the respective settlement cycle.

(b) Balance not exceeding US$ 100, for meeting any pipeline transactions till completion of respective settlement cycle, and

(c) Transaction fees and service tax payable in India in Rupees.

Prohibited Foreign Contributions

Sec. 4 of Foreign Contribution (Regulation) Act, 1976 (FCRA) prohibits acceptance of foreign contribution by any candidate for election, correspondent, columnist, cartoonist, editor, owner, printer or publisher of a registered newspaper, judges, government servants or employees of any corporation, members of any legislature, political party or its office bearers. Associations having a definite cultural, economic, educational, religious and social programme should get themselves registered with the Ministry of Home Affairs, before receiving any foreign contributions. These should be received only through a designated bank branch as specified in the application for registration. Those who are not registered with the ministry, may obtain prior permission of the Central Government. Indian citizens abroad do not fall in the purview of 'foreign source' and therefore do not attract the provisions of FCRA.

Capital Account Transactions

These are transactions altering assets or liabilities, including contingent liabilities, outside India of Residents or ROIs such as —

For Residents
(a) Investment in Foreign Securities.
(b) Forex loans raised in India and abroad.
(c) Transfer of immovable property outside India.
(d) Guarantee in favour of an ROI.
(e) Export, import and holding of currency or currency notes.
(f) Loans and overdrafts from and to an ROI.
(g) Maintenance of forex accounts in or outside India.
(h) Taking an insurance policy from an insurer outside India.
(i) Remittance outside India of capital assets.
(j) Sale and purchase of forex derivatives in India and abroad and commodity derivatives abroad.

For ROIs
(a) Investment in securities issued by a body corporate or an entity in India and contribution to the capital of a firm or a proprietorship concern or an AOP in India.
(b) Acquisition or transfer of immovable property in India.
(c) Guarantee in favour of an ROI.
(d) Import, export and holding of currency or currency notes.
(e) Forex accounts in India.
(f) Remittance outside India of capital assets in India.

Current Account Transactions

These are transactions other than a capital account transaction and include —
(a) Payments due in connection with foreign trade, other current business, services, and short-term banking and credit facilities

in the ordinary course of business.

(b) Payments due as interest on loans and as net income from investments.

(c) Remittances for living expenses of parents, spouse and children residing abroad, and

(d) Expenses in connection with foreign travel, education and medical care of parents, spouse and children.

Service Tax

Trade Notice 48/ST/2012 dt. 31.10.12 clarifies that there is no Service Tax *per se* on the amount of forex remitted to India from overseas. In case any fee or conversion charges are levied for sending such money, they are also not liable to Service Tax as the person sending the money and the company conducting the remittance are located outside India.

Even the Indian counterpart bank or financial institution who charges the foreign bank or any other entity for the services provided at the receiving end, is not liable to Service Tax as the place of provision of such service shall be the location of the recipient of the service, and this is outside India.

Master Circulars

Every year on 1st July, RBI issues a set of Circulars with a view to consolidate regulations related different subjects. To avoid repeated references to these circulars, we present hereunder a list of the Circulars in RBI/2014-15 series which are relevant to us.

No. 6 : Foreign Investment in India.

No. 7 : NRO Account.

No. 8 : Remittance Facilities for NRIs / PIOs / Foreign Nationals.

No. 9 : Immovable Property in India by NRIs/PIOs/Foreign Nationals.

No. 10 : Miscellaneous remittances from India.

No. 62 : FCNR(B) Accounts.

No. 64 : Loans and Advances.

No. 68 : Housing Finance.

2

Residential Status

When I read FEMA, I was reminded of a couplet —
I am the parliamentarian draftsman, I make the laws
For most of the litigations, I am the cause.

FEMA is a classic case of an armchair drafting of the legislation with little application of mind and no contact with reality.

Let us first study the definition of an NRI as conceived by the ITA.

RESIDENTIAL STATUS UNDER ITA

Tax liability in India is directly determined by residential status of an assessee under ITA and it depends on change in such status.

There are 3 statuses —
1. Resident and Ordinarily Resident (ROR)
2. Resident but Not Ordinarily Resident (RNOR), and
3. Non-Resident Indian (NRI).

An individual is treated as a Resident for the FY (April to March) if he satisfies, during the year, any one of the following 2 conditions: He is in India for at least a period or periods amounting in all to —

(a) 182 days in the FY, OR
(b) 365 days out of the preceding 4 FYs AND 60 days in the FY.

Most of those going for the first time may not be eligible to be an NRI because of the 'b' clause above which allows stay in India only for 60 days. Therefore, —

(i) Where an *Indian citizen* leaves India in any year for the purpose of employment, or as a member of a crew of an Indian merchant ship, the period of '60 days' is to be replaced by '182 days'.

Consequently, an Indian citizen going abroad for employment can stay in India up to 181 days for obtaining NRI status for that very year, even if he is in India for 365 days or more during the 4 preceding years.

(ii) When an *Indian citizen or a person of Indian Origin* (PIO) who is abroad comes to visit India, the period of '60 days' is to be replaced by 182 days.

Finally, an NRI is a person who is not a Resident.

Note that the condition-(i) above is applicable only to Indian Citizens and not PIOs whereas condition-(ii) is applicable to both of them. None of them is applicable to rank foreigners complicated.

We strongly feel that the word 'employment' has various shades of meaning. Dictionary defines it as 'work', 'occupation', ' keeping busy'. Therefore the period of 60 days can be replaced with 182 days, not only for rendering service to an employer but also for undertaking of business or profession.

Note also that for those who return to India permanently (not on a visit), the period of '60 days' is not replaced by 182 days. Consequently, anyone who has been in India for 365 days or more in the preceding 4 years and returns before February finds that his NRI status is lost right from the year of his return.

Crew Members on Ships with Indian & Foreign Flag
Most of the persons working on Indian ship, oscillate between NRI and RNOR because of the contractual nature of their job. For some years they may even become full-fledged Residents.

In the case of *CIT* v *Avtar Singh Wadhwan* (247ITR260), Bombay High Court has held that income from salary, in the case of crew of even an Indian vessel operating in international waters, is to be treated as having accrued outside India.

Members of a crew of a merchant ship with a foreign flag are treated as having left India for employment; not so for crew of an Indian ship. In an attempt to bring both of them on par with each other, FA90 extended the benefit of 182 days to Indian citizens who are members of the crew of an Indian ship. But again this was a shoddy correction. It merely states that if a crewman on an Indian ship passes the test of being an NRI, he will not be charged to tax on his foreign exchange earnings earned while working outside Indian waters. It is silent about the taxability in the hands of an individual when he travels from the status of an NRI to RNOR.

Moreover, as per Sec.10(*6viii*), salary of a Non-resident foreign national as a member of a ship's crew is exempt provided his stay in India does not exceed an aggregate period of 90 days in the FY. Therefore, the members of a crew of a merchant ship with an Indian flag are still not on par with those with a foreign flag.

In the case of foreign bound ships where the destination of the voyage is outside India, there is uncertainty with regard to the manner and basis of determination of the period of stay in India for crew members of such ships who are Indian citizens. Therefore, Sec. 6 has been amended by the recent FA15 to provide that in such cases the period of stay in India shall be notified by CBDT in due course.

RNOR

There are two types of Residents —

1. Resident but Not Ordinarily Resident (RNOR), and

2. Resident and Ordinarily Resident (ROR).

An RNOR is an individual who has been (a) an NRI in 9 out of the 10 previous years preceding that year, or (b) has, during the 7 previous years preceding that year, been in India for a period of, or periods amounting in all to 729 days or less.

If a Resident person is not an RNOR he is an ROR.

Consequently, those returning after being NRIs for 5 continuous years or less immediately become Residents. Those returning after 6 years may become RNORs for one year whereas others, including those after being NRIs, for say, 25 years may become RNOR for 2 years at the most. However, in rare cases where the individual has not come to India in any of the previous 5 years and has returned to India after 2nd April will be an RNOR for 3 years.

Miscellaneous

1. A person can be treated as a Resident of two or more countries at the same time.

2. India includes the territorial waters. Thus a person in a yacht moored around the shores of India would be staying in India.

3. Indian ships operating beyond the Indian territorial waters are treated as not in India.

Taxability Depends on Status

ROR : The total income of a person who is a Resident includes all income from whatever source derived which —

(a) is received or is deemed to be received in India in such year by or on behalf of such person; or

(b) accrues or arises or is deemed to accrue or arise to him in India during such year; or

(c) accrues or arises to him outside India during such year.

Many NRIs go in for cumulative deposits under the wrong impression that the tax becomes applicable in India only when the interest is actually received. The provision of Sec. 5(2) of ITA leaves no room for any doubt or ambiguity, that if an effective and final conclusion can be drawn, on the issue of accrual of income to a Non-resident, the actual date of receipt is inconsequential — *Smt. Trishla Jain v Income-tax Commissioner [ITR 43 to 48 of 1991].*

RNOR : Tax liability of an RNOR is the same as that of an NRI. In other words, his forex income is not taxable in India. There is only one exception. In the case of RNOR, income received and accrued outside India from a business controlled in or a profession set up in India continues to be taxable in India.

NRI : On the other hand, an NRI is not liable to tax on income accruing or arising outside India, even if it is remitted to India. As per Sec. 5, he is liable to pay tax only in respect of income received or deemed to be received in India or which accrues or arises or is deemed to accrue or arise in India by or on behalf of such person.

Income 'received or deemed to be received' in India has a strange and illogical aspect. You may be taken unawares if and when it bites. The receipt of income refers to the very first occasion when the recipient gets the money under his control. Once an amount is received as income abroad, any remittance or transmission of the amount to any other place, including India, does not result in receipt income at other place. The position will remain the same if income is received outside India by an agent of the assessee who later on remits it to India. The same income cannot be received by the same person twice, once outside India and once within India — *Keshav Mills Ltd.* v *CIT (1953) 23ITR230 (SC).*

Many employees request their employers to remit their salaries directly to their accounts in India. If you are one such an employee, take immediate corrective action.

Similarly, income which 'accrues or arises or is deemed to accrue or arise in India' has stranger effect. In the case of *Trishla Jain* v *CIT (310ITR274)*, decided by the Punjab & Haryana High Court, some NRIs had purchased debentures issued by Oswal Agro Mills Ltd., an Indian company. Interest was payable on July 1 and December 31 of every year.

The assessees declared the interest in their return for the FY 1987-88 in which they received the interest. The ITO took the view that the interest income was assessable on accrual basis in FY 1986-87. This was upheld by CIT (Appeals) and also by the Tribunal.

The High Court concluded that there is no room for any doubt or ambiguity that the actual date of receipt is inconsequential. Income of a Non-resident has to be included in the previous year on accrual basis, i.e. as and when such income arises (or is deemed to have arisen) to the assessee, in a specific, definite and crystallized manner.

RESIDENTIAL STATUS UNDER FEMA

This is very complicated. It varies from Rule to Rule. The complication gets further confounded because the definition as per ITA is different from that of FEMA.

Sec. 2(*u*) of FEMA defines a 'person' to include —
(a) an individual,
(b) an HUF,
(c) a company,
(d) a firm,
(e) an AOP or BOI, whether incorporated or not,
(f) every artificial juridical person, not falling within any of the preceding sub-classes, and
(g) any agency, office or branch owned or controlled by such a person.

Sec. 2(*v*) defines a person *Resident in India* to mean —
(i) A person residing in India for more than 182 days during the course of the *preceding* financial year but does not include,
　(A) A person who has gone out of India or who stays outside India, in either case, the following 3 purposes —
　　(a) for or on taking up employment outside India, or
　　(b) for carrying on outside India a business or vocation ,or
　　(c) for any other purpose, in such circumstances as would indicate his intention to stay outside India for an uncertain period.

　(B) A person who has come to or stay in India, in either case, otherwise than the following 3 purposes —
　　(a) for or on taking up employment in India, or
　　(b) for carrying on in India a business or vocation in India, or
　　(c) for any purpose, in such circumstances as would indicate his intention to stay in India for an uncertain period.

(ii) any person or body corporate registered or incorporated in India.

(iii) an office, branch or agency in India owned or controlled by a person Resident outside India.

(iv) an office, branch or agency outside India owned or controlled by a person Resident in India.

A person *Resident Outside India* (ROI) means a person who is not a Resident in India.

S*taying for uncertain period* connotes a fairly long period, if not permanent.

Hey! Wait a minute. ITA requires stay in India of '182 days or more' whereas FEMA requires 'more than 182 days'! Bad.

ITA deals with *previous year* and FEMA with *preceding year.*

Note carefully that for ITA the Residentship is always related with the entire FY. In other words, one cannot be a Resident for part of the year and a Non-resident for the rest of the year. That is not so for Residentship under FEMA. For instance, any person who goes abroad for any of the 3 purposes mentioned above, becomes an ROI from the day he leaves India and conversely he becomes a Resident from the day he arrives in India for any of the 3 purposes.

Also note that there is an innovative way to bypass this loss of status, which is followed by almost all who return to India permanently. They claim that they have not returned permanently and desire to go back, if an opportunity presents itself. Therefore, they behave as if they have come on short visit and this so-called 'visit' may extend for a few years, unless they have come on transfer of residence visa. We do not recommend this stance since the loss of ROI status for FEMA is hardly material, more so, if this person becomes an RNOR for ITA.

Yes, very complicated indeed. The following correspondence with one of my readers illustrates the situation adequately —

"I am a US Green Card holder since 2009, but my stay in US is limited as I have to visit India frequently to attend to my ailing parents and to look after my parental agricultural land. Consequently, my stay in US is normally 3 months and more than 6 months in a financial year in India. I get pension in India and file my Returns in the US as well as in India.

"Can I buy farm land in India as I am Resident of India for purpose of filing return, my stay in India in a financial year being more than 6 months and I am still not US citizen?"

— Harbaksh Singh, hkbs1988@gmail.com

No, you cannot buy any agricultural property in India. The residential status and citizenship are two different entities, totally separate from each other. Note that the provisions related with agricultural properties are contained in FEMA. Therefore, the residential status as defined by FEMA has to be applied.

You have not come to India for employment, business or vocation in India. Moreover you have not returned to India permanently.

You are not eligible to purchase any agricultural property in India.

Example

Let us take the instance of Mr. Wagh, an Indian Resident, who went to USA for the first time in his life on 1.11.2009 (FY 2009-10) for meeting his daughter who was working in the USA. He returned to India on 20.1.2012 (FY 2011-12). His Residentship for —

Income Tax —

FY 09-10 : Resident — He was in India for more than 182 days.

FY 10-11 : NRI — He was abroad for the entire FY. Had he come to India and stayed for more than 60 days, he would have been a Resident because he was also in India for 365 days out of the preceding 4 FYs.

FY 11-12 : Resident — He was in India for over 365 days out of the preceding 4 FYs and also for over 60 days during the current FY.

FEMA —

FY 09-10 : Resident — He was in India for more than 182 days during the preceding FY 2008-09.

FY 10-11 : Resident — Though he was abroad for the entire FY, he was in India for more than 182 days during the preceding FY 2009-10.

FY 11-12 : Resident — He has returned to India permanently.

Take the case of a crew member of a foreign ship or airline who, because of requirements of his job is regularly forced to stay in hotels in India for more than 182 days every year. Can he be treated as a Resident in India? Such a person is not *residing* in India but is only present in India and *staying* in a hotel. Therefore he continues to be an ROI.

There are two exceptions to the rules related with ROI —
1. A student going abroad is treated as an ROI.

2. There is a third status of *Resident but not Permanently Resident* related with deputies.

Both these subjects are covered in separate Chapters subsequently.

Person of Indian Origin (PIO)

FEMA defines a PIO to mean —

A citizen of any country other than Bangladesh or Pakistan, if —
(a) He at any time held an Indian passport, or

(b) He or either of his parents or any of his grand parents was a citizen of India by virtue of the Constitution of India or Citizenship Act, 1955.

(c) The person is a spouse of an Indian citizen or of a person referred to in (a) or (b) above.

The definition of PIO differs from Rule to Rule.

The provisions as stated above apply to 'Deposits' and 'Remittance of Assets' where the citizens (or an incorporated entity) of Bangladesh or Pakistan are excluded. This exclusion is expanded to citizens of Sri Lanka for the provisions related with 'Investment in Firm or Proprietary Concern in India' or 'Purchase shares or convertible debentures or preference shares of an Indian company' and further citizens of Afghanistan, China, Iran, Nepal or Bhutan for Rule related with 'Acquisition and Transfer of Immovable Property in India'.

Circular AP (DIR) 11 dt. 13.9.04 has lifted the restriction imposed on investment in Indian companies by Sri Lankan citizens. Accordingly, persons Resident outside India (other than a citizen of Bangladesh or Pakistan) including citizens of Sri Lanka would henceforth be eligible to purchase shares or convertible debentures of an Indian company under Foreign Direct Investment scheme subject to the specified terms and conditions. Moreover, as per notification GSR 713(E), dt. 23.10.07 a person who is a citizen of Bangladesh or an entity incorporated in Bangladesh may, with the prior approval of the Foreign Investment Promotion Board of the Government of India, purchase shares and convertible debentures of an Indian company under Foreign Direct Investment scheme.

For ITA, Explanation to Sec. 115C states that a person shall be deemed to be of Indian origin if he, or either of his parents or any of his grand parents, was born in undivided India.

What if such a person was born in divided India? Well, any person born in any place which was part of undivided India can be treated as born in undivided India even if the person was born after 15.7.47.

Sec. 2(*25A*) of ITA proclaims that India includes, for the purpose of Residentship, Dadra and Nagar Haveli, Goa, Daman and Diu, and Pondicherry in respect of any period. Even when these parts were not a part of India, still, by a fiction of law, these territories will be deemed to have been part of India and the question of residence will have to be decided on the basis of this fiction.

FEMA depends upon the Constitution of India or Citizenship Act. This may result in the same person being treated as PIO for ITA and not for FEMA and *vice versa*.

These small differences result in large confusions.

Borderline Cases — One More Difference
Where a person is in India only for a part of a day, the calculation of physical presence in India in respect of such broken period should be made on an hourly basis. A total of 24 hours of stay spread over a number of days is to be counted as being equivalent to the stay of one day — *Walkie* v *IRC [1952] 1AER92.*

Yet another case law, *223ITR462 (AAR) New Delhi* has a different view. The date of arrival as well as the date of departure have to be taken into account for calculating the period of stay in India, even if for some hours on these dates the person was in India on these dates, however short the period may be. The same view is reiterated by *P. 7 of 1995, In re (1997) 90Taxman62.*

These rulings may be applied even in the case of ITA where data is not available to calculate the period of stay of an individual in India in terms of hours.

The latest one decided on 29.6.12 is [2012] 24taxmann.com193 (Mumbai — Tribench F) *Income Tax Officer (IT)-1(1)* v *Fausta C. Cordeiro.* In this case, Commissioner (Appeals) found that the assessee generally arrived late in night after completing his work abroad and attended to work next day and generally left early in morning so as to attend work again after arriving at destination. It was held that such days of arrival was to be excluded and by doing so assessee's staying was less than 180 days in India and not 187 as claimed by the ITO. Therefore, the date of arrival was to be excluded as it was not a complete day.

RBI has not yet taken any decision related with residential status of a trust. It is reported that the following internal guidelines are issued by it —

1. Appointment of a Non-resident as a trustee in a trust in India does not require any approval under FEMA.
2. Revenue income of a trust for Non-resident beneficiaries, can be remitted outside India after payment of tax, subject to compliance with other provisions of FEMA.
3. Any trust in which an NRI is a beneficiary or a trustee, cannot enter into prohibited activities.

FOREIGN PRIVATE EQUITY FUNDS

The recent FA15 has brought about sea change in the definition of residential status of such Funds and for very good reasons.

This depended upon whether (i) the company had a Permanent Establishment in India and (ii) whole of control and management was situated in India and that too for whole of the year. Consequently, a foreign company could easily avoid becoming a Resident by simply holding a board meeting outside India.

In the case of offshore funds, there was an uncertainty on whether the presence of its fund manager in India constitutes a Permanent Establishment in India. Moreover, if the fund manager located in India undertakes investment activity outside India for an offshore fund, the profits made by the offshore fund from such investments could be claimed to be taxable in India. Further, presence of the fund manager could lead to the offshore fund being held to be Resident in India and its global income become taxable in India.

This is the reason why there are a large number of fund managers who manage investment activity in India on behalf of offshore funds without being located in India. This is inconvenient.

Therefore, a specific regime has now been adopted to provide that in the case of an eligible investment fund, the fund management activity carried out through an eligible fund manager acting on behalf of such fund shall not constitute business connection in India.

Further, an eligible investment fund shall not be said to be Resident in India merely because its fund manager is located in India. The basis of deciding the Indian Residency of entities incorporated outside India has been widened. Henceforth, only those foreign companies having a Place of Effective Management (PoEM) in India would be considered as tax Resident in India. PoEM has been further explained to mean a place where key management and commercial decisions that are necessary for the conduct of the business of an entity as a whole are, in substance made.

The offshore fund shall be required to fulfil the following conditions during the year for avoiding being treated as a Resident —
(i)   the fund is not a person Resident in India;
(ii) the fund is a Resident of a country or a specified territory with which a DTAA exists;
(iii) the aggregate participation or investment in the fund, directly or indirectly, by persons being Resident in India does not exceed 5% of the corpus of the fund;

(iv) the fund and its activities are subject to applicable investor protection regulations in the country or specified territory where it is established or incorporated or is a Resident;

(v) the fund has a minimum of 25 members who are, directly or indirectly, not connected persons;

(vi) any member of the fund along with connected persons shall not have any participation interest, directly or indirectly, in the fund exceeding 10%;

(vii) the aggregate participation interest, directly or indirectly, of 10 or less members along with their connected persons in the fund shall be less than 50%;

The above 3 conditions (v), (vi) and (vii), will not be applicable to an investment fund set-up by the Government or Central Bank of a foreign State or a sovereign fund or any other notified fund;

(viii) the investment by the fund in an entity shall not exceed 20% of the corpus of the fund;

(ix) no investment shall be made by the fund in its associate entity;

(x) the monthly average of the corpus of the fund shall not be less than ₹ 100 crore and if the fund has been established or incorporated in the previous year, the corpus of fund shall not be less than ₹ 100 crore at the end of such previous year;

(xi) the fund shall not carry on or control and manage, directly or indirectly, any business in India or from India;

(xii) the fund is neither engaged in any activity which constitutes a business connection in India nor has any person acting on its behalf whose activities constitute a business connection in India other than the activities undertaken by the eligible fund manager on its behalf, and

(xiii) the remuneration paid by the fund to an eligible fund manager in respect of fund management activity undertaken on its behalf is not less than the arm's length price of such activity.

In addition, the following conditions shall be required to be satisfied the fund manager for being an eligible fund manager:

(i) the person is not an employee of the eligible investment fund or a connected person of the fund;

(ii) the person is registered as a fund manager or investment advisor in accordance with the specified regulations;

(iii) the person is acting in the ordinary course of his business as a fund manager; and

(iv) the person along with his connected persons shall not be entitled, directly or indirectly, to more than 20% of the profits accruing or arising to the eligible investment fund from the transactions carried out by the fund through such fund manager.

Moreover, every eligible investment fund shall, in respect of its activities in an FY, furnish within 90 days from the end of the FY a statement in the prescribed form to the Department containing information relating to the fulfilment of the above conditions or any information or document which may be prescribed. In the case of non-furnishing of the prescribed information or document or statement, a penalty of ₹ 5 lakh shall be levied on the fund.

It is also clarified that this regime shall not have any impact on taxability of any income of the eligible investment fund which would have been chargeable to tax irrespective of whether the activity of the eligible fund manager constituted the business connection in India of such fund or not. Further, the regime shall not have any effect on the scope of total income or determination of total income in the case of the eligible fund manager.

Comments

All we have to say is that now, more than ever in the past, it would be difficult for the Private Equity Fund to station its Fund Manager in India, as a POEM or otherwise. Are we really inviting these companies to 'Make in India'?

3

Students Studying Abroad

Good news for students studying abroad. Through Circular 45 dt. 8.12.03, RBI has declared that for the purpose of FEMA, students will be treated as NRIs as soon as they go abroad for studies.

A student is a non-resident alien in the USA who is temporarily in the country on a 'F', 'J', 'M' or 'Q' visa and is not engaged in any activities that are prohibited by US immigration laws. If a non-resident alien receives a grant from outside sources, then it is not taxable in the USA. Students are, in reality, not dependent for a dominant part of their expenses on remittances from their households in India. Often they undertake certain employments.

Normally, the terms of a scholarship or fellowship grant specify that the amount or a part of it is to be used for tuition, enrolment fees, books and cost of supplies and equipment belonging to the institution that the student uses. This portion is not taxable but the portion representing payment for teaching, research or any service is taxable in the USA. It may also be taxable in India depending upon the residential status of the student as defined by ITA. Relief can be claimed from such tax under Article 21 of DTAA between India and the USA.

This benefit, in most cases, entitles a student to a refund of all or part of the money withheld. This can be exercised by filing a non-resident tax return in India. It is necessary to attach a covering note from the educational institution declaring that the whole or part of the scholarship or fellowship is an educational award and not money paid for personal services.

The greatest advantage lies in the fact that as non-residents, they will be eligible to receive remittances from India —

(i) up to US$ 100,000 from close relatives in India, on self declaration, towards maintenance, which could include remittances towards their studies also;

(ii) up to US$ 1 million per FY out of sale proceeds of assets / balances in their NRO account maintained with an Authorised Dealer bank in India, and

(iii) up to US$ 200,000 per FY under the Liberalized Remittance Scheme.

All other facilities available to NRIs under FEMA are equally applicable to the students. Educational and other loans availed of by them as residents in India will continue to be available.

We will be dealing with these facilities later in this book.

Students can open and maintain NRE, FCNR and NRO accounts. In the case of students proceeding to Russia and other Republics of CIS countries entire exchange admissible can be availed in the form of currency notes. The student need not necessarily avail of exchange facilities for the entire duration of the course from the same branch of the same AD.

We strongly feel that the ITA definition of NRI should have been changed simultaneously. A student does not go abroad for the purpose of employment. Therefore during the very first year of his going abroad, the clause '365 days out of the preceding 4 FYs AND 60 days in the FY' will sink its teeth into him and treat him as a Resident for ITA unless he is in India for less than 60 days.

Consequently, those who desired to send some money to their family members in India were forced to take recourse to the illegal hawala route. We are afraid that they will continue doing so.

Foreign Students in India

Anyone who had come to India for study or training and has completed it, may remit the balance in his accounts, provided such balance represents funds derived out of remittances received from abroad or rupee proceeds of forex brought and sold to an AD or out of stipend/scholarship received from the government or any organisation in India.

Students and Insurance

Foreign universities particularly in US and UK insist on students taking medical insurance and additional risk cover for mental or nervous disorders, alcoholism and drug dependency, pregnancy, sports injuries, cancer, child care, etc., for as much as US$ 2,50,000. The average premium for this is around US$ 900.

Indian insures offer such covers as per the specific needs of various universities at around US$ 350. Many US universities allow a student taking over from India. National Health Scheme in UK does not allow such waiver for treatment in government hospitals. Students can buy risk cover from India using UK private institutions.

ICICI Lombard insures students for US$ 100,000 for travelling. The premiums vary. For students going to the US or Canada the annual premium starts from ₹ 6,600 for the Bronze Plan and could go up to as high as ₹ 17,000 for the Gold Plus Plan. For UK or Europe, the premium is lower — at nearly ₹ 9,500 for the Gold Plus Plan. This plan offers medical cover worth US$ 50,000-250,000, in addition to covering dental treatment for US$ 250, baggage loss up to US$ 1,000, among various other accidents.

Bajaj Allianz's Student Companion Policy offers 3 different plans, Standard, Silver and Gold. Medical cover for these ranges between US$ 50,000 and US$ 200,000; baggage loss up to US$ 1,000 and personal liability cover up to US$ 100,000, compassionate visit up to US$ 7,500 and sponsor protection up to US$ 10,000.

Tata AIG offers similar cover, in addition to baggage loss up to US$ 1,000; personal liability cover up to US$ 100,000; study interruption up to US$ 7,500; compassionate visit up to US$ 7,000; bail bond up to US$ 5,000 and sponsor protection up to US$ 10,000.

Get the latest costs of insurance mentioned above, whenever needed.

Compassionate visit cover comprises of a round-trip economy class air ticket and accommodation expenses for an immediate family member if the student is hospitalised for 7 consecutive days. The student can visit his/her parents if either of them is critically ill.

4

Deputies — Hardships and Confusion

Thankfully, students are treated as NRIs. The authorities should have extended the same benefit to deputies (= employees sent on secondments) of Indian companies, placed abroad. The tax provisions on the income of the deputies is riddled with a lot of confusion and resultant hardships and litigations.

Hardship-1 : Residential Status

Some ITOs claim that a deputee cannot be considered as having gone abroad to take up an employment since he is already employed in India. Therefore '60 days' cannot be replaced by '182 days' in the rule for all deputies.

In the case of *ITR 218 AR, 2006 British Gas (I) (P) Ltd.* v *CIT*, the Indian company had deputed its employees to its group companies, including British Gas, UK. The Indian company also paid salary in India and recovered it from the UK company by raising a debit note. The employees were also given per diem by the UK company to meet their additional cost of living. Both the salary received in India and the allowance received in UK were taxed in UK since the employees were Tax Residents in UK. The AAR held that as per the Indo-UK DTAA agreement, since the employees are drawing their salary in respect of the employment being exercised in UK, the salary shall be taxable only in UK. Consequently, the Indian company need not apply TDS.

Unfortunately, AAR decisions are applicable only to the particular case and cannot be extrapolated to other same or similar situations. However, they have a persuasive value. It is pertinent to note the particular statement in the verdict having a universal application —

"An individual need not be an unemployed person who leaves India for employment outside India. Therefore, the fact that the deputee was already an employee at the time of leaving India is hardly material or relevant."

Hardship-2 : Tax on Salary Received in India

1. Income which is not attributable to services rendered in India is not taxable in India — Supreme Court in the case of *Sedco Forex Drilling International Inc (Civil Appeal No. 351-355 of 2005 and Others)* and also the Delhi Tribunal in the case of *DCIT* v *Vivek Paul (ITA 4236/Del/1997)*.

We strongly feel that this decision covers not only the salary received abroad even when the employee is a full-fledged Resident in India but also the salary received in India because both such salaries are paid for services not rendered in India.

2. U/s 9(1*ii*) salary payable for services rendered in India shall be regarded as income earned in India, even if paid outside India. It is not permissible to infer the corollary, viz., that in each and every case where services are rendered outside India, salary cannot be deemed to accrue or arise in India — *Capt. A. L. Fernandes* v *ITO [2002] 81ITD203 (Mum) (TM)*.

3. A Japanese deputee worked in India for 273 days during the FY. Since he was not a 'Resident' in India in any of nine out of ten previous years he was an RNOR. AO held that assessee was liable to tax in respect of salary received by him in Japan. Tribunal found that provisions of ITA were more beneficial to assessee, same should have been preferred over DTAA, and, thus income earned by assessee outside India could not be taxed in India.

On appeal, the High Court decided the case in favour of the assessee since he was an RNOR. Further it was held that Tribunal was right in holding that the rent-free accommodation provided by the Indian company to the assessee, was not a perquisite in the hands of the assessee u/s 17(2). Hence, the assessee was entitled to the benefit of the exemption provided by Section 10(*14*) — *CIT* v *Sakakibara Yutaka [2012] 25taxmann.com557 (HC Delhi)*.

Hardship-3 : Per Diem Allowance

Living allowance paid in addition to the regular salary to cover expenses incurred wholly, necessarily and exclusively in performance of office duties to the employees of Indian company who are on deputation are exempt from tax u/s 10(*14*)(*i*). Department wanted to tax any savings effected out of such allowances.

The ITAT held that it is not open to the revenue to call for the details of expenses actually incurred unless the specific allowance are disproportionately high compared to the salary received by him or unreasonable with reference to the nature of the duties performed by the taxpayer. It also held that ROIs coming to India and Indians going abroad are to be considered on same footing in respect of exemption u/s 10(14i) — *CIT v Sakakibara Yutaka [2012] 25taxmann.com557 (HC Delhi)*.

U/s 9(1*iii*) salary payable by the government to a citizen of India for services rendered outside India is deemed to have accrued or arisen in India irrespective of the place where it is paid.

Sec. 10(7) exempts any allowance or perquisite paid or allowed outside India. As per CBDT Circular 8/2005 dt. 29.8.05 the per diem allowance is exempt from tax u/s 10(*14*). Moreover, as per *[2011] 15taxmann.com328 (Kolkata - Trib)*, where, in addition to regular salaries and benefits in India, living allowance is given to employees of Indian company who are temporarily deployed in USA to work for Indian company, living allowance will be exempt.

Hardship-4 : Salary Received Abroad
A deputy would face tax in India on 'Residence' basis and in the overseas country on 'Source' basis.

The employee can claim a short stay exemption (less than 183 days during the FY) on salary paid by the Indian employer under the 'Dependent Personal Services', if the DTAA or the domestic tax laws of the host country have such a provision. If the employee is fully taxable abroad, he can claim credit for taxes paid abroad against his Indian tax liability for the same income.

Hardship-5 : TDS at Lower Rate
Can the employer consider the credit for foreign taxes to reduce the TDS on salary? Logical jurisprudence clearly gives the answer in the affirmative. However, unless the CBDT issues a clarification, the employers apply TDS to be on the safe side.

Hardship-6 : Employer Pays Tax

Many Indian employers pick up the Indian tax liability of a foreign deputy and pay him net of tax salary. In such cases a multiplier effect comes into play. For clarity suppose the tax payable is ₹ 10,000. Since the employer pays this tax, it is considered as additional salary and charged to tax @ 30.9% which works out at ₹ 3,090 and this is also paid by the employer. Now, this ₹ 3,090 is an additional salary, etc., etc., *ad infinitum*. Finally, the employer ends up paying ₹ 14,472!

Fortunately, The *ITAT Delhi Special Bench-F, in the case of RBF Rig Corpn. LIC (RBFRC)* v *ACI Circle I, Dehradun* held — "It may be a monetary gain or monetary benefit or a monetary allowance but definitely it is not a monetary payment to the assessee. If it is a payment to a third person like payment of taxes then such payment of taxes is not provided by way of monetary payment. Therefore, taxes paid by the employer can be added only once in the salary of the employee." As per this judicial view, tax payable works out at ₹ 13,090.

We fail to understand why the tax paid by the employer directly to the exchequer should be added even once.

Our prayers have been answered by HC Uttarakhand in the case of *DIT (International Taxation), Delhi-II* v *Sedco Forex International Drilling Inc* — taxmann.com 238. It observed that perquisites not provided by way of tax paid by employer on salaries/ remuneration of employees would constitute non-monetary benefits and, as such, same would be exempted u/s 10(*10CC*).

ITOs often take the stance that salary costs reimbursed by the Indian company under the secondment agreement are in the nature of technical service fees, warranting a withholding tax in India. Bangalore Tribunal has held that due consideration should be placed on the substance of the secondment agreement, which clearly proves that the real and economic employer of the seconded employees is the Indian company, even though they are on the payroll of the foreign company. Consequently, the services are not technical in nature.

Hardship-7 : Foreign Taxes

Payment of foreign taxes made by the Indian employer also has the same problems. Fortunately, it can be solved by giving a loan to the employee. The notional interest may be liable to tax in the hands of the employee. Consequently, as and when the employee receives the tax refund, he would need to repay it to his employer.

Hardship-8 : Filing Tax Returns Abroad

The financial year is April-March in India and January-December in most of the overseas countries. Consequently, the deadline for filing the returns in those countries is earlier than the one in India. Since some of the crucial data related with Indian tax is not available before this deadline, the deputies can experience delay in refund of the tax by the department. This problem is not yet satisfactorily resolved. Some countries grant an extension for filing the return on receiving such a request.

Hardship-9 : Returns of Spouses

Certain countries require spouses accompanying the employees to file overseas returns based on their stay abroad. There is also a possibility of joint filing of return by the employee and the spouse which may attract additional tax deductions. Since there is no such provision in India, the deputies are forced to forego the advantage. Yes, in the erstwhile states under the dominion of Portugal, viz., Goa, Daman, Diu, Dadra and Nagar Haveli system of 'Community of Property' prevails which is similar but not same.

The Worst Hardship-10 : Social Security

When a deputy of an Indian company goes abroad on an assignment for a few years, he has to contribute to the Social Security System, if it is prevalent in that country. It does not benefit him in any way as in most countries the minimum duration of contribution for deriving any benefit is 10 years. When the deputy returns to India before this period, he loses this amount *in toto*. According to an estimate, Indian IT professionals in the US contribute close to $1 billion every year to the Scheme.

Possibly to counter this atrocity, India had, w.e.f. 1.11.08 made it mandatory for International Workers (IWs) to contribute to

Employee Provident Fund and Employee Pension System, as for local workers. Previously, IWs were eligible to withdraw the accumulated EPF after the end of their employment in India. Now IWs can withdraw only after they have reached 58 years of age. The amount is taxable in India if the contributions are for less than 5 years unless such withdrawals are due to total incapacity to work or suffering from prescribed diseases or on grounds specified in the Social Security Agreement (SSA).

SSA is a reciprocal program that prevents double payment and equality of treatment with the host country workers to social security systems between countries. India has signed SSAs with 12 countries : Belgium, Germany, France, Switzerland, Luxembourg, Denmark, Korea, Netherlands, Hungary, Czech Republic, Finland and Norway. We may have missed some countries.

Generally, the PF office has to make payments to the IWs in their home countries. Now, w.e.f. 1.12.11, expatriates coming from SSA countries are allowed to withdraw on completion of the Indian assignment the amount in his bank account directly or through the employer. Moreover, the number of years of service in a SSA country will be combined with the services in India for determining pension eligibility. Expatriates and the employer can file a joint application in Form-19 which does not require any supporting documents. It is not clear whether provident fund contributions made prior to 1.12.11 can be withdrawn.

Government of India will no longer be contributing to the pension scheme of IWs. Currently, out of employer's contribution of 12%, ₹ 541 per month, viz., 8.33% of the salary (capped at ₹ 6,500) goes to the pension fund. The limit of ₹ 6,500 per month as indicated for domestic workers above is not applicable to IWs. This results in a bigger loss for the individuals from non-SSA countries. Even the individuals coming from SSA countries need to be careful as most SSAs only cover pension benefits but not EPF.

Now, huge amounts will get blocked in IWs EPF account for a very long time. Bad! Or is it really bad? Getting around 9% tax-free interest is a great boon.

It has been clarified that on reaching the superannuation age, the amount can be directly credited to a bank abroad. It will no longer be necessary for IWs to hold an Indian bank account to claim the PF withdrawal.

What follows is most scary. A new rule has come into effect from 1.4.11 whereby provident fund accounts inactive for more than 3 years will not earn any interest after this period. Contributions of employees from not SSA countries will surely remain inoperative for more than 3 years in most of the cases.

Good Solutions

To bypass such hardships, many proactive companies in India have got their offices abroad incorporated in that country. Salaries paid from such offices are not taxable in India if the employee happens to be an NRI for tax purposes. The employee can claim exemption if all the following conditions are satisfied —

◆ The employee becomes an NRI from ITA point of view.
◆ The employer transfers his service to his subsidiary incorporated abroad.
◆ The subsidiary in turn places the candidate on the project work and pays him salary directly, without getting reimbursement from the Indian company.
◆ The Indian company stops paying any salary or per diem abroad.

TDS not Applied when Applicable

Where the employer defaults in applying withholding tax when payments are made to non-residents, any interest, royalty, fees for technical services or other sum chargeable is not allowed as an expense if the entity making the payment does not deduct tax in respect of such payments. There was some doubt related with the quantum of disallowance arising out of the expression, 'other sum chargeable'. The Department has clarified vide Circular 3/2015 dt. 12.2.15 that the exposure of the tax withholder in his own income-tax assessment does not exceed the liability of the recipient of the income.

5

Not Permanently Resident in India

A person with a foreign passport, Resident in India for employment of specific duration, irrespective of its duration, or for non-specific duration not longer than 3 years, is defined by FEMA as a 'Person not Permanently Resident in India'.

Such a person has the following privileges or restrictions:

* He can own a normal Resident bank account and not NRI-related NRO, NRE or FCNR accounts. However, while leaving India after employment, he can re-designate such Resident account as NRO to enable him receive his legitimate dues. The debit to the account should be only for the purpose of repatriation abroad subject to the US$ 1 million per FY under the general facility for NRIs discussed in Chapter *Forex Remittances — NRIs*. There should not be any other inflow or credit to this account.

* He may possess forex, without any limit, in the form of currency notes, bank notes and travellers cheques, only provided he had acquired, held or owned it when he was an ROI and had brought it into India through legal channels, including baggage. It is absolutely necessary to fill the Currency Declaration Form (CDF) only if the total forex brought through baggage is above US$ 10,000. Nonetheless, it is advisable for him to file CDF. Similarly, for each subsequent inward remittance he should obtain an Encashment Certificate Form (ECF). Moreover, he should get Form-BCI from the banks while purchasing DDs, MTs, TTs, etc. Only then will he be able to repatriate any unspent forex without any hassles.

* He may purchase or sell foreign securities out of his forex resources abroad.

* He can hold an insurance policy issued by an insurer outside India only if he pays the premium out of his foreign resources.

* As per Notification FEMA 328/RB-2014 dt. 30.12.14, a citizen of a foreign state, Resident in India, being an employee of a foreign company or a citizen of India, employed by a foreign company on deputation to its office, branch, subsidiary, joint venture or group company in India may open, hold and maintain a forex account with a bank outside India and receive his whole salary for the services rendered in India, by credit to such account, provided that income tax is paid on the entire salary accrued in India. 'Company' shall include a 'Limited Liability Partnership'.

Any salary payable for rest or leave period which is both preceded or succeeded by service in India and forms part of the service contract is also regarded as income earned in India. The same rule is applicable to a citizen of India, employed by a foreign company on deputation outside India.

* No tax is payable in India only if the conditions relating to short stay exemption under the relevant tax treaty are met with. For example, under the Indo-US tax treaty, if the US Resident is deputed to India for less than 183 days in an FY and the salary is paid by the US company, such an employee would be taxable only in the US even with respect to salary relating to work carried out in India.

* ADs can allow a citizen of a foreign state other than Pakistan to remit for maintenance of his close relatives abroad, amount up to his net salary after deduction of taxes, contribution to PF, etc. The same facility is extended to a citizen of India, who is on deputation to India of a foreign company. A problem arises when the expatriate comes to India along with his family but still has to meet his personal liabilities abroad. Repatriation options for him then become limited. Remittance of only his salary and not other income in India for meeting his other liabilities is a concern.

* AP (DIR) Circular dt. 22-01-15 has clarified that the facility of remittance of salary outside India available to an employee of a company shall also be available to an employee who is deputed to a group company in India. In addition, the term 'company' referred to in the said regulation will include 'Limited Liability Partnership'.

* An entity in India may remit an amount being its contribution towards the provident, superannuation, pension fund in respect of an expatriate staff (means a person whose funds are maintained outside India by his principal employer outside India) in its employment who is a Resident but not Permanently Resident.

* In case the employee is tax equalised and his Indian tax liability is borne and paid by the employer in India, the employer can pay whole of his salary outside India. TDS is applicable on salary even if the employer is not Resident in India. If any refund becomes due to the employee after he has already left India and has no bank account in India by the time the assessment orders are passed, the refund can be issued to the Indian employer as the tax has been borne by him — Circular 707, dt. 11.7.95.

* Indian tax is levied for services rendered in India even if the employer is outside India and the salary is paid outside India.

* A deputy in India surely continues to earn non-employment income (such as dividends, interest on deposits, etc.) on his investments outside India. Subsequent transfer of the funds from his bank account outside India to his bank account in India will be tax neutral. However, such non-employment income directly remitted to the bank account in India is likely to be taxable in India.

* Most of the deputies outside India earn some side income by way of moonlighting assignments. Such incomes are taxable in India if the individual is a Resident as per ITA definition.

* When the expatriate comes to India as an employee of the Indian company, as opposed to his continuing on the foreign company payroll, keeping his salary outside India is riddled with problems. Indian companies can reimburse the expatriate's salary since it is a current account transaction, it involves a cost to the foreign company. A re-look at these regulations is urgently needed.

Unfortunately, AAR has held on the application made by Caterpillar, a US Company, that the salaries of the non-resident technicians paid in the US by the parent company for work carried out in India would be taxable in India. However, reimbursement of living expenses paid to non-resident technicians in India, by the Indian subsidiary or joint venture company would be exempt from tax u/s 10(14). Very confusing indeed!

MISCELLANEOUS

A foreign national is not permitted to take up employment in India unless he holds an Employment Visa. If he does not, his employment income received in India cannot be remitted abroad. If the period of engagement of such a person is up to 3 months, any other valid visa such as business, tourist, etc., will do.

Generally, extension of a visa is granted by the appropriate Indian Embassy/Indian Consulate abroad. Although an employment visa can be extended by the Ministry of Home Affairs, it is a time-consuming process. A business visa is normally not extended. The foreign national has to go back to his home country and apply to the Indian Embassy there to obtain an employment visa.

Upon arrival in India for employment purposes, one should apply for allotment of a Permanent Account Number (PAN).

While leaving India, at immigration, authorities may require a no objection certificate from the Indian tax authorities. If one does not have such a certificate he can furnish an undertaking, in the prescribed form, from the employer to the effect that the tax payable by employee, if any, shall be paid by the employer.

Registration for Foreigners
As per the provisions of the Registration of Foreigners Rules, 1939, any foreign national visiting India, who either has valid visa for more than 180 days or intending to stay for more than 180 days must register within 14 days of arrival with the 'Foreigners Regional Registration Office' with the following documents —
- Form A.
- Certificate from employer about Indian employment.
- 4 photographs.
- Original passport and Visa (returned after verification), and
- Proof of residence.

Thereafter, a 'Residential permit' will be issued to the foreigner.

To Sum

The considerations which should be kept in mind are — where salary should be delivered; if salary is to be paid outside India, would it be charged back to the Indian entity; current exchange control regulations for delivering salary; corporate tax implications (permanent establishment exposure), withholding tax, the transfer pricing regulations and service tax implications.

It is necessary to put in place a proper secondment structure. We hope that the authorities will smoothen and streamline the Indian tax and also the DTAA provisions to eliminate these hardships.

6

Income Tax

It is necessary for every NRI to have at least a handshake knowledge of the various tax provisions not only related with NRIs but also those related with Residents. He should also have a good insight into the investment avenues to be able to handle Indian assets acquired before leaving the Indian shores and to obtain more mileage from his investible funds.

The following is an attempt in that direction.

The recent FA14 has largely left the tax rates unchanged. However and thankfully, the threshold of income below which tax is not charged has been raised to ₹ 2,50,000 from ₹ 2,00,000.

INCOME TAX RATES

Income Tax Rates — Individuals & HUFs		
Net Taxable Income Slab ₹	Tax at Minimum ₹	Marginal rate %
Up to 2,50,000	Nil	Nil
2,50,001 – 5,00,000	Nil	10
5,00,001 – 10,00,000	25,000	20
Over 10,00,000	1,25,000	30
The tax amount is increased by cess @3%		

The threshold for Resident 'Senior Citizens' and 'Very Senior Citizens' is higher at ₹ 3,00,000 and ₹ 5,00,000 respectively. A senior citizen is an individual who is 60 years of age or more any time during the FY. For the Very Senior Citizens age is 80 or over. This concession is not available to NRIs.

This cess is applicable on normal tax, surcharge, TDS, advance tax, excise duty, custom duty as well as service tax. The 10% surcharge levied by FA13 if the total income of the assessee (after claiming all deductions) for the year exceeds ₹ 1 crore has been increased to 12%. There is a marginal relief, because of which, the total tax shall not exceed the excess over ₹ 1 crore.

₹	₹
Tax on 10,00,000	1,25,000
Tax on 2,20,000	66,000
Total 12,20,000	1,91,000
Cess @ 3%	5,730
Net Tax Payable	1,96,730

Example : Mr. Date, an NRI of 82 years of age has earned a total income, after deductions u/ss 80C, 80D, etc., of ₹ 12,20,000. His tax liability is as worked out in the alongside Table.

Note that the concession for senior citizen or very senior citizen is not available to him since he is an NRIs even though, being 82 years old, is a very senior citizen. Similarly, the concessions available for handicapped persons are not for NRIs.

Now, suppose his total income is ₹ 1 crore 3 lakh. The income tax thereon, without surcharge is ₹ 29,15,000. Surcharge thereon @12% works out at ₹ 3,49,800. Thanks to the marginal relief, his surcharge is limited at ₹ 3,00,000 and therefore, his tax liability works out at ₹ 32,15,000 (= 29,15,000 + 3,00,000). The break-even point where the excess income equals the extra liability works out at ₹ 3,51,660.

WHAT IS INDIAN INCOME

1. Salary paid in India including charges collected as payable for a service rendered in India.

2. Reimbursed by the government to a government employee or citizen of India for rendering any service outside India.

3. Dividend paid by an Indian company outside India to a Resident.

4. Interest payable by the government on all kinds of government securities and saving instruments like bonds.

5. Interest received from a Resident except if the borrower has borrowed money to pursue business activities outside India. This ensures positive cash flow into India.

6. Interest paid by a non-resident to a Resident except when the non-resident has used the money borrowed for business activities in India. This would be to boost investments in India.

7. The concepts of points 4, 5 and 6 are applicable for income generated from royalties, copyrights and fees for technical services.

Commission paid to non-resident for services rendered outside India is not chargeable to tax in India — *[2011] 16taxmann.com219 (Mum. - ITAT).*

Where the amounts are paid for preparatory study in a foreign country to a non-resident for services which are to be utilised in India, such amounts would be deemed to accrue or arise in India. There is no difference between fees for Engineering Services and amounts paid as living allowances and travel allowances — Authority for Advance Rulings in the case of *Steffen, Robertson & Kirsten Consulting Engineers & Scientists* v. *CIT* (1998) 230 ITR 206.

Royalty or Fees for Technical Services

U/s 115A in the case of a non-resident taxpayer, where the total income includes any income by way of Royalty or Fees for Technical Services received under an agreement entered after 31.03.1976 and which is not effectively connected with permanent establishment of the non-resident in India, the tax is payable on the gross amount of such income has been drastically reduced to 10% from @25% by the recent FA15. This action is slated to increase the flow of technology to India.

Sec. 40(ai) stipulates that any interest, royalty, fees for technical services or other sum chargeable under this Act, either payable in India to a non-resident (not being a company or a foreign company) or outside India shall not be allowed as a deduction if there has been a failure in deduction or payment of tax deducted.

INCOME EXEMPT FROM TAX

Some types of income are not treated as taxable income —
Agricultural Income : Sec. 10(1)
This income is tax-free but is aggregated with the other income only for rate, if it exceeds ₹ 5,000. NRIs are not allowed to purchase any agricultural land or farm house but they can continue to hold on to it if acquired before becoming NRI or inherited after becoming NRI. See the example at end of this Chapter for meaning of aggregation for rate.

Life Insurance : Sec. 10(10D)
Sums received under a life insurance policy are completely tax-free. Exceptions are (i) Keyman Insurance of LIC or like products of other insurance companies and (ii) Pension or annuity.

High-premium minimum-risk life policies are similar to deposits or bonds. The premium or other payment made on an insurance policy, other than a contract for a deferred annuity, is limited to 10% of the actual capital sum assured for the exemption. U/s 10(10D), where premium paid in any of the years during the term of the policy, exceeds 10% of the actual capital sum assured, the maturity value received by the policy holder will be fully taxable. However, any sum received under such policy on the death of the policy holder shall continue to be exempt. In calculating the actual capital sum, no account shall be taken of (i) the value of any premiums agreed to be returned or (ii) bonuses received.

Diplomatic Personnel
Remuneration of a foreign citizen (including a PIO) is exempt –
* U/s 10(*6ii*) working as an official of an embassy, high commission, legation, commission, consulate or trade representation of a foreign state or a member of the staff of such official if the corresponding Indian official in that foreign country enjoys a similar exemption. Such officers should not be engaged in any business or profession or employment in India otherwise than as members of such staff.

* U/s 10(6vi) for services rendered to a foreign enterprise during his stay in India provided (i) the foreign enterprise is not engaged in any business or trade in India, (ii) his stay in India does not exceed aggregate period of 90 days in the FY and (iii) such remuneration is not liable to be deducted from income of the employer.

* U/s 10(6xi) if the remuneration is received for training in an undertaking or office owned by (i) the government or (ii) a company owned by the Central or State Government or its subsidiary or (iii) a statutory corporation or (iv) a co-operative society, wholly financed by the Central or State Government.

Allowance or Perquisite Paid by Government : Sec. 10(7)
Any allowances or perquisites, paid or allowed as such outside
India by the Government to a citizen of India for rendering service
outside India is exempt.

Co-operative Technical Programme : Sec. 10(8)
The remuneration of an individual serving in India, received
directly or indirectly, from a foreign Government in connection
with any co-operative technical assistance programme in
accordance with an agreement entered into by the Central
Government and a foreign Government, is exempt from tax.

Remuneration of Consultant : Sec. 10(8A & 8B)
Any remuneration or fee received by a consultant directly or
indirectly out of the funds made available to an international
organisation under a technical assistance grant agreement between
it and the Government of a foreign State is exempt. — Sec. 10(8A).

Similarly, the remuneration received by an employee of the
consultant is also exempt, provided the employee is either not a
citizen of India or is an RNOR — Sec. 10(8B).

Family Member of Employee : Sec. 10(9)
Foreign income of any family member of an employee referred to
in Sec. 10(*8*) or 10(*8A*) or 10(*8B*) referred to above, accompanying
him to India is exempt if the family member is required to pay
income tax (including social security tax) to the foreign Government.

Allowance Received from UNO
Staff Assessment is an amount appropriated by the UN for its own
expenses. This money does not belong to the employee of the UN.
U/s 2 of the UN (Privileges and Immunities) Act, 1947 (read with
Sec. 18 of the Schedule thereto) the rest of the salary and emolument
is exempt from tax in India.

Consequently any pension received by an ex-employee after his
retirement is also exempt from tax — Circular 293 dt. 10.2.81.

The exemption is limited only to the salary and pension received
from UN. The rest of the income will be treated as normal income,
on par with other incomes.

The salaries may have been structured by the UN after factoring in this appropriation of monthly staff assessment. Yes, Staff Assessment is tantamount to deduction at source. However, there are no tax concessions on the Indian income earned from the financial assets in India of the employee. The two are unconnected.

Dividend is Tax-free and Capital Gains Exempt

Both these matters are dealt with in detail in Chapter *Capital Gains*.

DEDUCTIONS

Some specified deductions are available on income from some specified sources. Contributions made out of income chargeable to tax is deductible from gross total income for arriving at the total income on which tax is required to be computed.

Salaries

Professional tax paid, if any, is deductible.

Family Pension

Where any family member of a deceased employee gets a pension from the employer, Sec. 57(*iia*) grants deduction of $33^1/_3\%$ with a ceiling of ₹ 15,000.

Contributions to Specified Schemes : Sec. 80C

Contributions by an individual or HUF to specified schemes u/s 80C qualify for a deduction up to an aggregate ceiling of ₹ 1.5 lakh from gross total income. There are no ceilings on deductions u/s 80C for individual schemes, unless the Rules of the schemes provide for their own limits. These schemes are —

1. Life Insurance Premiums.

2. Unit Linked Insurance Plan of UTI, Dhanaraksha of LIC.

3. Equity-Linked Tax-Saving Schemes.

4. Tuition fees paid, whether at the time of admission or thereafter, to any university, college, school or other educational institution situated within India for the purpose of full-time education of any two children of the individual. However, the eligible amount shall not include any payment towards any development fees or donation

or payment of a similar nature.

The concession is available to each of the parents, if eligible, even in respect of the same child, on their respective payments.

5. Payment by an individual or HUF towards cost of purchase or construction of a residential house (not necessarily self-occupied) in respect of —

* Instalment or part payment due under (i) any self-financing or other schemes of any development authority, housing board or other similar authority engaged in the construction and sale of house property on ownership basis OR (ii) any company or co-operative society of which the assessee is a shareholder or member towards cost of house property allotted to him.

* Repayment of housing loans from (i) Central or State Government, (ii) any bank including a co-operative bank, (iii) deposits in HLA of NHB, (iv) LIC, (v) a housing finance public limited company, (vi) any co-operative society engaged in providing long-term finance for construction or purchase of houses in India, (vii) employer, if the employer is a public company, (viii) PSU, (ix) university and its affiliated colleges, (ix) a local authority or (x) a co-operative society and (xi) an employer being an authority, board, corporation, or any other body established under a Central or State Act.

* Stamp duty, registration fee and other expenses incurred on transfer. This payment need not flow from borrowed funds.

These expenses shall not include :
(i) admission fee, cost of share or initial deposit,

(ii) cost of any addition, alteration, renovation or repairs carried out after the issue of the completion certificate or the house is occupied by the assessee or it has been let out, and

(iii) expenditure where a deduction is separately allowed u/s 24.

Such a house is required to be held for a minimum period of 5 years from the end of the FY in which its possession was taken. If the house is sold earlier, aggregate deduction claimed shall be added to the normal income of the assessee for the year during which the house is sold. The same tenet is applicable when the assessee receives the money back whether by way of refund or otherwise.

6. Specified 5-year term deposit of a scheduled bank eligible for deduction u/s 80C(2xxi).

Contributions to (i) any life insurance company for life cover, (ii) LIC deferred annuity, (iii) Equity-linked Savings Scheme (ELSS) of MFs and (iv) ULIP and Dhanaraksha in the name of spouse and all children, major or minor, married or otherwise (including married daughters), but not parents dependent or not, are also eligible for the deduction. Sums paid or deposited to effect or to keep in force a contract for a deferred annuity is eligible for deduction provided that such contract does not contain a provision for the exercise by the insured of an option to receive a cash payment in lieu of the payment of the annuity. If the premium payment exceeds 10% of the actual capital sum assured, only 10% will be eligible u/s 80C(3).

Where a taxpayer discontinues an LIC policy before premiums for two years have been paid, the deduction allowed during earlier years shall be withdrawn and shall be deemed to be the income of the year in which the policy is discontinued.

In the case of *Life Annuity*, the amount of annuity installments will be treated as *Income from Other Sources*. In the case of *Annuity Certain*, the interest portion of the annuity installment is treated as income. If *Cash Option* is exercised, the difference between the amount of cash option received and the total amount of premiums paid is treated as taxable income.

Life insurance policies or deferred annuities taken in the name of spouse or any child, major or minor, even a married daughter by an individual are eligible for the deduction. Same is the case for such instruments taken in the name of any member of HUF by an HUF.

The aggregate deduction from income chargeable to tax from all such schemes has a ceiling of ₹ 1,50,000.

Limit on Deductions u/s 80D Enhanced — Mediclaim

For obvious reasons, health insurance on self from an Indian insurer is not useful to NRIs. However, they can claim the deduction on such insurance taken for their family members in India.

The ceiling on deduction on health insurance premia paid, and also on expenses incurred on preventive health check-up, by an individual for himself and his family members has been raised from ₹ 15,000 to ₹ 20,000. The additional deduction on the health of his parents has also been raised from ₹ 15,000 to ₹ 20,000. In both these cases, if the insured person happens to be a senior citizen, the deduction has been raised from ₹ 20,000 to ₹ 30,000. However, the aggregate deduction available to any individual has been limited to ₹ 30,000. Similarly aggregate deduction for health insurance premia and medical expenditure incurred in respect of parents has also been limited to ₹ 30,000.

A similar deduction is also available to HUF for any of its member.

Loan for Studies Abroad : Sec. 80E

Deduction of interest on loan taken by the student or his parents, the spouse, or his legal guardian for full time studies in all fields of studies (including vocational studies) pursued after Senior Secondary Examination from a bank or an approved financial and charitable institution is available for 8 successive years.

If someone takes a loan from his employer for higher studies, he will not be entitled to the deduction, unless the employer himself falls within the category of an approved source.

Donations : Sec. 80G

An assessee is entitled to a deduction of 50% and in some cases 100% of donations made to approved charitable purposes. Some of these donations attract a ceiling of 10% of the total income of the assessee, as reduced by the amount deductible under any other provision of Chapter VI-A.

Such donations must be in the form of money and not in kind, unless the donor is the manufacturer of the items donated — *(178ITR171 Saraswati Industrial Syndicate).*

Any payment exceeding ₹ 10,000 shall only be allowed as a deduction only if such sum is paid by any mode other than cash.

Donations to Political Parties : 80GGC
Donations to an electoral trust or a political parties are eligible for 100% deduction, provided the donation is not made in cash.

Interest on Savings Bank Accounts : Sec. 80TTA
A deduction up to ₹ 10,000 is available in respect of any interest on a savings account of an individual or HUF (but not a firm, AOP or BOI) with a banking company or a co-operative society engaged in carrying on the business of banking (including a co-operative land mortgage bank or a co-operative land development bank.

TDS @30.9% is applicable on interest on NRO accounts. Now, interest up to ₹ 10,000 from NRO savings is deductible. This gives an impression that where such interest is under ₹ 10,000, no TDS is applicable. This is not so. Refer Chapter *Tedious TDS*.

It is earnestly hoped that CBDT takes a corrective action.

Interest on Housing Loans Deductible u/s 24
Refer Chapter *Immovable Property*.

ADVANCE TAX

All taxpayers are required to pay advance tax in spite of the fact that most of their income is subject to TDS.

If the tax payable for the year is ₹ 10,000 or more advance tax is payable without having to submit any estimate or statement of income to the ITO in 3 installments during each FY as follows :

On or before	15th September	:	30% of estimated tax.
	15th December	:	60% less tax already paid.
	15th March	:	100% less tax already paid.

TDS is treated as advance tax paid.

TAX RETURNS

U/s 139(1), returns must be filed if the income chargeable to tax is over the tax threshold, even if it comes below the threshold after claiming deductions under Chapter VI-A. This is so, even if the TDS covers the tax payable liability.

Where a Resident individual has any asset (including financial interest in any entity) located outside India or signing authority in any account (bank account, demat account, etc.) located outside India, filing of tax return is compulsory irrespective of whether such individual has taxable income below the threshold or not.

Expatriate employees and their accompanying family members who come into India generally qualify to be RNORs for the first 2 to 3 years. Such individuals may have to provide details of their overseas investments and bank details even though their overseas income is not taxable in India. Accompanying family may not even have taxable income in India, yet they have the filing obligation.

Though NRIs are not mandatorily required to possess PAN, it is desirable to have one. This subject is covered in detail in Chapter, *PAN is PAIN*.

The due date for furnishing the returns is 30th September for (i) companies and (ii) assessees as well as working partners of a firm whose accounts are required to be audited. For other assessees the date continues to be 31st July.

Sec. 288B requires any amount payable and the amount of refund due, to be rounded off to the nearest multiple of ₹ 10.

Penalty is imposable if the returns are not filed before the end of the next FY. Consequently, it is okay even if the returns are not filed by the due date if correct taxes are paid. However, late filing suffers from an embargo on carry forward of loss earned during the current year, from business (speculative or otherwise), capital loss and loss from the activity of owning and maintaining race horses. The ITO has no powers to condone such a lapse. Already carried forward losses from the earlier years suffer no damage.

Sec. 139(9) asserts that the return of income shall be regarded as defective unless the tax together with interest, if any, payable in accordance with Sec. 140A has been paid on or before the date of furnishing of the return. The AO may intimate the defect to the assessee and give him an opportunity to rectify it within 15 days. The return shall be treated as invalid if it is not rectified within the time allowed.

Filing Returns through Representative Assessee

Sec. 163 defines such a person as any person in India —
  (a) who is employed by or on behalf of the NRI; or
  (b) who has any business connection with the NRI; or
  (c) from or through whom the NRI is in receipt of any income whether directly or indirectly; or
  (d) who is a trustee of the NRI; and
  (e) any other person who has acquired by means of transfer a capital asset in India.

No person is to be treated as an agent of an NRI unless he has had an opportunity of being heard by the Assessing Officer as to his liability to be treated as such. An NRI may also appoint an authorised representative to act as his agent.

Payment of Income Tax through Internet

Some banks, particularly IDBI and ICICI have extended the facility of on-line payment of income-tax to their account holders who are registered for net banking with the bank. All that is required is to log on to www.incometaxindia.gov.in or http://tin.tin.nsdl.com and follow the instructions. After payment, account holders would be able to generate the taxpayers' counterfoil containing the Challan Identification Number (CIN). Other banks are likely to follow.

Business Process Outsourcing

Circular 1/2004 dt. 2.1.04 deals with NRIs carrying on manufacture and sale of goods or merchandise or provision of services outside India and who outsource some of its incidental activities. A typical activity is conclusion of contracts and procurement of orders (which enable the core activities to be carried on abroad) to an IT-enabled entity in India, which constitutes a permanent establishment of the non-resident principal. The insignificant profit attributable to the conclusion of such contracts or procurement of such orders is difficult to determine and can be considered to be embedded in the income of the permanent establishment taxable in India. The only condition is that the price charged for such services by the permanent establishment should be at arm's length and related with fair market price. In such a situation, therefore, no income shall separately accrue or arise or be deemed to accrue or arise to the non-resident principal in India.

Advance Ruling

An NRI has been given a special privilege by Sec. 245Q of seeking for an advance ruling on subjects which pertain to determination of any question of law or fact, tax liability of NRI arising out of a transaction undertaken or proposed to be undertaken by a Resident or computation of total income in respect of an issue pending before any tax authority or Tribunal.

Application can be filed before the Authority for Advance Rulings, accompanied by a fee of ₹ 2,500. A person who is an NRI in the previous year preceding the financial year in which the application is filed is eligible to seek the ruling.

Applications will not be entertained for (i) determination of fair market value of property, (ii) any transaction which is designed *prima facie* for avoidance of income tax and (iii) matter already pending before any income-tax authority, tribunal or court.

The application cannot be rejected merely because the Appellate Tribunal, in another case, has decided a similar issue in favour of the revenue — *Burmah Castrol Plc (2008) 174 Taxman 95 (AAR - New Delhi)*.

U/s 245S, the advance ruling shall be binding only on the applicant and on the Department in respect of the specific transaction, unless there is a change in law or facts of the case.

Application for advance ruling cannot be admitted if applicant has already filed return of income — *[2011] 16 taxmann.com 195 (AAR - New Delhi)*.

How to Compute Tax

The example on following page elucidates the method of computing tax. Note that if there were no agricultural income the tax on normal income of ₹ 3,50,000 would be only ₹ 10,000. The agricultural income is actually, not tax-free. This is in addition to the agricultural tax charged by some of the State Governments.

	₹	₹	₹
Business Income	4,17,000	4,17,000	
House Property			
Self Occupied	NIL		
Property Given on Rent	1,50,000		
Less : Interest on Loan	1,20,000	30,000	
Capital Gains			
Short-term on debt-based MF		11,000	
Other Sources			
Interest on Bank Deposits	42,000	42,000	
Total Gross Income		5,00,000	
Deductions			
Equity Linked Saving Scheme	1,30,000		
Housing Loan Repayment	50,000		
	1,80,000		
Limited to		1,50,000	
Taxable Income		**3,50,000**	
Agricultural income			
Non-agricultural Income	3,50,000		
Add : Agricultural Income	3,00,000		
TOTAL Income	6,50,000		
Tax on ₹ 6,50,000		55,000	
Agricultural Income	3,00,000		
Add : Threshold	2,50,000		
	5,50,000		
Less : Tax on ₹ 5,50,000		35,000	20,000
Long-term Capital Gains			
Total Sale Proceeds	1,50,000		
Less : Indexed Cost	90,000		
Capital Gains		60,000	
Contribution to Sec. 54EC		50,000	
		10,000	
Tax on Capital Gains of ₹ 10,000 @ 20%			2,000
Sub-total			22,000
Add Cess @ 3%			660
Tax Payable			**22,660**
Less : Advance tax Paid		17,000	
TDS		5,000	22,000
Tax Liability			**660**

7

Wealth Tax

Wealth tax is virtually non-existent in India. Tax is levied only on 'unproductive assets' and therefore investments in shares, debentures, MFs, Banks, etc., are exempt from wealth tax. Moreover, wealth tax is charged @1% of the amount by which the net wealth exceeds ₹ 30 lakh. The cess of 3% is not applicable on wealth tax.

This above para has been extracted from our last edition. The authorities realised that the cost of collection is not worth the effort and therefore, the recent FA15 has abolished the wealth tax!

The other reason presented is that this action is to counterbalance increase in the surcharge on super rich directly from 10% to 12%. Unfortunately, this hike in the surcharge takes the maximum marginal tax rate at 33.99% to 34.608%, higher by 0.618%. It is this maximum marginal tax rate which is applicable on —

Sec. 115-O   : Distributed profits of domestic companies
Sec. 115-QA : Buy-back of shares by domestic companies
Sec. 115-R   : Distributed income to Unit holders, and
Sec. 115 TA : Distributed income by Securitisation trusts.

Consequently, the exchequer is slated to get more revenue from the poor you and me through the above mentioned Sections rather than the super rich through surcharge.

A direct outcome of this provision is that the stated intention of the government to increase the investment in financial assets rather than physical assets (gold, real estate, etc.) will surely take a beating.

Yes, wealth tax is abolished but the Income Tax Returns Form will be suitably modified to capture the information relating to the relevant assets. Consequently, we will have to give this detail even when the total value of these assets owned by us is less than ₹ 30 lakh. And God forbid! If it is found that value was over ₹ 30 lakh in the past ....

Only the following assets were considered for wealth tax —

* Any building or land appurtenant thereto used as residential, commercial, guest or a farm house situated within 25 kilometres from the local limit of any municipality, but does not include —

  (a) Residential house of a company allotted to its employee or a whole-time director with a gross annual salary of under ₹ 10 lakh.

  (b) Houses forming part of stock-in-trade.

  (c) Houses used for his business or profession.

  (d) Residential property let out for minimum of 300 days in a year.

  (e) Commercial establishments and complexes.

  (f) One house or part of a house or a plot of land not exceeding 500 square meters, belonging to an individual or an HUF.

* Motor cars, yachts, boats, aircrafts and also jewellery, bullion, furniture, utensils or any other article made wholly or partly of precious metals other than cars used in the business of running them on hire or as stock-in-trade used for commercial purposes.

* Cash in hand in excess of ₹ 50,000 of individuals and HUFs and in other cases, amounts not recorded in the books of account. Note that current/savings account balances are not cash in hand.

* Urban Land.

* Archaeological collections, drawings, paintings, sculptures and any work of art.

* Any asset, including financial interest in any entity located outside India.

'Net Wealth' was the aggregate value on the valuation date of all these assets in excess of the debts outstanding on such assets. It is necessary for us to declare the details related with all such assets through the revised Returns Forms related with income tax.

Take care.

8

Gift Tax Has Come Back

FA98 had deleted Gift Tax Act (GTA) which charged gift tax to the donor. Good! FA04 amended Sec. 56 of Income Tax Act and charged income tax to donee. Bad!!

Accordingly, if an individual or an HUF receives from any person any sum of money and/or some specified assets without any or with some inadequate consideration, the aggregate value of which exceeds ₹ 50,000, the whole of such amount will be treated as *Income from Other Sources*. If it does not exceed ₹ 50,000, it will not be treated as income.

Consequently if the amount of gift received by the donee from all the sources is ₹ 50,000 or less, there is no tax. However, if such gift is higher even by a small margin, The entire amount of gift is to be treated as income of the donee.

The specified assets are only — 1. Land and building. 2. Shares and securities. 3. Jewellery and bullion. 4. Archaeological collections. 5. Drawings, paintings, sculptures or any work of art.

Movable property and immovable property will be considered at its fair market value and stamp duty value respectively. If it is received with inadequate consideration, the difference between the fair market value or stamp duty, and the inadequate consideration shall be taxed as the income of the recipient, if it exceeds ₹ 50,000.

Gifts received from following sources are exempt from the tax —
(a) any relative; or
(b) on the occasion of the marriage of the individual; or
(c) under a Will or by way of inheritance; or
(d) in contemplation of death of the payer;
(e) from any local authority;

(f) from any fund or foundation or university or other educational institution or hospital or other medical institution or any trust or institution referred to in Sec. 10(23); and

(g) from any charitable trust or institution.

For ITA 'relative' means (differs from FEMA definition for which refer Chapter *General Provisions*) —

(i)   spouse of the individual;

(ii) brother or sister of the individual;

(iii) brother or sister of spouse of the individual;

(iv) brother or sister of either parents of the individual;

(v)   any lineal ascendant or descendant of the individual; and

(vi) any lineal ascendant or descendant of the spouse of the individual; and

(vii) spouse of the persons referred in clauses (ii) to (vi).

Definition of relative is a paradox. Suppose I am your mother's brother. In that case, I am your relative but you are not my relative since you are my sister's daughter. Yes, I am your relative but you are not my relative. Strange!.

More strangely, and for no particular reason, SCRA and Companies Act define 'relative' separately and not consistent either with each other or with ITA.

Clubbing Provision

Yes, the GTA was omitted but not the clubbing provisions which require income and wealth from assets transferred directly or indirectly without adequate consideration to minor children, the spouse (otherwise than in connection with an agreement to live apart) or daughter-in-law will continue to be deemed income and wealth of the transferor. Same is the case when assets are held by a person or an AOP for benefit of the assessee, the spouse, daughter-in-law and minor children.

Gifts to a daughter-in-law are clubbed but not gifts to a son-in-law. Male chauvinistic law makers indeed!

The entire income of a minor is to be included in the income of that parent whose total income (excluding the income includible) is higher. Where the marriage of the parents does not subsist, the income of the minor will be included in the income of that parent who maintains the minor child. Once the income is included in the hands of one of the parents based on the above criteria, it shall continue to be included, even if the criteria change, unless the AO is satisfied that it is necessary to do so. Where the income of an individual includes the income of his minor children, an exemption up to ₹ 1,500 in respect of each minor child can be claimed by the individual u/s 10(32).

Where a minor is admitted to the benefits of a partnership firm, the value of the interest of such minor in the firm shall be included in the net income of the parent of the minor.

All the income of a physically or mentally handicapped minor child is directly assessed in the hands of the child. Again a minor earning income by way of manual work or an activity involving application of his skill, talent or specialised knowledge and experience, is directly assessed in the hands of the child. Unfortunately, the income arising from all his investments suffer clubbing.

Income on Income
The main advantage of gifts accrues from the fact that in the case of spouse or daughter-in-law, income on income is not clubbed. If the spouse has no other income, no tax is payable unless the interest on interest crosses the minimum tax threshold of ₹ 2.50 lakh. In other words, instead of investing in your own name it is better to give a gift, pay tax on the income arising from the original corpus gifted and keep on building a corpus for your spouse or daughter-in-law. Yes, it is cumbersome to keep track of what is clubbable and what is not but it may be worth the effort.

Some Useful Tips
1. Contributions to PPF standing in the name of spouse or minor children attract clubbing. The interest is tax-free, whether clubbed or otherwise. NRIs cannot open a PPF account in their own names, but if the spouse or minor child is a Resident, surely the NRI can contribute to accounts in their names and claim deduction u/s 80C.

2. Income of minors up to ₹ 1,500 is free from clubbing. More the number of minors, better is the benefit. Forget family planning.

3. Savings made by the wife out of household expenses given by her husband would be separate property of the wife. Any income arising therefrom is not aggregated with the income of the husband.

4. Give gifts to close Resident relatives to take advantage of higher interest obtainable from schemes which are not available to NRIs.

5. Before the GTA was abolished, aggregate gifts over ₹ 30,000 in an FY was taxable at the penal rate of 30% and therefore, it was a wise strategy to give a gift up to ₹ 30,000 per year and build up a corpus for the children and spouse. Now that you can give need-based gifts as and when they arise, without attracting any tax, there is no need to build a corpus and take the risk of the child running away (and worse, the spouse eloping) with your money.

Do not Purchase House in Wife's Name
Purchasing a house in the name of the wife by applying your own funds means that you are using her as a name-lender and this is a 'benami transaction'. This is illegal. It can be made legal by gifting the money to the wife to enable her purchase the property in her name. An alternative is to gift your house to her, but this will attract stamp duty and registration charges. It is also necessary for you to follow the procedure for gifting. The utility, if any, is lost because of the clubbing provisions.

Moreover, if you take a housing loan in your name, you would not be entitled to claim any tax benefits associated with the loan, because the house belongs to the wife. Further, once you have gifted any repatriable asset, whether cash or the house, you have lost the right to repatriate it.

In short, do not buy a house property (or any other asset) in the name of the wife. The tax concessions on housing loan can be availed only by the person who owns the house.

Power of Attorney (PoA)
The same tenet holds for buying housing properties through PoA. This system is quite prevalent in Delhi and Haryana and is slowly percolating to other parts of India. It has the advantage of avoiding the hefty stamp duty. We do not approve this route because —

EMIs paid by a PoA holder are on behalf of the original allottee and therefore, the PoA holder cannot claim deduction of interest u/s 24 and capital repayment u/s 80C. The original allottee cannot claim these benefits because he has not incurred the costs.

Gift Procedure

To safeguard against any hassles, it is advisable to follow proper gift procedure. All that is required is an offer by the donor and acceptance thereof by the donee in black and white. The donee should request the donor for a gift and then the donor should remit the amount to the donee. Alternatively, the donor can offer the gift. In either case, it is necessary for the donee to accept the gift in writing (may be through a thank you note). Only then it would be considered as a gift in India. It is preferable to mention the relationship between the donor and the donee.

Note that the Department has a right to inquire into the genuineness of the gift to ensure that it is not a payment made for any hawala or smuggling transaction or services rendered.

It is better to prepare a gift deed and get it registered (with related stamp duty) but such a precaution is normally needed in the case of high-value gifts, particularly those of real estate.

9

Bank Accounts

RBI does not involve itself directly in routine operations and has passed on its own responsibility to monitor and control to the ADs and kept the regulatory authority with itself.

Opening of accounts by individuals, entities of Pakistan nationality or ownership and entities of Bangladesh ownership requires prior RBI approval. All such requests may be referred to the Chief General Manager-in-Charge, Foreign Exchange Department, Foreign Investment Division, Reserve Bank of India, Central Office, Mumbai - 400 001. Circular AP (DIR) 82 dt. 11.2.13 has allowed ADs to open NRO accounts of any individual of Bangladesh nationality if the bank ensures that the individual is holding valid visa and valid residential permit. This relaxation does not apply to entities of Bangladesh ownership.

COMMON FEATURES

Opening Accounts

Documents required to open any new account are Passport (Copy of Name, Address and Photo pages along with issue and expiry page). If it is an Indian passport, copy of Visa/resident permit is also necessary. In case the place of birth is outside India, OCI card is required, irrespective of the nature of the passport along with as many as the following self-attested documents, either original or its notorised copy —

1. Electricity/Landline telephone bill – Not over 3 months old.

2. Latest 3 months transaction of passbook with a cancelled cheque.

3. Banker's verification, only from a scheduled commercial Indian bank required on bank letterhead with bank employee name, signature, employee code and designation.

4. Driving licence with name, address and photo pages along with issue and expiry date pages.

5. In case of Merchant Navy NRI persons, Mariner's declaration or certified copy of CDC (Continuous Discharge Certificate) is to be submitted.

In rare cases where there is a difficulty in submitting such details, a person can open a Basic Savings Bank Deposit Account (BSBDA) which is available at all the scheduled commercial banks, including foreign banks having branches in India. It does not have a mandatory minimum balance. There is no cap on number of deposits but withdrawals are capped at four a month, including withdrawals through ATMs. A BSBDA holder is not eligible to open any other savings account. Anyone desiring opening such an account will do well to carefully check the rate (large amounts attract higher rates) and its structure of different banks.

Interest Rates
Banks are free to determine their interest rates on both savings and term deposits under NRE and NRO accounts but in no case, such rates should be higher than those on comparable domestic rupee deposits. Circular DBOD.Dir.BC. 39 /13.03.00/2013-14 dt. 14.8.13 has allowed banks to offer interest rates without any ceiling on NRE deposits (but not on NRO) with maturity of 3 years and above. Anyone desiring opening an account will do well to carefully check the rate and structure of interest of different banks.

Interest is paid at quarterly or longer rests. In the case of SB, interest is calculated on daily basis and credited regularly whether the account is operative or not.

On deposits repayable in less than 3 months or where the terminal quarter is incomplete, interest is paid proportionately for the actual number of days reckoning the year at 365 days. Some banks reckon the year at 366 days in a leap year. While banks are free to adopt their methodology, they should intimate this to their prospects.

If a Fixed Deposit Receipt matures and the amount is left unclaimed, it attracts savings bank rate of interest.

Conversion of NRE into FCNR(B) deposit and *vice versa* before maturity would be subject to the penal provisions.

In the case of conversion of NRE or FCNR term deposits into RFC account, the bank should not levy any penalty. If such a deposit has not run for a minimum period of 1 year, the bank may, at its discretion, pay interest at a rate not exceeding the rate payable on savings deposits held in RFC accounts.

A bank should allow premature withdrawal of a term deposit. It can determine its own penal interest. Interest on the deposit for the period that it has remained with the bank will be paid at the rate applicable to that period and not at the contracted rate. No interest is payable where premature withdrawal takes place before completion of the minimum period prescribed. However, the bank, at its discretion, may disallow premature withdrawal of large deposits held by entities other than individuals and HUFs. The depositors should be made aware of the applicable deposit rate, penal rate and also possibility of disallowing premature withdrawal of large deposits while accepting such deposits.

Joint Accounts
A Resident PoA holder—

(a) Can make all local payments in rupees including payments for eligible investments through NRO accounts.

(b) Can effect remittance outside India through normal banking channels, funds out of the balances in NRE and FCNR accounts to the NRI's account abroad provided specific powers for the purpose have been given to that effect, and

(c) Shall not make payment by way of gift to a Resident or transfer funds from one NRE/NRO account to another account of a different person.

An easier structure in terms of a Letter of Authority (LoA) of banks can be used for allowing the LoA holder to withdraw funds for local payments. Better still is to have a Resident joint holder.

An NRI can have Resident close relative/s to be joint holder on 'former or survivor' basis. However, the relative shall operate the account as if he is a PoA holder during the life time of the NRI— Circular GSR 893(E), dt. 25.9.12

A Resident can include NRI close relative as joint holder in his resident bank accounts including EEFC/RFC on 'former or survivor' basis though nomination facility is available.

However, such a joint holder was not eligible to operate the account during the life time of the Resident. Now, Circular AP (DIR) 87 dt. 9.1.14 has allowed an NRI close relative to be a joint holder on 'either or survivor' basis for all types of resident accounts including savings bank account subject to :

(a) It will be treated as resident bank account for all purposes.
(b) Cheques, instruments, remittances, cash, card or any other proceeds belonging to the NRI shall not be eligible for credit to this account.
(c) The NRI shall operate such account only for and on behalf of the Resident for domestic payment and not for creating any beneficial interest for himself.
(d) Where the NRI becomes a joint holder with more than one Resident in such account, such NRI should be the close relative of all the resident bank account holders.
(e) Where the non-resident account holder becomes the sole survivor of such an account, the NRI shall inform the bank and get the account categorised as NRO.
(f) While extending this facility the AD bank should satisfy itself about the actual need for such a facility.

At the request of all the joint account holders, the bank may, at its discretion, allow deletion of existing or add the name of another person as a joint holder. In no case the term and the aggregate amount of the deposit should undergo any change. This should not be construed as premature withdrawal of the term deposit.

Deceased Depositor
In the case of current account of a deceased individual depositor or sole proprietorship concern, interest should be paid from the date of death of the depositor, till the date of payment to the claimant at interest rate applicable to SB as on the date of payment.

In the case of an NRE, when the claimants are Residents, the deposit on maturity should be treated as a domestic rupee deposit and interest should be paid for the subsequent period at a rate applicable to a domestic deposit of similar maturity.

In the case of a term deposit standing in the name of (i) a deceased individual depositor, or (ii) two or more joint depositors, where one of the depositors has died, interest should be paid —

(a) At the contracted rate on the maturity of the deposit.

(b) If the deposit is claimed before maturity, interest should be paid at the applicable rate for the period elapsed prevailing on the date of placement of the deposit, without charging penalty.

(c) In the case of death after maturity, interest should be paid at a RFC SB rate operative on the date of maturity from the date of maturity till the date of payment.

(d) If on request, the bank agrees to split the amount of term deposit and issues two or more receipts, no penalty should be levied provided the period and aggregate amount of the deposit do not undergo any change.

(e) If the claimant is a Resident, the maturity proceeds may be converted into Indian rupees on the date of maturity and interest be paid for the subsequent period at the rate applicable to a deposit of similar maturity under the domestic deposit scheme.

(f) In the case of NRO, the amount due or payable to an ROI nominee shall be credited to his NRO account. If the nominee is a Resident, it shall be credited to his resident account.

(g) A Resident nominee can remit funds outside India for meeting the liabilities abroad of the deceased account holder.

TAX ON NRE & FCNR INTEREST

The interest on NRE is tax-free u/s 10(4ii) of ITA. Schedule-II (10) of the FEMR states, "When an account holder becomes a person Resident in India, deposits may be allowed to continue till maturity at the contracted rate of interest, if so desired by him. However, . . . such deposits shall be treated as resident deposits from the date of return of the account holder to India."

Sec. 10(15fa) of ITA exempts interest "by a scheduled bank to a non-resident or to a person who is not ordinarily resident within

the meaning of Sec. 6(6) on deposits in foreign currency . . . ."
FCNR and RFC are the two accounts covered by this Section.

Consequently, from the date of returning to India permanently, both NRE and FCNR would be treated as resident accounts, even if they are not redesignated as such. These can run up to their maturity but the interest on NRE becomes taxable from the date of the return whereas the FCNR interest is tax-free as long as the holder remains an RNOR. Alternatively, both NRE and FCNR can be converted into RFC without any penalty. RFC interest is taxable in the hands of Residents but not RNORs but it suffers TDS.

Miscellaneous
ADs can convert Indian Rupees into the designated forex at the clean TT selling rate and convert forex at clean TT buying rates ruling on the date.

NRO and RFC interest suffers TDS @30.9% even though interest on RFC is tax-free only for RNORs and not for Residents.

NRE ACCOUNT

The account may be opened only by the NRI himself. The AD should obtain an undertaking from the NRI that he would intimate the AD when he becomes a Resident.

The term of NRE FD is normally 1 to 3 years. However, banks are allowed to accept deposits up to 5 years provided the rate of interest is not higher than the one applicable to 3 years deposits.

Renewal of Overdue Deposits
All aspects concerning renewal of overdue deposits may be decided by individual banks subject to the customers being notified of the terms and conditions of renewal including interest rates, at the time of acceptance of deposit. The policy should be non-discretionary and non-discriminatory.

Permitted Credits
◆ Remittances to India in any permitted currency through normal banking channels.
◆ Foreign currency notes or coins tendered by account holder during

his temporary visit to India, provided the amount is declared on a Currency Declaration Form (CDF), where applicable, and tendered to the AD in person by the account holder himself.

◆ Cheques drawn on his forex account, travellers' cheques or bank drafts issued outside India payable in any permitted forex and even in INR for which reimbursement is receivable in forex. These should be deposited by the account holder in person during his temporary visit to India.

◆ Transfers from other NRE/FCNR accounts.

◆ Transfer from NRO up to US$ 1 million per FY. Refer Chapter, *Forex Remittances NRIs.*

◆ AP (DIR) Circular 21 dt. 23.9.03 has allowed the balances in the EEFC and RFCD accounts to be transferred to his NRE account at the option of the account holder consequent upon a Resident becoming an NRI.

◆ Interest accruing on the funds held in the account.

◆ Maturity proceeds and interest/dividend on government securities and MFs.

◆ Refund of share/debenture subscriptions to new issues of Indian companies or portion thereof.

◆ Refund of application or earnest money made by the house building agencies on account of non-allotment of flat/plot, together with interest, if any (net of income tax payable thereon).

◆ Cancellation of deals for purchase of residential or commercial property.

◆ Demand draft or banker's cheque issued against encashment of forex supported by encashment certificate.

◆ Current income like rent, dividend, pension, interest, etc.

◆ Sale proceeds of assets including immovable property acquired out of rupee or foreign currency funds or by way of inheritance.

Permitted Debits

◆ Remittances outside India of current income like rent, dividend, pension, interest, etc., net of applicable taxes.

◆ Local disbursements.

◆ Transfer to NRE accounts of the account holder or any other person, if eligible.

◆ Investment in shares, securities, CPs, or immovable property.
◆ Any other transaction covered under general or special permission granted by the RBI.

ADs may at their discretion allow for a period of not more than two weeks, overdrawing in NRE SB accounts, up to a limit of ₹ 50,000 subject to the condition that such overdrawing together with the interest payable thereon are cleared within two weeks by inward remittances through normal banking channels or by transfer of funds from other NRE/FCNR accounts in India.

FCNR ACCOUNT

FCNR(A) scheme was introduced in 1975, where the foreign exchange risk was borne by the government of India. It was withdrawn in August 1994 in view of its quasi-fiscal costs to the government. The FCNR(B) was introduced w.e.f. 15.5.93. To begin with, the FCNR(B) scheme was applicable to deposits accepted in four currencies, viz., Pound Sterling, US Dollar, Deutsche Mark and Japanese Yen. On 4.11.00 it was extended to cover EURO while deposits in Deutsche Mark were accepted only up to 31.12.01. Maturity proceeds after this date on deposits in Deutsche Mark were payable only in EURO. On 26.7.05 the scheme was extended to cover Canadian and Australian dollars.

AP (DIR) Circular 36 dt. 19.10.11 has permitted opening of FCNR(B) deposits in any permitted foreign currency which is freely convertible. This is indeed a good move since earlier, NRIs/PIOs from other countries had to convert their remittances into one of the six permissible currencies while depositing and repatriating. This incurred exchange/swap losses and also bank charges.

FCNR may be opened only as term deposit for (a) 1 year and above but less than 2 years, (b) 2 years and above but less than 3 years, (c) 3 years and above but less than 4 years, (d) 4 years and above but less than 5 years and (e) 5 years only. No SB or RD please.

Banks are free to determine the interest rates (fixed or floating with an interest reset of 6 months) subject to prescribed ceiling.

On deposits of maturities, 1 year to less than 3 years interest shall be paid within the ceiling rate of LIBOR/SWAP plus 200 basis points for the respective currency and corresponding maturity. On deposits with maturity of 3-5 years it will be plus 300 basis points. On floating rate deposits, interest shall be paid within the ceiling of SWAP rates for the respective currency/maturity plus 200 bps/ 300 bps as the case may be. For floating rate deposits, the interest reset period shall be six months.

The interest on the deposits should be paid on the basis of 360 days to a year and be calculated and paid at intervals of 180 days each and thereafter for the remaining actual number of days. The depositor has the option to receive the interest at maturity with compounding effect and also to get the interest credited to any NRI-related accounts, existing or to be opened afresh.

Overdue FCNR Deposits

Banks have discretion to renew an overdue deposit or a portion thereof provided the overdue period from the date of maturity till the date of renewal (both days inclusive) does not exceed 14 days. The interest rate on renewal should be the appropriate rate for the period of renewal as prevailing on the date of maturity or when the depositor seeks renewal, whichever is lower. If the overdue period exceeds 14 days and if the depositor renews a portion or whole amount as a fresh deposit, banks may fix their own interest rate for the overdue period. However, if the deposit is withdrawn before completion of minimum stipulated period after renewal, banks are free to withdraw the overdue interest paid.

Other Conditions

The terms and conditions as applicable to NRE deposits in respect of joint holdings, opening accounts during temporary visit, operation by PoA/LoA, debits/credits, loans, overdrafts, change of Residential status, repatriation of funds, transfer of EEFC/RFC balances, etc., shall apply *mutatis mutandis* to FCNR deposits. Moreover, as per AP (DIR) Circular 57 dt. 18.5.07, remittance of the maturity proceeds of FCNR deposits to third parties outside India is permitted if the transaction is specifically authorised by the account holder and the AD is satisfied about its bona fides.

Inland Movement of Funds
Any inland movement of funds for opening these accounts as well as for repatriation outside India will be free of inland exchange or commission. RBI has now allowed remittance of the maturity proceeds of FCNR to third parties outside India, provided the transaction is specifically authorised by the account holder and the AD is satisfied about the bonafide of the transaction.

Withdrawal from FCNR
Such withdrawal faces 2 hurdles — 1. It is an FD from which cash payouts are not made as a rule. 2. The branches do not have any forex and will direct you to its HO. You may be able to withdraw cash up to a limited amount from your NRE account with the branch though you may have to collect the forex from their HO. However, traveller's cheques can be obtained without any limit.

Taxability of Interest in the Host Country
The interest on NRE and FCNR is free from Indian taxes in the hands of NRI. However, you will have to check on the taxability of this income in your host country.

In the USA all the banks and financial institutions report to the IRS (income tax authority of USA) all the interest or dividend income earned by any person. IRS has the right to ask for such information only from Indian branches of banks incorporated in the USA. Normally, it cannot do so from the Indian banks, such as all the nationalised banks, UTI Bank, ICICI Bank, HDFC Bank, etc. However, in rare cases, it might ask and then the answer will have to be provided by the banks. The bank will provide the statement of interest income if you ask for it.

NRO ACCOUNT

This is the only so called 'non-repatriable' account. In practice, it is repatriable — well, almost. Interest is remittable subject to tax compliance and corpus is also remittable up to US$ 1 million per FY under some conditions. Refer Chapter *Forex Remittances, NRIs*.

It is mandatory for a Resident to inform his bank within a *reasonable time* when he becomes an NRI as per FEMA. What is reasonable is not defined. In practice, the number of persons who fail to inform their banks is so large that the default is mostly overlooked, unless the authorities suspect foul play. On receipt of the information from the NRI, the bank will redesignate his accounts as NRO.

On the other hand, when an NRI becomes a Resident, his NRO account should be redesignated as resident account. Where the account holder is only on a temporary visit to India, the account can continue as NRO.

NRO can be opened and maintained with ADs or some designated post offices in India as current, savings, RDs or FDs.

Even a foreign national of non-Indian origin visiting India can do so with funds remitted from outside India or by sale of foreign exchange brought by him to India when he is in India on holidays or short tour. The account can be freely operated by the account holder or the joint holder for bona fide transactions. At the time of his departure from India, the amount can be converted into forex provided the account has been maintained for a period not exceeding 6 months and the account has not been credited with any local funds, other than interest accrued thereon. For accounts maintained beyond this period, application for repatriation should be made on plain paper to the related RBI Regional Office.

The minimum tenor of domestic and NRO term deposits, irrespective of its quantum of the deposit, is 7 days. Since the NRO accounts are designated in Indian rupees, the exchange risk on such deposits is borne by the depositors themselves.

W.e.f. 16.12.11 the interest rate on NRO are deregulated. At present it is between 4% to 7% p.a. Scheduled commercial banks have been advised to calculate interest on savings bank accounts on a daily product basis. Interest should be paid at quarterly or longer rests. Interest on savings bank accounts should be credited on regular basis whether the account is operative or not.

Conversion into Cash Rupees
As per AP (DIR) Circular 14 dt. 17.10.07, requests for payment in cash by ROIs may be acceded to the extent of US$ 3,000 or its equivalent. For higher amounts, the money changers should make

payments through account payee cheques or demand drafts.

Permissible Credits

◆ Remittances from abroad in freely convertible foreign currency through normal banking channels.

◆ Freely convertible foreign currency tendered by the account holder during his temporary visit to India or transfers from rupee accounts of non-resident banks. Foreign currency exceeding US$ 5,000 or its equivalent in form of cash should be supported by Currency Declaration Form. Rupee funds should be supported by Encashment Certificate, if they represent funds brought from outside India.

◆ Transfer from rupee accounts of non-resident banks.

◆ Legitimate dues in India of the account holder such as rent, dividend, pension, interest, etc.

◆ Sale proceeds of assets including immovable property acquired out of rupee/forex funds or by way of legacy/inheritance.

◆ Gifts and/or loans from a close relative within the overall limit of US$ 75,000 per FY as permitted under the Liberalised Remittance Scheme (LRS). Refer Chapter, *Forex Availability — Residents* for details.

Permissible Debits

◆ All local payments in rupees including payments for investments subject to compliance with the relevant RBI regulations.

◆ Remittance outside India of current income like rent, dividend, pension, interest, etc., of the account holder net of taxes.

◆ Remittance up to US$ 1 million per FY for all bona fide purposes. (Refer Chapter *Forex Remittances — NRIs*).

◆ Loans to non-resident account holders and to third parties may be granted in Rupees by Authorized Dealer/bank against the security of fixed deposits subject to certain terms and conditions. (Refer Chapter, *Loans & Overdrafts* for details.)

Rank Foreigners on a Visit to India

NRO (current/savings) account can be opened by a rank foreign national visiting India, with funds remitted from outside India through normal banking channels or forex brought by him. The balance in the NRO may be converted back into forex at the time of his departure provided the account has been maintained for 6 months or less and the account has not been credited with any local funds other than interest. Account maintained for over 6 months require applications for repatriation on plain paper to the concerned Regional Office of the RBI.

RESIDENT FOREIGN CURRENCY (RFC)

Any person who was an NRI returning only from External Group of countries and now has become a Resident is eligible to open a RFC account, mainly for transferring his NRE and FCNR balances and the proceeds of assets held outside India to this account. The important aspect of RFC is that the funds are free from all restrictions regarding utilisation of foreign currency balances, including any restriction on investment in any form outside India.

RFC accounts can be maintained in the form of current or savings or term deposit accounts, where the account holder is an individual and in the form of current or term deposits in all other cases. No loans or overdrafts will be permitted in these accounts. If and when the account holder again becomes an NRI he can transfer the funds from his RFC to NRE.

Permissible Credits

◆ FE amounts remitted from abroad.
◆ Sale proceeds of FE Assets held in India.
◆ Incomes or sale proceeds from assets, including immovable property held abroad.
◆ Pension, superannuation or other monetary benefits from former employer outside India.
◆ Transfer from NRE or FCNR accounts of the account holder.
◆ Proceeds of foreign currency notes and foreign travellers' cheques brought in by the account holder.
◆ Transfers from other RFC accounts of the account holder.
◆ Interest earned on RFC accounts.
◆ Gifts or inheritance received from an ROI.

Permissible Debits

◆ Remittance abroad for any bona fide purpose of the account holder or for his dependents. This may include purchase of a foreign security.

◆ Transfers to other RFC accounts of the account holder.

◆ All local disbursements and bank charges.

The scheme of importing gold and silver is extended to RFC and EEFC account holders.

RFCD ACCOUNT

A Resident individual can use this Resident Foreign Currency (Domestic) Account for crediting forex in the form of currency notes, bank notes and travellers cheques acquired by him —

* While on a visit to abroad, for services rendered abroad not arising from any business in or anything done in India.

* As honorarium, gift, services rendered or in settlement of any lawful obligation, whether earned in India or abroad, from any person not Resident in India.

* As unspent amount of forex for travel abroad

* Gift from a close relative.

* Forex received from life insurance policy of an Indian insurer.

* Earnings through export of goods or services, royalty, honorarium or any other legal means.

* Disinvestment proceeds received on conversion of shares to ADRs/GDRs under sponsored and approved ADR/GDR Scheme.

The account will be maintained as only current account and shall not bear any interest. Cheque facility is available. There is no ceiling on the balances.

Debits to the account shall be for payment towards current or capital account transactions which are eligible for Residents.

Existing facility of retention of US$ 2,000 or its equivalent in forex by Residents continues provided that such forex is in the form of currency notes, bank notes and traveller's cheques.

EEFC ACCOUNT

All categories of Resident forex earners, including SEZ developers, can credit up to 100% of their forex earnings to Exchange Earner's Foreign Currency accounts as non-interest bearing accounts. ADs are no more permitted to grant any credit facilities, both fund based and non-fund based, against balances in EEFC.

Exporters are permitted to grant trade related loans or advances from their EEFC to their overseas importer customer without any ceiling. Where the amount of loan exceeds US$ 1 lakh a guarantee of a bank of international repute situated outside India is required to be provided by the overseas borrower in favour of the lender.

Permissible Credits

* Inward remittance other than the remittance received pursuant to any undertaking given to the RBI or which represents forex loan raised or investment received from outside India or those received for meeting specific obligations of the account holder.
* Payments received in forex by a 100% Export Oriented unit, unit in Export Processing Zone, Software Technological Park, Electronic Hardware Technological Park, etc.
* Forex receipts of a unit in Domestic Tariff Area for supply of goods to a unit in SEZ.
* Payment received by an exporter from an account maintained with an AD for the purpose of counter trade. Counter trade is an arrangement involving adjustment of value of goods imported into India against exported from India.
* Advance remittance received by an exporter towards export of goods or services.
* Professional earnings including director's fees, consultancy fees, lecture fees, honorarium and similar other earnings received by a professional by rendering services in his individual capacity.
* Interest earned on the funds held in EEFC.
* Recredit of unutilised forex earlier withdrawn from the account.
* Amount representing repayment by the account holder's importer customer, of loan/advances granted by the account holder.

Permissible Debits

* Permissible current account and capital account transactions.

* Payment in forex towards cost of goods purchased from a 100% Export Oriented Unit or a unit in Export Processing Zone, Software Technological Park, Electronic Hardware Technological Park, etc.

* Payments towards certain trade-related purchases, loans/ advances to importer customer outside India, customs duty, etc.

* Travel, miscellaneous expenses towards exports, meeting the expenses of studies abroad of students sponsored by the account holder, etc.

* Payment in forex to a Resident for supply of goods and services including airfare and hotel expenditure.

* Following remittances outside India —

  ■ Reimbursement of pre-incorporation expenses up to US$ 1,00,000.

  ■ Gifts and donations up to US$ 5,000 each, per FY per remitter per donor.

  ■ Commission per transaction to agent abroad for sale of residential flats or commercial plots in India up to US$ 25,000 or 5% of the inward remittances, whichever is more.

It is obvious that the utility of RFC, RFCD and EEFC has been much diluted ever since the Residents can legally purchase sufficient forex for bona fide reasons. Moreover, NRIs as well as Residents are allowed to continue to hold bank accounts and investments abroad.

MISCELLANEOUS

Foreign Currency International Deposits (FCID)
Some banks in India having their overseas banking units accept FCIDs which are essentially FCNRs but are free from the FEMA regulations. Consequently, the rate of interest is higher and so is the flexibility for the term of the deposit. Since the interest is paid by an Indian bank, it is taxable in India with the associated TDS applicability and the DTAA provisions.

Duplicate Demand Draft

Issue of duplicate demand draft can be effected up to ₹ 5,000 even before obtaining non-payment advice from the drawee branch on the basis of adequate indemnity. The drawee office may merely be cautioned in this regard. If the draft is for more than ₹ 5,000, non-payment certificate should be called for from drawee office by telex/telegraph at applicant's cost and other formalities completed.

A duplicate demand draft should be issued within a fortnight from the receipt of such request. For delay in issuing duplicate draft beyond the stipulated period, banks should pay interest at the rate applicable for fixed deposit of corresponding maturity.

Foreign Currency Rupee Options

In terms of AP (DIR) Circular 108 dt. 21.6.03 as a part of developing the derivative market in India and adding to the spectrum of hedge products available to Residents and NRIs for hedging currency exposures, foreign currency rupee options are permitted w.e.f. 7.7.03 subject to certain conditions.

Residents and Bank Accounts in Foreign Countries

RBI has granted general permission to open the accounts to those who go abroad temporarily for business, medical treatment, higher studies, training, etc. Deposits into such accounts can be made only out of foreign exchange obtained from an AD in India or foreign exchange received outside India by way of scholarship, salary or payment for services not arising from any business in India or anything done while in India. The general permission also applies to Residents for accounts abroad opened prior to 8.7.47. Such persons need not submit any annual returns related with funds held in or interest remitted from such accounts.

Money Transfer Service Scheme (MTSS)

Master Circular 1/2012-13 dt. 2.7.12 deals with MTSS which is a quick and easy way of transferring personal remittances from abroad to beneficiaries in India. Only inward (and not outward) personal remittances into India by individuals to individuals towards family maintenance and remittances favouring foreign tourists visiting India are permissible. Any remittances related with trade, purchase of property, investments or credit to NRE accounts shall not be made through this arrangement. MTSS envisages a tie-up between reputed money transfer companies abroad and agents in India who would disburse the funds to the beneficiaries in India at ongoing exchange rates.

There is a cap of US$ 2,500 on individual remittances under the scheme. Amounts up to ₹ 50,000 may be paid in cash to a beneficiary in India. Any amount over this limit shall be paid through an account payee cheque, demand draft, payment order, etc.

Facilities for NRIs on Repatriation Basis — Summary

1. Government dated securities/Treasury bills.
2. Units of domestic mutual funds.
3. Non-convertible Debentures of Indian companies.
4. Shares and convertible debentures of Indian companies through stock exchange under Portfolio Investment Scheme.
5. Shares and Convertible Debentures of Indian companies under the FDI scheme (including automatic route and FIPB).
6. Perpetual debt instruments and debt capital instruments issued by banks in India.
7. Bonds issued by Public Sector Undertakings.
8. Shares in Public Sector Enterprises being disinvested by the Government of India.

Facilities for NRIs on Non-Repatriation Basis — Summary

1. The first 4 items listed above.
2. Units of Money Market Mutual Funds
3. SEBI approved Exchange traded derivative contracts out of INR funds held in India on non-repatriable basis, subject to the limits prescribed by the SEBI.

Note : NRIs are not permitted to invest in small savings or Public Provident Fund (PPF).

10

Capital Gains

It hurts to pay tax on capital gains. A large part of these gains is due to the endemic inflation. In terms of real money value, the actual gains may be negative. Yet, tax is levied on these gains. To counter this atrocity, we have to examine carefully the various tax-saving devices and take as much shelter behind them as possible.

Definition : Capital Asset and Transfer
The term *capital asset* does not include personal effects such as wearing apparel, furniture, air conditioners, refrigerators, etc., held for personal use by the assessee. Even cars, scooters, cycles, motorcycles owned and used by the assessee are personal effects. Therefore, the sale of personal effects do not attract any capital gains tax. However, a car is exigible to wealth tax. Strange!

FA13 has changed the definition of rural land (Refer Chapter *Wealth Tax*) which depends upon the population and distance from local limits of any municipality, cantonment board, etc. Rural agricultural land is not a capital asset. Consequently, its sale would not attract provisions of capital gains tax. Looking at it from another angle, sale of all lands, agricultural or not, located in urban areas and non-agricultural land located in rural areas would attract the tax.

However, gains arising out of compulsory acquisition under any law or as approved by the Central Government or the RBI of such an agricultural land, irrespective of its location, have been made exempt by Sec. 10(37).

Transactions not Regarded as Transfer
Following transactions are not considered as transfers :
◆ Distribution of assets on partition of an HUF [Sec. 47(i)].
◆ Assets transferred under a gift or a Will or an irrevocable trust. [Sec. 47(iii)].
◆ Transfer of any work of art, archaeological, scientific or art collection, etc., to the government or a university or the National

Museum, National Art Gallery, etc. [Sec. 47(ix)].

◆ Conversion of debentures, debenture stock or deposit certificates of a company into shares or debentures [Sec. 47(x)]. However, conversion of preference share into ordinary shares amounts to transfer in hands of the shareholders — *CIT v Motors and General Stores P Ltd (1967) 66ITR692 (SC)*.

◆ Transfer of bonds or GDR made outside India by an NRI to another NRI is not a transfer. [Sec. 47(viia)].

◆ Switch from one scheme to another of the same MF or from one option of the same scheme to another, is a transfer. However, dividend payment to dividend reinvestment and *vice versa* of the same scheme is not a transfer.

◆ Bona fide realignment of interest by way of effecting family arrangements among the family members does not amount to transfer — *CIT v A L Ramanathan (2000) 245ITR494 (Mad)*.

◆ Transfer presumes existence of both the asset and the transferee. When the property is destroyed both these criteria are not satisfied — *Vania Silk Mills (Pvt) Ltd. v CIT* (1991) 59Taxman3 (SC) had laid down this principle. It was negated by inserting Sec. 45(1A) asserting that, tax will be charged on any gains arising from money or other assets received under an insurance arising out of damage or destruction of any capital asset, as a result of (i) flood, typhoon, hurricane, cyclone, earthquake or other convulsion of nature or (ii) riot or civil disturbance or (iii) accidental fire or explosion or (iv) action by an enemy or action taken in combating an enemy (with or without a declaration of war).

Assets Acquired at Nil Cost : Sec. 55

The Supreme Court had held in the case of *B. C. Srinivasa Shetty, 128ITR294* that no tax is chargeable on transfer of capital assets in respect of which there is no cost of acquisition. This decision has been negated steadily by ordaining that the cost of acquisition should be taken as nil in the following cases —

(a) Goodwill of a business (not of a profession).

(b) Trademark or brand name associated with the business.

(c) Patent, copyright, formula, design, etc.

(d) Right to carry on any business.

(e) Tenancy rights, Route permits, Loom hours, etc.

Cost Inflation Indexation

Starting with FY 81-82 as the base year, the RBI notifies 'Cost Inflation Index' (CII) every year as given in the Table-1.

LT gains are computed by deducting from the full value of the consideration (i) any expenditure (brokerage, stamp duty, etc.) incurred in connection with the transfer, (ii) indexed cost of acquisition and (iii) indexed cost of improvement. Indexed cost is computed by multiplying the cost of acquisition or improvement of the asset by the ratio of the CIIs for the years of sale and acquisition.

For assets acquired prior to 1.4.81, the option of substituting the fair market value (FMV) in place of original cost is possible. In other words, if the cost of acquisition is lower than FMV as on 1.4.81, the assessee may adopt the FMV as his cost. If it is higher, he may adopt it as his cost of acquisition. The CII based on 81-82 only will be taken into account, whatever be the choice. Note that

Table-1 : Cost Inflation Index

Financial year	Inflation Index	Growth %	Financial year	Inflation Index	Growth %
1981-82	100		1998-99	351	6.04
1982-83	109	9.00	1999-00	389	10.83
1983-84	116	6.42	2000-01	406	4.37
1984-85	125	7.76	2001-02	426	4.93
1985-86	133	6.40	2002-03	447	4.93
1986-87	140	5.26	2003-04	463	3.58
1987-88	150	7.14	2004-05	480	3.67
1988-89	161	7.33	2005-06	497	3.54
1989-90	172	6.83	2006-07	519	4.43
1990-91	182	5.81	2007-08	551	6.17
1991-92	199	9.34	2008-09	582	5.63
1992-93	223	12.06	2009-10	632	8.59
1993-94	244	9.42	2010-11	711	12.50
1994-95	259	6.15	2011-12	785	10.41
1995-96	281	8.49	2012-13	852	8.53
1996-97	305	8.54	2013-14	939	10.21
1997-98	331	8.52	2014-15	1024	9.05

Note : The CII for FY 2015-16 is expected to be declared in July '15.

an assessee has the right to take the FMV as on 1.4.81 even for bonus shares allotted to him prior to that date. Same is true for other assets, normally required to be taken at nil value.

Sale Value for Stamp Duty — Sec. 50C

Where the consideration declared by the assessee for transfer of land or building or both, is less than the value adopted or assessed for stamp duty, the latter shall be deemed to be the full value of the consideration. If the assessee claims that this deemed value exceeds the fair market value (FMV) the ITO may ask a valuation officer of the Department to assess the FMV. If it turns out to be less than the value adopted for stamp duty, the ITO shall take the FMV to be the full value of consideration. Otherwise, the original duty shall prevail, subject to revision in any appeal.

This results in the buyer paying higher stamp duty and the seller paying higher tax on capital gains. Unfortunately, when the buyer sells the property at a later date, he is forced to adopt the original value declared by him and not the stamp duty valuation.

Stock-in-trade

Several courts had held that since immovable property held as stock-in-trade is not a 'capital asset', Sec. 50C cannot be applied to transfer land, flats, buildings, etc., constructed and sold by builders and developers which are 'stock-in-trade' in their business, could not be brought u/s 50C.

To negate such judicial decisions, FA13 has inserted a new Sec. 43CA to take the stamp duty value of stock-in-trade on its transfer, as deemed to be the full value of the consideration for the purposes of computing capital gains. Surely, the builders will jack up their prices which are already sky high.

Where the date of the agreement fixing the amount of consideration for the transfer of the immovable property and the date of registration are not the same, the stamp duty value may be taken as on the date of the agreement, instead of that on the date of registration. This exception shall, however, apply only in a case where the amount of consideration, or a part thereof, has been paid by any mode other than cash on or before the date of the agreement.

Advance for Transfer of a Capital Asset

Amount confiscated by the seller cannot be treated as his capital gain, since no transfer of any capital asset has actually taken place. — *CIT* v *Sterling Investment Corp Ltd.* [1980] 123ITR441 (Bom).

Such forfeited amount was treated as a capital receipt not chargeable to tax during the year of forfeiture. This amount was reduced from the cost of acquisition of the property so that tax would get collected during the year of sale. This provision was ingeniously used by some persons to convert their black money into white by entering into a sham agreement to sell a property, usually held for the long term, with an accommodating party on the understanding that the earnest money will be forfeited as per the terms of the agreement.

To counter this situation, FA14 amended Sec. 56 to provide that any advance money taken against sale of an asset and forfeited because the negotiations did not result in transfer shall be chargeable to tax under the head 'Income from Other Sources'.

This has resulted in a situation for the buyer. Though it is a pecuniary loss, he cannot claim it as a capital loss u/s 45 as he neither ever owned nor relinquished the capital asset in question. We hope that he would be permitted to claim it as a loss under the head 'Income from Other Sources'. Now, a CBDT clarification is necessary to avoid litigations.

FA12 has curtailed the practice of receiving a very high premium against the issue of shares.

Business of Dealing in Shares

Where dealings in shares is a business of the person, all capital gains (or losses) are charged to tax under the head, 'Profits and gains of business or profession'. Sec. 36 provides that STT paid on transactions entered into in the course of the business shall be allowable as deduction.

Shares & FIIs

Currently FIIs pay a concessional 10% tax on LTCG from transfer of unlisted securities. In contrast, other sections of NRIs such as individuals and foreign companies (not FIIs) pay a higher 20% tax on similar gains. FA12 u/s 112(ciii) has brought parity by taxing all NRIs at a concessional rate of 10% on LTCG (without indexation) from sale of unlisted securities. Note that the reduced rate is applicable to securities covered under the Securities Contracts (Regulation) Act, 1956. Therefore this reduced rate may not be applicable to transfer of shares of private companies, as they are not governed by SCRA.

Exchange Rate Risk

Protection provided by First Proviso to Sec. 48 has become meaningless for NRIs because of total freedom from tax on long-term capital gains. However, it still is applicable to short-term gains on shares or debentures of an Indian company (private or public) acquired by utilising foreign currency.

In such cases, capital gains shall be computed by deducting the cost of acquisition from the net value of the consideration received or accruing into the same foreign currency as was initially utilised for the purchase of shares or debentures. The capital gains so computed in such foreign currency shall be reconverted into Indian currency. Thus the NRI is protected against the exchange risk.

The method of conversion into foreign currency is specified by Rule 115A and are dealt with in Chapter *Tedious TDS*.

Treatment of Losses

U/s 74 losses under the head 'Capital Gains' cannot be set off against income under any other head. Though short-term loss can be set off against both short-term or long-term gain, any long-term loss shall be set off against long-term gain only. If there are no sufficient gains during the year, the balance loss, short-term or long-term, can be carried forward for 8 successive years for similar set off.

TAX & FA14 AMENDMENTS

Capital Gains Tax : Sec. 112

A 'Short-Term capital asset' (ST) is a financial asset held for 36 months or less immediately preceding the date of transfer. The holding period is only 12 months for shares of a company, units of

MFs, zero coupon bonds and listed scrips, bonds, debentures, etc.

An asset which is not ST is LT (Long-term).

FA14 has taken away debt-based MF schemes from this concessional lower period of 12 months and w.e.f. 1.4.14, the normal period of 36 months will be applicable.

Note the word 'held' in this provision. The assessee need not be a owner of the property and can hold it as a lessee, as a mortgagee, under a hire purchase agreement, or on account of part performance of an agreement.

In the case of other financial assets like houses, jewellery, etc., STCG is taxed like any other income at the rates applicable to the assessee. LTCG is taken as a separate block, charged to tax at a flat rate of 20% with indexation benefit.

Shares & Securities

Security Transaction Tax (STT) is a minuscule amount of tax collected from the following transactions taking place in a recognised stock exchange in India —

(a) Purchase and sale of shares.
(b) Sale of equity-based MFs.
(c) Sale of Options in securities.
(d) Sale of Futures in securities.

STT is also charged on redemption of equity-based units of MFs, (but not on debt-based) directly with the fund house which had issued these units.

The LTCG arising out of any transaction which has suffered STT is exempt and STCG is taxed at a concessional rate of 15% only.

There are two hidden bombs in this provision. 1. If the gains are exempt, the loss is also exempt and cannot be set off against any other short-term or long-term gain. 2. Tax on STCG @15% is beneficial only to those who are in 20% or 30% zone; not to 10%.

The requirement to have the deal in a recognised stock exchange in India applies only to sales and not purchases. Therefore, when bonus shares issued are sold in the market, the tax concessions apply. These used to attract heavy tax since their cost of acquisition was required to be taken as nil. Same is the case for IPOs and right issues but to a lesser extent. Those who have lost the record of cost and date of acquisition need not now worry.

10%-or-20% Option

In the case of listed shares and securities which are not sold on any recognised stock exchange in India, such as a 'buy-back' of its own shares by the company or direct transaction between two persons, as well as Zero Coupon Bonds (alternatively termed as Deep Discount Bonds) which do not suffer any STT, LT gains is charged to tax @10% without indexation (= sale - cost = profit) or 20% with indexation (= sale - indexed cost), whichever is lower. ST gains are to be added to the normal income of the assessee and charged to tax at the rate applicable to his slab of income.

Debt-based schemes of MFs were in the same league. FA14 has taken away the option of 10% without indexation from the debt-based units of MFs. Now, such units have joined the league of all other assets, such as houses, jewellery, etc., including unlisted shares, where LTCG is taken as a separate block, charged to tax @20% with indexation and STCG is taxed like any other income at the rates applicable to the assessee.

Capital Gains & Tax Threshold

For a Resident individual or an HUF, where the total income as reduced by (a) STCG which is charged to tax @15% and (b) LTCG which is charged to tax with 10% or 20% option, no deduction is allowed under Chapter VIA (Secs. 80C, 80D, etc.).

There is an additional benefit only for Residents. Where the normal income falls below the tax threshold, the gains can be reduced by the gap between the total income and the threshold.

Dividend Distribution Tax (DDT)

U/s 10(34), dividend received from a domestic company and u/s 10(35) income distributed by any MF, is tax-free. However, this dividend suffers DDT @15%, payable by the company before distributing the dividend to its stakeholders. With the surcharge of 12% (raised from 10% by the recent FA15), and educational cess of 3%, the effective rate works out at 17.304% (= 15×1.12×1.03).

In other words, if the company desires to pay ₹ 100 as dividend, it can pay ₹ 82.696 to the shareholder and pay ₹ 17.304 (= 16.995% of 86.0419) to the exchequer.

This DDT is in addition to the normal income tax.

In the case of MFs, the equity-based schemes are exempt from this DDT u/s 115R(2). For individuals & HUFs, on all debt-based funds of MFs, DDT rate is 25%. With surcharge of 12% and 3% education cess, the rates work out at 28.84%. For all other categories of taxpayers, the rate is 30% (= 34.608%).

Many investors feel that this is an atrocity. We do not. As a matter of fact, we are thankful to the FM for raising the rate on DDT. Surprised? Well, here are our reasons.

Dividends suffer DDT; Growth does not. Yes, growth attracts tax on capital gains. But in the case of MFs, it works out at almost nothing. Let us examine this aspect carefully.

Suppose you have invested in FY 13-14, ₹ 10,000 in a Fixed Maturity Plan (FMP) which is a close-ended debt-based scheme, with a term of 370 days (just over one year) and it has yielded a modest return of 8%, giving a redemption value of ₹ 10,800.

The dividend option attracts DDT of ₹ 230.72 (= 0.2884×800).

Now, let us see the result of growth option.

The Cost Inflation Index for FY 14-15 is 1,024 and for FY 13-14 it is 939. Therefore the indexed cost works out at ₹ 900.52 (= (10,000 × (1,024 / 939) = 11,203. The LTCG has resulted in a loss of ₹ 403 (= 10,800 − 11,203). The 10%-or-20% option is meaningless.

This was unpalatable to the revenue.

The MFs used to play a slick trick by launching an FMP at the fag end of the year to obtain the benefit of double indexation.

This was more unpalatable to the revenue.

FA14 has raised the period of 1 year to 3 years for getting the colour of long-term on all debt-based schemes. Let us see the effect of this diktat.

₹ 10,000 grow @ 8% p.a., at ₹ 12,597 (= 1.08^3 × 10,000). Three years ago for FY 11-12 the index is 785. The LTCG results in a loss of ₹ 447. Though it is inconsequential, the MFs can play the same slick trick to obtain the benefit of quadruple indexation.

This was also the situation when the DDT was introduced way back in FY99. We had placed this very solution of opting for growth and not dividend before our readers at that time. Our success was perhaps limited to only those elite readers who understood our message with clarity.

Way back in 2003, we were appointed by UTI to design their 'UTI Bond Fund'. We had structured the scheme without the (or dividend reinvestment) option. "Give the investors what is good for them" we told UTI, "and not what they want". UTI accepted the suggestion and launched the scheme with aplomb. Unfortunately, in due course, UTI was forced to introduce dividend option because it found that there were a large number of investors who shunned the scheme only because they did not understand that they can, opt for 'Systematic Withdrawal Plan' at the frequency they desire.

In the case of our example, if ₹ 800 are withdrawn every year, it *ipso facto* becomes the real tax-free income –- no normal tax, no TDS and no DDT. Dividend on shares suffers DDT and therefore it is not really tax-free.

Mr. Arun Jaitley deserves kudos for punishing the investors if they opt for dividend option in MF schemes by —
(i) deleting the option of 10% which was useless in any case,
(ii) raising the period from 1 year to 3 years for entitling it to be LT, and
(iii) raising the DDT rates on dividends paid.

MFs have become the best investment avenue for one and all.

If you have risk appetite, go for equity-based schemes. The dividend is tax-free and there is no DDT.

Otherwise, go for close-ended growth-based FMPs. These are almost devoid of any volatility because the fund manager invests in investment-graded assured returns schemes.

Finally, allow us to reiterate what we have been saying right from the very first edition of this book — We do not understand why any investor goes to any bank for any investment when MF schemes giving better take-home returns with similar safety are available.

Exemption from LTCG Tax : NHAI & REC Bonds

Sec. 54EC offers exemption of long-term capital gains on all assets, if the LT gains are invested in Bonds of National Highway Authority of India (NHAI) or Rural Electrification Corporation (REC) within 6 months from the date of earning capital gain. These Bonds come with a lock-in period of 3 years.

There is a ceiling of ₹ 50 lakh per FY on deposits in these Bonds.

Those who had earned higher capital gains on or after 2nd October of any year could contribute ₹ 50 lakh to these Bonds during the current FY and another ₹ 50 lakh during the next FY, both within 6 months and claim exemption up to ₹ 1 crore! Since this was not the intention of the legislation, FA14 has taken a corrective action by providing that the total relief obtained in such cases shall not exceed ₹ 50 lakh though investment can be made during the FY when the CG occurs and the subsequent FY but within the stipulated period of 6 months.

Exemption from LTCG Tax : Residential House

The ITA provides other opportunities for saving tax on long-term capital gains such as by way of Sec. 54 & Sec. 54F. Sec. 54 gives exemption from tax on capital gains arising out of sale (or transfer) of a residential house, self-occupied or not, provided the assessee has purchased within 1 year before or 2 years after the date of sale or has constructed within 3 years after that date, a residential house. If only a part of the LTCG is used, the exemption would be pro-rata and the excess will be taxed.

Two points are worthy of careful note —
1. For construction, there is no restriction on commencement date. It could have begun even more than 20 years before the sale.
2. The assessee need not apply the amount from the sale proceeds for purchasing another residential house. He can take a loan for

the purchase or construction and use the sale proceeds for investment elsewhere, if it is beneficial for him to do so.

Sec. 54F deals with capital gains arising out of assets other than residential houses. The stipulations are essentially the same but with 3 differences —

1. The assessee should not be an owner of more than one residential premises on the date of transfer.

2. Sec. 54F requires reinvestment of the net consideration (sale value less expenses) whereas Sec. 54 is content with reinvestment of only the amount of capital gains.

3. In the case of Sec. 54, the assessee is required not to sell the new house within 3 years. If this condition is not satisfied, the cost of the new asset is to be reduced by the amount of long-term capital gains exempted from tax on the original asset and the difference between its sale price and such reduced cost will be chargeable as short-term capital gain earned during the year in which the new asset is sold.

Sec. 54F also requires the assessee not to sell the new house within 3 years. In addition, he is expected not to purchase within 1 year or construct within 3 years, another residential house. If any of these conditions are not satisfied, the capital gain originally exempted shall be treated as long-term capital gain of the year in which the house is sold or another house is purchased or constructed.

This penalty is different from that of Sec. 54 and creates confusion. We do not comprehend the wisdom of imposing different punishments for the same offence.

'A' House is 'One' House

Sec. 54 states "... where, ... the capital gains arises from the transfer of a long-term capital asset being ... a residential house, and the assessee has ... purchased a residential house, then ...."

There were a flood of litigations revolving around the meaning of 'purchased a residential house' and the judiciary pronouncements were contradictory and inconsistent with one another.

Additional flood arose because of faulty language used in the legislation which made it possible to claim the benefit even on a house purchased abroad.

FA14 has settled both the problems at one stroke by replacing the phrase 'purchased a residential house' with 'purchased one residential house in India'.

Hereunder are some difficulties arising out of these amendments.

Difficulty-1: An assessee sells two houses, either on the same date or different dates. Can he buy one large house and claim deduction for both the houses together?

The amendment has replaced the word 'a' associated with purchase of new house by the word 'one'. The word 'a' associated with transfer of a long-term capital asset has not been replaced.

It appears that for claiming exemption arising from transfer of 'a' house, the assessee has to purchase one house. If he sells yet another 'a' house, he has to buy another one house.

Prior to this amendment, he could sell two houses and buy one. *DCIT Central Circle-32 v Ranjit Vithaldas [2012] 23taxmann.com 226 ITAT Mumbai Bench 'A'* — If two flats are sold even in different years and capital gains from both flats is invested in one residential house, exemption will be available for each flat sold provided the time-limit for construction or purchase of new house is satisfied.

Difficulty-2 : Similar amendments are carried out in the case of Sec. 54F which deals with LTCG arising from transfer of capital assets other than residential houses. If the assessee is required to purchase one residential house, per one item on which capital gains have been incurred, the Section becomes impotent.

Difficulty-3 : If 'a' is 'one' it is also not 'half'. Can an assessee purchase the new house jointly with his wife who has also contributed a share of the cost?

ITO v Rasiklal N. Satra (280ITR243 dt 19.9.05) — Ownership of a residential house, means ownership to the exclusion of all others. Therefore, where a house is jointly owned by two or more persons, none of them can be said to be the owner of that house.

Difficulty-4 : Sec. 54F allowing the assessee to own one house, other than the new house on the date of sale of the underlying assets. The Section is now not applicable if the assessee possesses more than one house. Does one-and-half house mean more than one house?

Difficulty-5 : U/s 80C(xviii) deduction on repayment of capital amount of housing loan is available — "for the purposes of purchase or construction of 'a' residential house property . . . ."

Does this mean that if a person has taken two houses financed through housing loans, he cannot claim deduction on installments towards part payment of the loan against only one house. Strangely, the interest paid on the same loans can be claimed as deduction even against more than one house!

Now perhaps there will be more litigations than ever before unless the CBDT issues a clarification.

CAPITAL GAINS ACCOUNTS SCHEME, 1988 (CGAS)

For ascertaining that the assessee really intends to purchase a new residential house within the stipulated time, all scheduled banks have a special bank account designated as CGAS. The amount deposited in such an account before the last date of furnishing returns of income or actual date, if earlier, along with the amount already utilised, is deemed to be the amount utilised for the purpose. This means that the assessee can utilise this amount for any purpose whatsoever during intervening period — *ACIT v Smt Uma Budhia (2004) 141 Taxman 39 (Kol.)*.

If the amount is not utilised wholly or partly for the stipulated purpose, then, the amount of capital gains related with the unutilised portion of the deposit in CGAS shall be charged as the capital gains of the year in which the period expires.

Circular 743 dt. 6.5.96 states that when the account holder expires, the unutilised amount in CGAS account is not taxable in the hands of the legal heirs or nominees as the unutilised portion of the deposit does not partake the character of income in their hands but is only a part of the estate devolving upon them.

MISCELLANEOUS

CG on Car

Capital asset, as defined by Sec. 2(14) of ITA does not include items held for personal use such as furniture, air-conditioners, refrigerators, motor cars, etc. Therefore, a car used for personal purpose (depreciation is not charged), is not a capital asset. When it is sold, no capital gains, either short-term or long-term can arise. The profit or loss cannot be brought to income tax.

It is obvious that all the returning NRIs will do well by bringing their cars with them and sell these in due course.

Bonds & GDRs

Transfer of a capital asset, being bonds or GDRs outside India by an NRI to another NRI is not regarded as a transfer.

Sale of Listed Indian Shares by a Foreign Company

The benefit of lesser rate of tax conferred by Sec. 112(1) can be invoked by NR foreign company as well; the expression 'before giving effect to 2nd proviso to Sec. 48' cannot be construed as a condition precedent for invoking the proviso to Sec. 112(1); hence, the applicant foreign company is liable to pay tax at the lesser rate of 10% as per the proviso to Sec. 112(1) — *Fujitsu Services Ltd., In re [AAR 800 of 2009].*

Merger/Demerger of Foreign & Indian Companies

Transfer of shares by a foreign company to another foreign company where the transferred shares have underneath assets in India, the controversy of the eligibility of levying capital gains tax arose in the Vodafone's case.

The recent FA15 has now declared that such transactions would be tax-free subject to some specified conditions.

Sec. 47(viab) has been inserted to provide that any amalgamation, of a share of a foreign company, which derives, directly or indirectly, its value substantially from the share or shares of an Indian company, held by the amalgamating foreign company to the amalgamated foreign company, if— at least 25% of the shareholders of the amalgamating foreign company continue to remain shareholders of the amalgamated foreign company.

Sec. 47 (vicc) has been inserted to provide that any demerger, of a share of a foreign company, which derives, directly or indirectly, its value substantially from the share or shares of an Indian company, held by the demerged foreign company to the resulting foreign company, if — the shareholders, holding not less than 75% in value of the shares of the demerged foreign company, continue to remain shareholders of the resulting foreign company.

Such transfers would not attract tax on capital gains in the country in which the merged or demerged foreign company is incorporated.

Until now, there was no enabling provision for carry forward of the period of holding by a demerged company to the resulting company. The proposed amendment reckoning this period of holding and the cost of acquisition would clear these uncertainties.

Indirect Transfer of Shares of an Indian Company
Explanation 5 to Sec. 9(1i) retrospectively to clarify that any share or interest in a company or entity registered or incorporated outside India shall be deemed to be situated in India if the share or interest derives, directly or indirectly, its value substantially from the assets located in India. The meaning of 'substantial value' was neither explained nor could be inferred from the statute book.

Now Explanation 6 has been inserted by the recent FA15 to provide that a share or interest of a foreign entity shall be deemed to be deriving its value substantially from Indian assets (tangible or intangible) only if the value of Indian assets as on the specified date (a) exceeds ₹ 10 crore and (b) represents at least 50% of the value of all the assets owned by the foreign entity. The liabilities (even if identifiable) will not be reduced from the asset values for reckoning the monetary limit.

Further, exemption has been provided for shareholders holding non-controlling interest up to 5% of a foreign company, which derives value substantially from Indian assets. It has also exempted overseas amalgamations and demergers undertaken, subject to certain conditions, which results in transfer of another foreign company shares deriving, directly or indirectly, its value substantially from the share or shares of an Indian company exceeding the aforesaid thresholds.

There are still some unaddressed issues relating to indirect transfers. Firstly, the taxability for shareholders of the amalgamating or demerged foreign company has not been considered. Secondly, step-up in the cost base is not granted pursuant to tax being levied on the indirect transfer and hence, subsequent direct transfer may lead to double taxation to the extent of value accretion taxed in the case of first transfer.

For instance, if a US company holds significant interest in a German company, which derives value substantially from Indian company shares, the proportionate gains realised by the US company from transfer of German company shares would be taxed in India. Subsequently, if German company transfers Indian company shares, the gains would again be taxed in India without any step up in the cost basis pursuant to the Indian taxes paid on the earlier transfer. Further, the threshold for excluding small investors which is kept at 5% as against 26% as recommended by the Expert Committee may not be adequate. The reporting obligations cast in case of indirect transfers, especially on widely held Indian companies appear to be out of place, considering the impracticality of gathering information for all the offshore transactions by the foreign indirect shareholders and hence, the provision of penalty seems to be harsh.

Incidentally, CBDT Circular 4/2015 dt. 26.3.15 has clarified that declaration of dividend by a foreign company outside India does not have the effect of transfer of any underlying assets located in India and therefore, the dividends declared and paid by a foreign company outside India in respect of shares which derive their value substantially from assets situated in India would not be deemed to be income accruing or arising in India by virtue of the provisions of Explanation 5 to Sec. 9(1i).

MINIMUM ALTERNATE TAX (MAT)

Way back in 2002 the authorities discovered that their own plethora of tax concessions, offering certain specified incomes as tax-free or deductible or earning rebates, has enabled many companies to bring their tax liabilities almost to a negligibly low, if not nil level. This, in spite of their performance being super excellent. This was not strangely palatable to the authorities though all such concessions were and are being offered with a specific purpose of boosting and supporting some certain economic and/or social objectives.

Sec. 115JB was introduced w.e.f. 1-4-2002 requiring all such companies to pay MAT at a reasonable rate of as low as 7.5% of its book profit if the tax as per ITA worked out at lower than this level. The phrase 'book profit' means the net profit as shown in the P&L account prepared in accordance with the provisions of the Companies Act as adjusted by certain specified amounts. The difference between the MAT and actual tax payable is treated as deferred tax, which, as and when the company becomes liable to actually pay any tax over the level of MAT as per the provisions of the ITA, can be adjusted and continue to be adjusted at least for 8 years or until it becomes nil, whichever is earlier.

Over the years, this reasonable rate of 7.5% slowly and steadily became unreasonable due to it being raised to 10% by FA06, 15% by FA09, 18% by FA10 and 18½% by FA11. The actual rate after taking cognizance of cess of 3% and surcharge of 5% (for companies) works out at 20.00775%.

Now, after 13 years, the Department is taking a stand that MAT was and is applicable to Foreign Portfolio Investors (FPIs = Foreign Institutional Investors (FIIs)) and foreign Private Equity firms (PEs) structured as corporate entities.

This stand appears to have ignored the fact that the budget speech related with the year of introduction of MAT as well as the accompanying explanatory memoranda had indicated that this Section will be applicable only to Indian Companies. Moreover, most of such companies are governed by the DTAA between India and the foreign country of which the foreign companies is a Resident. The local Acts of both the countries cannot override the provisions of the DTAA. Therefore, the income computed in accordance with the tax treaty cannot form a part of the book profits for applying MAT.

FA14 has amended Sec. 2(14) to characterise the securities held by FPIs as capital asset. This was a welcome move since the sale of listed securities is free from levy of Capital Gains Tax.

Almost all the income of any FPI arises from transactions in securities and therefore it would be in the nature of capital gains. Consequently, such companies, (assuming that MAT is applicable to them) would never be able to take advantage of the provision of the 'deferred tax' since their tax liability would never cross this current limit of 20.01%. Recognising this fact, the recent FA15 has amended Sec. 115JB so as to provide that income from transactions in securities (other than short-term capital gains arising on transactions on which STT is not chargeable) arising to an FPI shall be excluded from the chargeability of MAT and the profit corresponding to such income shall be reduced from the book profit. The expenditures, if any, debited to the profit & loss account, corresponding to such income (which will be excluded from the MAT liability) are to be added back to the book profit for the purpose of computation of MAT. Good!

Now come several bad aspects —

1. The amendment is to take effect from 1.4.15 leaving FPIs exposed to MAT on all their income for preceding periods.
2. Those FPIs who invest in debt will continue to face the old problems which the amendment intends to resolve.
3. FPIs receiving interest income on government securities and corporate bonds are currently taxed at only 5%. MAT will increase the rate of tax on such interest at 20.00775%.
4. All FPIs will face higher compliance burden such as preparing books of account for its Indian operations as specified by the Companies Act and obtaining a tax certificate from a chartered accountant
5. Offshore funds not registered as FPIs will possibly still be subject to MAT. What about those FPIs with no Permanent Establishment in India? What about all other non- resident investors? At present, none of these draw up any India specific P&L account.

FM, in his recent Budget speech had said that MAT would not be levied for investments of non-residents from 1.4.15. No one realised that, as he explained in one of his subsequent press conference, that he is sticking to his promise of not making any amendments retrospectively. Consequently, if the tax was applicable in the past, it will have to be paid. Newspaper reports indicate that CBDT has already sent out notices to FPIs defaulting on such payment of MAT and the collective demand adds up at about ₹ 40,000 crore!

We feel that the fear and uncertainty surrounding the levying of taxes in general and MAT in particular will not auger well for the 'Make in India' campaign of Mody. All this may lead to a flood of litigations in future.

Thankfully, while passing the Finance Bill by the parliament, FM clarified that capital gains from transfer of securities, interest, royalty and technical service fees accruing or arising even to a foreign company has been excluded from chargeability of MAT if tax payable on such income is less than 18½%.

NRI Selling Shares to NRI

FA12 has clarified (thanks to the Vodafone episode) that overseas transfer of shares between two NRIs of an Indian company would be deemed to be a transfer of capital asset situated in India and therefore, subject to tax on capital gains. This naturally scared the foreign investors who began withdrawing money from India to shift to other countries with stable tax regime. To redeem the lost ground, the Finance Minister has declared —

(a) The clarificatory amendments do not override the provisions of DTAA which India has with 82 countries. It would impact only those cases where the transaction has been routed through low tax or no tax countries with whom India does not have a DTAA.

(b) These will not be used to reopen any cases where assessment orders have already been finalized.

This means that old cases which have not been finalised and new cases which are yet to be filed in a court of law will continue to haunt such investors abroad.

Very scary indeed!

11

Shares and Securities

There are two kinds of investors — those who don't know where the market is headed, and those who don't know that they don't know. Then again, there is a third type — the investment professional, who indeed knows that he or she doesn't know, but whose livelihood depends upon appearing to know.

--- Bernstein William in his book '*The Intelligent Asset Allocator*'

Investment in India, particularly in shares of Indian companies is known to be more rewarding than elsewhere in the global markets since the returns are significantly high and safe. It has become higher and safer particularly under the aegis of the Modi Government. The economic health of the industries at large has improved considerably because of the policy of liberalisation and globalisation. The GDP is slated to rise by over 8% in the current fiscal. The inflation is under control. Therefore, NRIs should invest in India (= Make in India) not only for their own benefit but also to boost the economy of their motherland.

General Conditions
For this discussion, shares include fully and mandatorily Convertible Debentures (CDs). Any NRI can seek RBI permission for any deed which is not covered by general permission, unless, it is specifically prohibited (such as purchasing agricultural land).

ROIs cannot purchase, hold, receive as a gift or by any other means shares of Financial Services Sector which covers Banks, NBFC, Insurance, ARCs, CICs, Stock Exchanges, Clearing Corporations, Depositories, Commodity Exchanges, etc., without approval of RBI.

NRIs (other than citizens of Pakistan or an entity in Pakistan) are allowed to invest in shares of Indian companies listed in recognised stock exchanges in India. Circular AP (DIR) 22 dt. 19.12.07 allows a citizen of Bangladesh or an entity incorporated in Bangladesh to purchase shares of an Indian company under FDI with the prior approval of the FIPB.

RBI Circular (DIR) 1 dt. 13.9.04 has lifted the restriction on dealing in Indian shares by Sri Lankan citizens.

An NRI can purchase shares, debentures, units of MFs, dated central and state government securities (other than bearer securities), treasury bills, units of domestic MFs, bonds issued by a Public Sector Undertaking (PSU) in India and shares in public sector enterprises being disinvested by the Government of India through stock exchanges, either directly or through a Resident trustworthy person, including stock broker as his agent in India.

An NRI should operate through only one AD. Separate DP accounts and also bank accounts are required for handling all these 3 cases. Moreover, separate DP accounts are also required for 'repatriable' and 'non-repatriable' securities. Mostly the shares held prior to becoming an NRI or out of Indian assets earned or received thereafter, are non-repatriable. The system provides the facility to freeze the DP accounts for any debits, or for both, debits and credits.

On returning to India permanently, it is the responsibility of the NRI to inform the change of status to the AD bank and also the DP. Subsequently, a new Resident demat account will have to be opened and the securities transferred to Resident demat account before closing the NRI demat account.

An NRI wishing to purchase shares of an Indian company, outside PIS, especially of non-listed shares, will have to seek RBI approval in the prescribed form.

Citizens of Nepal and Bhutan and also NRI Residents therein are permitted to invest in shares of Indian companies on repatriation basis under FDI. The consideration will be paid only in forex.

The recent FA15 has merged FDI with FPI.

Buy-back of Unlisted Shares
A company, having distributable reserves, has 2 options to distribute the same to its shareholders —

1. Payment of dividends to the shareholders. Such a dividend is subject to DDT and it is exempt in the hands of shareholders.

The current rate of DDT has been raised to 17.304% from 16.995% by the recent FA15.

2. Purchase of its own shares (buy-back) at a consideration fixed by it. This income is taxed in the hands of shareholder as long-term capital gains on which the rate of tax is 20.6%.

The tax of 20.6% on LTCG computed after indexation is lower than the 17.304% of DDT. Therefore, many unlisted companies resorted to distribute dividends through buy-back for avoiding DDT.

FA13 has inserted a new Sec. 115QA to provide that the consideration paid by an unlisted company for purchase of its own shares in excess of the sum received by the company at the time of issue of such shares(= distributed income) will be charged to additional income tax @20% of the distributed income paid to the shareholder. The additional income tax payable by the company shall be the final tax on similar lines as DDT.

No credit or deduction or allowance of such additional tax will be available to the company or the shareholder. Such income would be exempt in the hands of the shareholders.

This loophole has now been effectively plugged.

PORTFOLIO INVESTMENT SCHEME (PIS)

An NRI should operate only through one AD. He shall open a separate NRE(PIS) account for investment on repatriation basis and NRO(PIS) account for non-repatriable basis. He shall take delivery of the shares purchased and give delivery of shares sold. In other words, short selling is not permitted. The limit of holding, both on repatriable and non-repatriable is 5% of the paid-up capital of the company. Moreover, the aggregate paid-up value of shares held by all the NRIs cannot exceed 10% of the paid-up capital of the company. This aggregate ceiling of 10% can be raised to 24% after the General Body of the company passes a special resolution.

All this limit business need not bother you. RBI monitors this limit assiduously on a case-by-case basis and puts the scrip on 'Caution List' when the trigger limit is very near the cap. Thereafter it grants permission on first-come first-served basis. When the limit is reached, such shares are kept on banned-for-purchase list.

The bank shall ensure that amounts due to sale proceeds of shares acquired by modes other than PIS, such as underlying shares acquired on conversion of ADRs/GDRs, shares purchased outside India from other NRIs, shares acquired under private arrangement, shares purchased while he was a Resident in India, do not get credited/debited in the PIS accounts.

NRIs can invest in SEBI approved Exchange Traded Derivative Contracts on non-repatriable basis, subject to the limits prescribed.

Shares acquired by an NRI under PIS shall not be transferred by way of gift except to his close relatives or Charitable Trusts or by way of sale under private arrangement or pledged for giving loan to a third party. The value of securities thus transferred during a *calendar year* should not exceed the rupee equivalent of US$ 50,000 — AP (DIR) Circular 14 dt. 15.9.11.

ADR, GDR & IDR OF INDIAN COMPANIES

Global Depository Receipts (GDRs) are negotiable securities issued outside India by a Depository bank, on behalf of an Indian company, which represent the local Rupee denominated equity shares of the company held as deposit by a Custodian bank in India. GDRs are traded on Stock Exchanges in the US, Singapore, Luxembourg, London, etc. GDRs listed and traded in the US markets are specially referred to as American Depository Receipts (ADRs). In the Indian context, GDRs are treated as FDI.

RBI permits purchase of shares of a JV/WOS abroad of the Indian promoter company which is engaged in the fields of software, by its employees/directors provided —

(i) The consideration for purchase does not exceed US$ 10,000 per employee in a block of 5 calendar years.

(ii) The shares so acquired do not exceed 5% of the paid-up capital of the JV or WOS outside India, and

(iii) After allotment of such shares, the percentage of shares held by the Indian promoter company, together with shares allotted to its employees is not less than the percentage of shares held by the Indian promoter company prior to such allotment.

Proceeds from sale of shares so acquired have to be repatriated to India. In most cases, foreign companies with a stake of more than 51% are listed. So employees are given ESOPs on the local shares.

Sec. 115ACA inserted originally by the FA99 was applicable to a Resident employee of an Indian company, including its Indian and foreign subsidiaries, engaged in the specified knowledge based industry such as Information Technology. It taxed @10% the Residents deriving income by way of dividends or LTCG arising from GDRs purchased under its ESOP.

The recent FA15 has changed the definition of GDR so as to realign it from 'Depository Receipt Mechanism Scheme, 1993, to the new 'Depository Receipts Scheme, 2014'. Earlier, DRs were based on the underlying shares of the company (i.e., sponsored GDR) or Foreign Currency Convertible Bonds (FCCB) of the issuing company and where the company was either a listed company or was to list simultaneously. Besides, the holder of such DRs had to be a Non-Resident only.

As per this new scheme, DRs can be issued against the securities of listed or unlisted and private or public companies against underlying securities which can be debt instruments, shares or units. Further, now the DRs can also be issued by shareholders without involving the company, through the so called unsponsored DR route. DRs can be freely held and transferred by both Residents and Non-residents. Since the tax benefits were intended to be provided in respect of sponsored GDRs and listed companies only, the provisions are amended in such a fashion that the tax benefits continue to be applicable only in respect of such sponsored GDRs and listed companies as defined in the earlier depository scheme.

The move is likely to affect appetite for shares of unlisted companies looking to raise capital abroad.

The ambiguity related with tax implications of DRs (of both listed and unlisted companies) when they are converted to shares is still unresolved. Moreover, the method for determining the cost of acquisition of shares converted from DRs is not provided. This is what we had observed in our last edition, Even this issue has been resolved by the recent FA15. Section 2(42A) of the Act was silent on the computation of period of holding in case of shares which are acquired on redemption of GDRs as referred to in Section 115AC(1b). Now, the period of holding in such a case shall be reckoned from the date on which a request for redemption is made by the assessee. Sec 49(2ABB) has been inserted to provide that the cost of acquisition of shares acquired by a non-resident on redemption of GDRs shall be the price of such shares as prevailing on any recognized stock exchange on the date on which a request for redemption is made by the assessee.

The proceeds so raised have to be kept abroad till actually required in India. Pending repatriation or utilisation of the proceeds, the Indian company can invest the funds in —

(a) Deposits with or Certificate of Deposit or other instruments offered by banks who have been rated by Standard & Poor, Fitch, IBCA, Moody's, etc., and such rating should not below the eligible rating stipulated by RBI. Current eligibility is at AA-

(b) Deposits with branches of ADs outside India, and

(c) Treasury bills and other monetary instruments with a maturity or unexpired maturity of one year or less.

There are no end-use restrictions except for a ban on deployment or investment of such funds in real estate or the stock market. There is no monetary limit on raising of GDRs.

The GDR proceeds can be utilised for the first stage acquisition of shares in the disinvestment process of PSUs and also in the mandatory second stage offer to the public.

A Limited Two-way Fungibility

Under this scheme, a SEBI-registered stock broker in India can purchase shares of an Indian company from the market for conversion into GDRs as required by overseas investors. Re-issuance of GDRs would be permitted to the extent of GDRs which have been redeemed into underlying shares and sold in Indian market.

Sponsored GDR Issue

An Indian company can also sponsor an issue of GDRs where the company offers its Resident shareholders a choice to submit their shares to the company enabling it to issue these abroad. The proceeds of the issue are distributed amongst those Residents who offered their rupee denominated shares for conversion. The proceeds can be credited to EEFC or RFCD or SB rupee account in India. Moreover, where a Resident who has offered his shares as above and has since become an NRI, the sale proceeds can be credited to his foreign currency accounts abroad or in India.

Indian Depository Receipts (IDR)

IDRs, denominated in Indian Rupees, can be issued in India by eligible companies Resident outside India through any Domestic Depository to Residents, NRIs and also SEBI registered FIIs. For raising of funds through issuances of IDRs by financial and banking companies having presence in India, either through a branch or subsidiary, prior approval of the sectoral regulators is necessary.

There is an overall cap of US$ 5 billion for raising capital through IDRs. This cap is akin to the cap imposed on FIIs for investment in debt securities.

The FEMA Regulations shall not be applicable to Residents for investing in IDRs and subsequent transfer arising out of transaction on a recognized stock exchange in India.

To encourage greater foreign participation in the Indian capital market and to retain the domestic liquidity, SEBI has allowed partial fungibility to the extent of redemption of IDRs into underlying equity shares and re-conversion of equity shares of a foreign issuer (which has already listed their IDRs) into IDRs up to 25% of the IDRs originally issued. IDRs shall not be redeemed into underlying equity shares before the expiry of 1 year.

Following guidelines shall be followed on redemption of IDRs —

(i) Listed Indian companies may either sell or continue to hold the underlying shares subject to Regulations 6B and 7 of

Notification FEMA 120/RB-2004 dt. 7.7.04, as amended from time to time.

(ii) Indian MFs may either sell or continue to hold the underlying shares subject to Regulation 6C of above FEMA Notification.

(iii)Other Residents can hold the underlying shares only for sale within 30 days from the date of conversion of the IDRs into underlying shares.

(iv) FEMA provisions shall not apply to the holding of the underlying shares, on redemption of IDRs by the FIIs including SEBI approved sub-accounts of the FIIs and NRIs.

(v) Proceeds of the issue of IDRs shall be immediately repatriated outside India by the eligible companies issuing such IDRs.

Incidentally, gains arising on redemptions of IDR into the underlying equity shares if not specifically exempt would lead to the holder being subjected to tax in the absence of any realised gains, making any redemption unattractive — A point for CBDT to note.

MISCELLANEOUS PROVISIONS

* Transfer of sale of not listed or thinly traded shares under private arrangement are subject to guidelines related with fixing of price, collection of proceeds, documentation, etc.

* A Resident can sell shares (including subscriber's shares), of an Indian company under private arrangement to an ROI, unless the shares are of an Indian company engaged in financial sector.

* Notification FEMA 4/2000-RB dt. 3.5.2000, gives general permission to companies incorporated in India to borrow in rupees by way of issue of Non-Convertible Debentures (NCDs) to NRIs on non-repatriation or repatriation basis.

* RBI ADMA Circular 27 dt. 31.8.99 has granted general permission to Indian Proprietorship Concerns, Firms, Companies for issue of CPs to NRIs on non-repatriable, non-transferable basis.

Dividend & Interest

U/s 9(1iv) any dividend paid by an Indian company outside India, is taxable in India unless it is exempt u/s 10(34). Moreover, u/s 9(1v) interest payable by the following entities is taxable in India—

(a) The Government, or

(b) A Resident, except where the interest is payable in respect of any debt incurred or moneys borrowed and used for business or profession carried on outside India or for earning any income from any source outside India.

(c) An NRI, where the interest is payable on any debt incurred or moneys borrowed and used for a business or profession in India.

Transfer of Shares — Summary

General permission has been granted to rank foreigners and NRIs for acquisition of shares by way of transfer as follows —

* An ROI requires prior permission of RBI to transfer shares, government dated securities, treasury bills, bonds, and units of MFs to any ROI.

* An ROI has to obtain prior approval from RBI for gifting any security to an ROI close relative.

* The application to RBI should indicate (i) relationship between the transferor and the transferee, (ii) reason for the gift and (iii) market value of the securities as certified by a CA or the MF as the case may be. Moreover a certificate from the concerned Indian company certifying that the proposed transfer shall not breach the applicable sectoral cap or the FDI limit and also 5% of its paid up capital.

* The value of security to be transferred together with any security already transferred by the transferor, as gift, to any ROI should not exceed the rupee equivalent of US$ 50,000 during a calendar year — AP (Dir) Circular 14 dt. 15.9.11.

* An ROI can sell the shares of an Indian company on a recognised stock exchange in India through a stock broker registered with stock exchange or a merchant banker registered with SEBI.

* A Resident can sell shares (including transfer of subscriber's shares) of an Indian company.

* Sale under private arrangement by ROI to a Resident is possible.

Investment in Partnership Firm/Proprietary Concern
An NRI (other than a citizen of Bangladesh, Pakistan or Sri Lanka) can contribute capital of a firm or a proprietary concern in India or any association of persons in India on non-repatriation basis. Contribution on repatriation basis requires RBI permission.

Offshore Funds of Foreign MFs
India-dedicated offshore funds invest in the shares of Indian companies but are priced in a foreign currency. Such funds offer a lot of advantages to overseas investors —
1. Currency risk is absent.

2. Any income earned either through dividends or capital gains from offshore funds registered in Mauritius and other extremely tax-friendly regimes will not be taxed in India.

3. Offshore funds have a lower expense ratio of around 1.75% against 2% on domestic funds, thanks to over-regulation.

   Yes, there are some problems —
1. Some offshore funds are priced on a weekly basis limiting the entry and exit facilities to once a week, causing liquidity problems.

2. Usual currency risk also exists for funds which maintain their portfolios in rupees but the NAV is marked to market in US$.

3. The time involved for the fund to sell the underlying investments in India can cause delays.

4. The shares redeemed on any valuation day may be limited to 10% of the total number of shares prior to the valuation day.

Exchange Traded Derivatives Contracts
FIIs and NRIs may invest out of Rupee funds held in India on non-repatriation basis in such contracts subject to the limits prescribed by SEBI. Accordingly, the position limits for FIIs and NRIs shall be the same as the client level position limits.

For Index-based contracts, there is a disclosure requirement for any person or persons acting in concert who together own 15% or more, of the open interest of all derivative contracts on a particular underlying index. For stock option and single stock futures contracts, the gross open position across all derivative contracts on a particular underlying security of an NRI shall not exceed the higher of – 1% of the free float market capitalisation in terms of number of shares, or 5% of the open interest in the derivative contracts on a particular underlying stock in terms of number of contracts.

These position limits would be applicable on the combined position in all derivative contracts on an underlying stock at an exchange.

An NRI is required to notify to the Exchange the names of the Clearing Member/s through whom he would clear his derivative trades. The Exchange would then assign a unique client code to the NRI and monitor his position limits.

ALTERNATIVE INVESTMENT FUNDS (AIFs)

These are privately-pooled investment vehicles, which collects funds from Indian and foreign investors and are primarily established in India for making investments as per a defined investment policy laid out for the benefit of its investors. AIFs can be set up as a trust, company, limited liability partnership or any other body corporate. Similarly, the investment by AIFs can be in entities which can be a company, firm, etc., including another AIF.

In order to regulate AIFs, in May 2012, SEBI had categorized the funds into 3 categories :

Category-I : Funds which invest in start-ups, early stage ventures, social ventures and includes certain venture capital funds (VCF) / venture capital companies (VCC).

Category-II : Funds including PEs or debt which do not fall in Category-I and Category-III which generally are not leveraged.

Category-III : AIFs which employ diverse or complex trading strategies including leveraging and dealings in listed or unlisted derivatives.

AIFs are now available to Foreign Portfolio Investors (FPI) and Foreign Direct Investment (FDI) and for this purpose the distinction between FPI and FDI has been done away with. The present separate caps for both would be merged into one.

To bring about clarity in taxation in the hands of the AIFs as well as their unit holders, a new Sec. 115-UA has been inserted by the recent FA15 providing a special tax regime of a pass-through tax status to Category-I and Category-II AIFs. Consequently —

1. Any income (other than 'Profits & Gains from Business') earned by the AIF shall be chargeable to tax in the hands of the unit holder. Such income shall be completely exempt from tax in the hands of AIF.

2. The income in the nature of 'profits and gains of business or profession' shall be taxable in the hands of AIF. Such income shall be completely exempt in the hands of unit holder.

3. The income paid or credited by the AIF to the unit holder shall be deemed to be of the same nature and in the same proportion in the hands of the unit holder as it had accrued to or received by the AIF.

4. The income paid by an investment fund to its unit-holders shall not be subject to DDT.

5. Where any income (other than business income, which is taxable at AIF level) is payable to a unit holder by an AIF, the fund shall deduct income tax @10%.

6. The income received by the AIF is exempt from the TDS requirement u/s 197A(1F).

7. If in any year, AIF incurs a loss, whether business loss or otherwise, such loss shall not be passed through to the unit holders but would be carried over at AIF level to be set off against income of the next year in accordance with the provisions relating to carry-forward and setoff of losses.

The AIF is required to provide the details of various components of income to the prescribed tax authority and the unit holders.

The existing pass-through regime for VCF and VCC u/s 115-U, which is somewhat different from the proposed regime for AIF will continue to be applied to existing VCFs and VCCs which are registered under SEBI (VCF) Regulations, 1996.

The remaining VCFs and VCCs, being part of Category-I AIFs, shall mandatorily have to follow the new regime.

Now that there is enough clarity in respect of this new tax regime, it is hoped that it will bring in considerable growth in long-term foreign investment and Private Equity (PE) investment in India.

NRI Director of Indian Companies

RBI permission is not required for appointment as a director or to continue as a director of Indian companies, unless the sitting fees, commission, travel fare, etc., are to be paid to him in forex. For seeking RBI permission, there is no prescribed form. Only the Memorandum and Articles of Association and proof of directorship, is required to be submitted.

For Dividend Stripping, see Chapter *Mutual Funds*.

12

Employees' Stock Options

A listed Indian company may issue shares under ESOP to its employees or employees of its joint venture or wholly owned subsidiary abroad who are ROIs, directly or through a trust. Unlisted companies have to follow Companies Act. The face value of the shares should not exceed 5% of the paid-up capital of the company.

The equities should be issued within 180 days from the date of receipt of the inward remittance or by debit to the NRE/FCNR account. Transgression without prior permission of RBI, attracts penal provisions, unless the amount is refunded within this period.

Residents & Foreign Shares

Under AP (DIR) Circular 16 dt. 15.12.01, a Resident employee or a director of an Indian office, branch, subsidiary or a JV (based on the foreign shareholding in the JV) of a foreign company can acquire foreign securities under ESOP without any monetary limit provided (i) the share holding of the foreign company is not less than 51%, (ii) annual return is submitted by the Indian company to RBI through the AD giving details of remittances, beneficiaries, etc., and (iii) the ESOP is offered globally on uniform basis. AP (DIR) Circular 97 dt. 28.3.12 has dropped the condition-(i) above and therefore, such shares can be acquired irrespective of the percentage of the direct or indirect equity stake in the Indian company, subject to the fulfilment of the other two conditions.

AP (DIR) Circular 30 dt. 5.4.06 permits AD banks to allow remittances without any monetary limit for acquiring shares under ESOP irrespective of whether the ESOP is offered directly by the issuing company or indirectly through a trust, SPV, or a Step Down Subsidiary, etc.

General permission is granted to foreign companies for repurchasing the shares issued to Residents under any ESOP provided —

(i) The shares were issued in accordance with the Rules and Regulations framed under FEMA and the shares are being repurchased in terms of the initial offer document, and

(ii) The proceeds thereof are repatriated to India not later than 90 days from the date of their sale.

A Resident who has acquired or holds such foreign securities, may transfer them by way of pledge for obtaining fund-based or non-fund-based facilities in India from an AD.

ADR-GDR of Knowledge-based Indian Companies

RBI may permit an Indian company engaged in the field of software to allow its resident employees, including working directors, to purchase foreign securities under a GDR-linked ESOP, provided the consideration for purchase does not exceed US$ 50,000 or its equivalent in a block of five calendar years.

Cashless ESOP

Under Cashless ESOP issued by a company outside India, the employees can hold stock options and shares granted by the parent organisation without any restrictions on its monetary value, provided it does not involve any remittance from India. However, the employees are bound to sell the shares immediately on the date of exercise. The difference between the sale consideration and the exercise price needs to be promptly repatriated to India. This scheme does not involve any cash outflow and therefore the RBI does not control the implementation of cashless ESOP.

Do cashless ESOP permit acquisition of stock options by employee of subsidiaries, branches, JVs of foreign corporations or is it restricted to employees of the parent corporations working in India? Can these be continued to be held post-retirement or on termination of employment? What about the legal heirs? Clarity is required.

ESOP & Income Tax

FA09 has abolished Fringe Benefit Tax (FBT) under which ESOP was taxed as a perk. Yes, FBT has been abolished but Rule-3 has not been correspondingly amended. This means that beginning from FY 09-10, all the employees, irrespective of the type of the employer, will be taxed on all the fringe benefits.

Accordingly, where the share is listed on a recognised stock exchange, its value shall be the average of the opening price and closing price on that date. If it is listed on more than one recognised stock exchange, the value shall be governed by the exchange which records the highest volume of trading in the share. Where the exchange quotes both 'buy' and 'sell' prices, the 'sell' prices of the first and the last settlement would be taken into account. If there is no trading on that date, the 'sell' price quoted nearest to immediately preceding such date shall be the value.

In the case of non-listed shares, the value shall be determined by a category-I merchant banker registered with SEBI. To avoid multiple valuations depending upon the vesting dates of different employees, the valuation done earlier, not exceeding 180 days, can be taken for the purpose. Thus, the company may have to ask for valuation from the merchant banker, at the most twice in one year.

Foreign ESOPs
Several multinational companies listed on an overseas stock exchange have issued stock options to employees of their Indian subsidiaries. Possibly the new Rule has meticulously avoided the words 'listed in India' following 'recognised stock exchange' to rope in such companies. However, the good work is undone by defining a 'recognised stock exchange' to have the same meaning assigned to it in Sec. 2(f) of the Securities Contracts (Regulation) Act, 1956. This raises some queries. Is FBT payable or not on such ESOPs and if payable, would these have to be treated as 'unlisted'? Can a merchant banker situated abroad do the valuation by registering itself with SEBI? Unless these issues are addressed with clarity, we are in for a large number of litigations. Indian companies listed abroad, also carry these question marks.

Since the sale does not take place in a recognised stock exchange in India, the LTCG gets taxed @20.6% with indexation benefits and STCG at rates applicable to the assessee.

If the employee does not have enough funds to exercise the option, he may use the 'cashless exercise' also known as 'flipping the option' by effecting the sale and purchase on the same day and pay the cost of acquisition out of the sale proceeds.

Such a transaction gives rise to short-term capital gains. A bit of aggression on the employee's part can prevent this from happening. The employee should exercise the option by paying for the shares through a loan, if necessary, one year before effecting the sale. Of course, the cost benefit analysis of the tax saved *vis-a-vis* the interest paid on the loan will have to be carried out.

Where shares, debentures or warrants, are allotted by a company, directly or indirectly, to its employees under ESOP and such shares are transferred by the employee by way of gift or irrevocable transfer, the market value on the date of such transfer shall be deemed to be the full value of the consideration. Such gift would attract provisions of capital gains.

The industry was clamouring for a roll back in FBT which essentially is an expenditure tax. Instead, a fresh item that basically encourages employees to stick to the job and put in that much extra effort has been effectively discouraged.

One step forward, One step backward.

13

Mutual Funds

There are only two investment avenues, besides Banks, where a retail NRI can invest freely with repatriation benefits. One is the share market. Those who do not have time, energy and inclination to study the market may invest in the market through MFs. As a matter of fact, even those who have time, should invest through MFs, because an individual will never be able to compete with the team of researchers the MF employs.

All the MFs have the twin objectives of mobilising the savings of the masses in order to channelise them into productive corporate investments, and providing facilities to persons of even modest means of owning indirectly, equity shares, company bonds, debentures and government securities. An MF is a financial intermediary between investors and the markets (stock and debt). It protects the investor against capital risk by giving him the benefit of its professional expertise in investment management. MF's constant supervision on the portfolio, which it holds on behalf of the investor and the diversification of large funds over a large portfolio throughout the spectrum of industries, is of great value to the investor.

STT & DDT
The matter related with Securities Transaction Tax and Dividend Distribution Tax is covered in Chapter *Capital Gains.*

Dividend & Bonus Stripping for Shares & Units
The 4 conditions applicable for Sec. 94(7) to be operational are —
1. The purchase of shares or units is within 3 months before the record date for dividends.

2. The sale of shares is within 3 months after the record date for dividends or bonuses. In the case of units this period is 9 months.

3. The dividend is tax-free.

4. The transaction results in a loss.

If all these conditions are simultaneously satisfied, loss arising to the taxpayer on the sale, to the extent it does not exceed the dividend, has to be ignored.

Sec. 94(8) deals with bonus stripping, only of MFs and not equities. The stipulation for its applicability is identical with that of dividend stripping with one difference. The loss, if any will also be ignored for the purposes of computing the income chargeable to tax. However, the amount of loss so ignored shall be deemed to be the cost of purchase or acquisition of the bonus units.

This is indeed very unkind to the MF industry.

WHICH SCHEME TO OPT FOR?

All MFs normally offer 3 schemes — Equity-based, Balanced and Debt-based, each with three options, Dividend paying, Dividend reinvestment and Pure-growth. Thus there are nine options.

We do not like the Balanced scheme since the investor can choose his own ratio, by going in separately for the Equity-based and Debt-based scheme. We also do not like the dividend reinvestment plan since it forces you to buy additional units of the same scheme with the amount of dividend. The dividend on equity-based is no more subjected to the DDT. Therefore, the growth option has lost its advantage. Moreover, the debt-based dividend attracts DDT and therefore, it is unattractive. This leaves us with only 2 options — (i) debt-based growth and (ii) equity-based dividend.

Mark to Market
Strange but true, interest rates and prices of fixed income instruments have an inverse relationship. In other words, when the overall interest rates in the economy rise, the prices of fixed income earning instruments fall and *vice versa*.

To illustrate, let us assume that the current NAV of the MF is ₹ 10 and its corpus is ₹ 1,000 crore. This means that if the fund sells all the assets of the scheme and distributes the money on equitable basis to all the unit holders, they will receive Rs. 10 per unit. Now suppose, the interest rate falls from 6.0% to 5.4%. Immediately thereafter you wish to invest ₹ 1 lakh in the scheme. Realise that the entire corpus of the fund stands invested at an average return of 6.0%. If the Fund sells the units to you at it's current NAV of ₹ 10, you will be allotted 10,000 units. This will benefit you immensely. You will be a partner in sharing the benefit of the higher returns of 6.0%, though the fund will be forced to invest your ₹ 1 lakh at the lower rate of 5.4%.

This is injustice to the existing investors. Therefore, comes the 'mark to market' concept. The fund raises its NAV to ₹ 11.11. You will be allotted only 9,000 units and not 10,000. The returns on 9,000 units @ 6.0% would be identical with the returns on 10,000 units @ 5.4%.

In other words, NAV rises when the interest falls and *vice versa*.

CAPITAL ASSURED SCHEMES

The retail investor wants some kind of guarantee, any guarantee. In the past, in their effort to garner as many investors in their fold, the MFs chose the simple way out by giving some assurance or the other, instead of launching on educating the investor. The way the MFs tried to take advantage of this weakness for assurance and their analytical ignorance is manifest from the fact that for one of their schemes, UTI assured respectable dividends but not the capital. All such MFs faced bad problems when the market went into a prolonged bear phase. The parents of the MFs had to rescue their children by funding the deficit.

In spite of all this, there are still many investors who have fallen in love with some assurance without realising that the decision-oriented criteria should only be the brand image, the parentage and the ability of fund manager of the MF and not any assurance.

The MFs have discovered a way to guarantee capital and also derive some benefit from the share market. The idea is simple yet effective. Invest the entire capital in fixed income schemes and invest the interest received therefrom in equities. This way the capital remains intact while participating in equity upside, if any.

Numbers being easier to understand, let us assume that you have investible funds of ₹ 5 lakh. Here is what you do. Out of ₹ 5 lakh invest around ₹ 2 lakh in a bank 10-yr cumulative FD which gives 9.5% interest. Invest the rest ₹ 3 lakh in an equity-based MF. This ₹ 2 lakh FD would grow to ₹ 5 lakh in 10 years. Now, no matter what happens to the money invested in the MFs, at the end of 10 years, you will certainly have ₹ 5 lakh which is what you originally started with. The market value of ₹ 3 lakh of equity-based MF is an additional icing on the cake.

For ease of understanding and not to compromise simplicity over accuracy, we have left out the tax angle.

Surely, the MFs have a vast field from which they can choose guaranteed returns, and this would be much higher than the market rate. Moreover, there are tax benefits for MFs and not for others.

No wonder they say, a steady job and an MF is still the best defence against social security.

FIXED MATURITY PLAN (FMP)

We never liked the close-ended schemes (having a fixed tenure) of MFs because —

1. At redemption scrips in large quantity had to be sold, even when the fundamentals scream for a 'buy'. This would spell disaster for the share market and consequently for the Indian economy.

2. At redemption the investor is forced willy-nilly to pay tax, if any, and reinvest the remaining funds, possibly in similar schemes and possibly in those launched by the same MF. This is a national waste. Longer the term, lesser is this wastage.

   Open-ended funds have the longest term.

3. At present, the debt market is experiencing an upward pressure on the interest rates causing concerns about the rate risk.

The MFs have discovered a new product, Fixed Maturity Plan

(FMP) with varying terms of maturity. These invest in instruments that mature at the same time their scheme term ends. So a 90-day FMP will invest in debt instruments that mature within 90 days. Holding the underlying instruments up to their maturity effectively eliminates the interest rate risk as the value of the instruments at their redemption is known at the time of investment itself. At this particular juncture, it is possible to pick up papers which give a little higher than a yield of 9.70%!!

The MF declares a dividend which is tax-free a day or two in advance of the date of maturity.

Yes, for the short-term FMP, there is this tax arbitrage. For growth FMP schemes with a term of over one year, there is the concessional tax on long-term capital gains. Moreover, the benefit of double indexation can be pocketed.

Double indexation is a neat trick where you hold an investment for a little more than one year but get the benefit of the index multiple of two years. Let us take an example for clarity.

An FMP of a term of 370 days, is launched on 29.3.10, i.e. FY 09-10 and the date of maturity is 3.4.11, i.e., FY 11-12. Let us assume you have invested ₹ 1,00,000 and it has grown by 8.0% to ₹ 1,08,000. The CII for FY 09-10 was 632 and it was 785 for FY 11-12. The indexed cost is ₹ 1,24,209 (= 1,00,000*785/632). The capital gains work out at a loss of ₹ 16,209 (= 1,08,000 − 1,24,209)! This loss is available for set off.

Sadly the retail investor requires guarantee; not double indexation.

To protect the MFs against any unreasonable run on close-ended schemes as happened during the 3rd quarter of 08, SEBI has made it compulsory for all close-ended schemes (except ELSS) to be mandatorily listed. Now, the investor has an exit route only through the markets where he will have to pay a price for the distress sale.

EQUITY-BASED MF SCHEMES

Equity-based schemes of MFs have evolved as the best parking place for all investible funds. These have become more attractive than ever before because of —

(a) Freedom from tax on dividends in the hands of the investor.

(b) No dividend distribution tax required to be paid by the MFs.

(c) Freedom from long-term capital gains tax.

(d) Short-term capital gains taxed at the concessional rate of 10%.

The one and the only disadvantage is the risk factor. The fortunes of equity-based schemes are linked closely with the market and its associated volatility. One can get very good rewards but the possibility of losing one's shirt (and also, in some cases, more intimate garments) cannot be lost sight of.

At this particular post-election juncture, the markets have hit an all time high, and are still looking up, thanks to the Modi factor. The entire country is confident of a robust market growth. The GDP is stated to grow at over 6%.

Perhaps this is the right time to go for equity-based.

OTHER ADVANTAGES

MFs schemes have become more flexible than flexibonds.

1. *Savings Bank Account* : Deposit and withdraw whenever you feel like. Withdrawal takes less than 5 working days against less than 5 minutes in a bank. Banks permit issue of cheques to third parties whereas withdrawal slips (= self-cheques) are for MF schemes. The difference is inconsequential. Such schemes are essentially SB accounts with much higher returns.

2. *Systematic Withdrawal Plan (SWP)* : You can give standing instructions to receive some amount of your choice at a periodicity of your choice — annual, 6-monthly, quarterly or even monthly! That is not all. You can ask for additional withdrawals whenever you need more funds. This becomes a pension plan.

3. *Systematic Investment Plan (SIP)* : You can make investments of an equal amount of money at regular intervals (monthly/quarterly) until you cancel the facility. You may either submit post-dated cheques covering a period of your choice or opt for the auto-debit facility. If you adopt this strategy, you will be averaging out the market movements and this is really a great advantage.

However, we do not advocate this plan. The investor can and should invest regularly but without any commitment. This would enable him to invest higher or lower amounts depending upon the money in hand and also grab new opportunities such as good IPOs. Moreover, keeping track of submitting additional cheques when due or the requisite balance in the bank is a difficult proposition.

4. *One Plan Equals All* : Can be converted into Tax-free Savings Bonds, Children's Gift Growth Plan, Children's College and Career Fund, Marriage Endowment Plan, etc.

5. *Crisis Management* : No need to keep a large amount in savings bank for unforeseen calamities.

MF investments of NRIs

Any NRI or a PIO is allowed to invest in MF schemes on a repatriable basis if the amount invested is forex in nature. It is the internal regulation of some of the countries such as the USA and UK who do not approve of such investments. The MFs accept the investments as long as the address mentioned in the application is not of such countries.

Repatriable DP Account

Normally, investments made by either direct remittance of forex from abroad or by applying NRE funds are repatriable and can be credited to NRE account. This is true in the case of investment in shares, MFs and immovable property in India. The income in India of an NRI from any source can be repatriated abroad after taxes are paid thereon.

However, in the case of shares, the transactions have to be carried out from a Repatriable DP account. In other words, an NRI is required to have, if need be, separate DP accounts, one repatriable and the other non-repatriable.

In the case of MFs, on redemption, MFs issue a certificate indicating that the original amount was invested through an NRE account or direct remittance from abroad.

Tax Neutrality on Merger of MF Schemes

In the USA, very strangely, the number of MF Schemes is much higher than the number of listed shares. India is moving in that direction mainly because of the uncanny attraction of the retail investor to NFOs (=IPOs). In spite of millions of rupees spent on the so called 'investor education' the investor brings money to the Fund only when it floats a new scheme. He refuses to look at the old schemes, even those which have performed very well.

The fund manager is forced to offer brand new schemes with regular ferocity for garnering funds for his house. A natural outcome of this situation is that every fund house has many schemes which are clones. Since long, it had become urgently necessary to merge some of such schemes for better governance. Unfortunately such mergers attracted provisions of capital gains and therefore any attempt in that direction by SEBI received lukewarm response.

Thankfully Sec. 47(viii) has now been inserted to provide tax neutrality when two or more schemes of equity oriented fund or of other than equity oriented fund get merged or consolidated.

Tax on Dividends & Capital Gains

This matter has been covered in Chapter *Capital Gains.*

14

Immovable Property

For most transactions in immovable property of an ROI, RBI has granted its general permission to ADs for administering and monitoring it. All situations not falling under the general permissions, including requests for acquisition of agricultural land by any ROI may be made to the Chief General Manager, Reserve Bank of India, Exchange Control Department, Central Office (External Payments Division), Amar Building, Fort, Mumbai 400001.

Rank Foreigners

Foreign nationals of non-Indian origin resident outside India are not permitted to acquire any immovable property in India unless such property is acquired by way of inheritance (but not as a gift) from a person who was a Resident. However, they can acquire or transfer immovable property in India, on lease, not exceeding five years without the prior permission of the RBI. He needs to seek prior approval of RBI for selling or gifting an agricultural land, plantation property and farm houses held by him in India. He cannot even be a joint 2nd holder along with an NRI or a PIO.

Such persons who have acquired immovable property in India by way of inheritance or have purchased it with the specific approval of the RBI cannot transfer it without prior permission of RBI.

In any case, a citizen of Pakistan, Bangladesh, Sri Lanka, Afghanistan, China, Iran, Nepal or Bhutan, Macau or Hong Kong, can acquire or transfer immovable property in India without prior permission of the RBI other than lease, not exceeding 5 years. This list curbing transaction in real estate has been extended to citizens of Macau and Hong Kong by Notification FEMA 335 / 2015-RB 4.2.15 since these happen to be under special administrative control of China.

For acquiring lease of up to 5 years, they do not need any RBI permission, but approvals, if any, required by other authorities such as the concerned State Government will have to be obtained. The visa should clearly indicate his intention to stay in India for an uncertain period to determine his residential status.

Foreign Embassy, Diplomat or Consulate General can purchase/ sell immovable property in India other than agricultural land/ plantation property/farm house provided (i) clearance from Government of India, Ministry of External Affairs is obtained and (ii) the consideration for acquisition is paid out of funds remitted from abroad through banking normal channels.

Permanent Establishment

An ROI, including a foreign company, who has been permitted to establish a branch or office or place of business in India (excluding a liaison office) can acquire an immovable property in India which is necessary for or incidental to his business. The payment for acquiring such a property should be made by way of forex. A declaration, in Form-IPI is required to be filed with the RBI within 90 days of the acquisition of the property.

Such a property can also be mortgaged with an AD as a security for other borrowings. On winding up of the business, the sale proceeds of such property can be repatriated only with the prior approval of RBI.

However, if the foreign company has established a Liaison Office, it cannot acquire immovable property. In such cases, Liaison Offices, can take property by way of lease not exceeding 5 years.

Transactions Allowed in India

An NRI may purchase, sell, receive gift from or give gift of property to an NRI, PIO or Resident. A PIO also has similar rights except that he cannot sell property to either an NRI or PIO.

If the property is agricultural land or plantation property or farm house, an NRI can sell the property or give gift to a Resident. A PIO has also similar rights but he can sell or gift the property only to Indian citizens permanently residing in India. No other transactions are permitted.

An NRI and PIO (or even a rank foreigner) can receive inheritance of any immovable property with specific approval of RBI provided he had inherited it or had acquired it in accordance with the provisions of the then existing forex law in force.

An NRI or PIO who has acquired any immovable property under the general permission of RBI need not file any papers with RBI.

Refer Table-1 for clarity.

Mortgaging property to party abroad requires RBI's prior approval.

The payment of purchase price, should be made out of funds received in India through normal banking channels by way of inward remittance from any place outside India or funds held in

Table-1 : Transactions of Immovable Property

	NRI	PIO	Resident	Note
Indian Citizen Resident Outside India May				
Purchase Property From	Yes	Yes	Yes	
Sell Property To	Yes	Yes	Yes	
Receive Gift From	Yes	Yes	Yes	
Give Gift To	Yes	Yes	Yes	
Agricultural Property				
Purchase Property From	No	No	No	
Sell Property To	No	No	Yes	
Receive Gift From	No	No	No	
Give Gift To	No	No	Yes	
Person of Indian Origin Resident Outside India May				
Purchase Property From	Yes	Yes	Yes	# 1
Sell Property To	No	No	Yes	
Receive Gift From	Yes	Yes	Yes	
Give Gift To	Yes	Yes	Yes	# 2
Agricultural Property				
Purchase Property From	No	No	No	
Sell Property To	No	No	Yes	# 3
Receive Gift From	No	No	No	
Give Gift To	No	No	Yes	# 3

1. Out of Forex remitted from abroad or NRE or NRO accounts in India.
2. Residential House or Commercial Property.
3. Citizen of India.

any non-resident account maintained in India and no other mode such as traveller's cheque, foreign currency notes, etc. No payment can be made outside India.

Repatriation of Sale Proceeds
Repatriation of sale proceeds of residential property purchased by NRI/PIO is permitted to the extent of the amount paid for acquisition of immovable property in forex. Such repatriation is restricted to not more than 2 such properties. There is no restriction on repatriation of number of commercial properties. The balance amount, if any, can be credited to the NRO account and can be remitted under US$ one million facility.

Where the funds were raised by way of loans from ADs or housing finance institutions, repatriation is allowed to the extent of such loans were repaid in forex.

Repatriation of amounts representing the refund of application or earnest money, purchase consideration made by the house building agencies, seller on account of non-allotment of the property, cancellation of bookings or deals, together with interest (net of income tax payable) may be allowed by the AD provided the original payment was made in forex.

If these provisions are examined carefully it will be noticed that the right to repatriate is acquired by a person who was an NRI/PIO at the time of acquisition and who is an NRI/PIO at the time of the sale. The residential status between these two periods is immaterial.

If the sale takes place on or before the expiry of 3 years, provisions of STCG and if after 3 years LTCG will be attracted.

The remittance facility in respect of sale proceeds of immovable property is not available to citizens of Pakistan, Bangladesh, Sri Lanka, China, Afghanistan, Iran, Nepal and Bhutan. The facility of remittance of sale proceeds of other financial assets is not available to citizens of Pakistan, Bangladesh, Nepal and Bhutan.

Commission to Agents
AP (DIR) Circular 76 dt. 24.2.04 permits ADs to freely allow, without RBI permission, remittance by way of commission to

agents abroad for sale of residential flats or commercial plots in India up to US$ 25,000 or 5% of the inward remittance, per transaction, whichever is higher.

Remittance of Rent
The rental income being a current account transaction is repatriable irrespective of whether the property was purchased through forex or otherwise, subject to tax compliance.

Where the house is purchased through housing finance and it is rented out, the entire rental income, even if it is more than the prescribed instalment, should be first applied towards repayment of the loan. If it is less than the prescribed instalment, the borrower should remit the amount to the extent of the shortfall from abroad or pay it out of his NRE or NRO accounts in India.

Cash Used During Transfer of Real Estate
Sec. 269SS and Sec. 269T have been amended to mandate that no person shall accept or repay from any person any loan or deposit or any sum of money, whether as advance or otherwise, in relation to transfer of an immovable property, otherwise than by an account payee cheque or account payee bank draft or by electronic clearing system , if the amount of such loan, deposit or specified advance is ₹ 20,000 or more. The specified advance means any sum of money in the nature of an advance, by whatever name called, whether or not the transfer of the immovable property takes place. Related penalties are contained in Secs 271D and 271E.

We were under the impression that almost all the transactions of real estate involve a large portion of black money and this fact is known to the lawmakers. Do they feel that this limit of ₹ 20,000 in the legislation will curb black money?

HOUSING FINANCE

The loans can be procured even to (i) purchase a piece of land, (ii) pay stamp duty and (iii) extend or improve an existing house. The security for the loan is always by way of creating equitable mortgage of the property in favour of the lender. Additionally, any existing or a new life insurance policy equal to the loan amount sanctioned should be assigned as collateral security.

The sanction is around 85% of the property cost and starts from a minimum of ₹ 25,000.

Equated Monthly Installments (EMI) is the fixed amount, required to be paid by the borrower every month till the end of the loan tenure. It consists of part principal and part interest. At start, the component of interest is understandably high. As time passes, it reduces and the component towards repayment of capital correspondingly increases.

Housing loan in rupees availed of by NRIs from ADs or Housing Financial Institutions in India can be repaid by the close relatives in India of the borrower.

Tax Provisions
The interest is deductible up to ₹ 2.0 lakh (raised from ₹ 1.5 lakh) by the recent FA14 on loans taken after 1.4.99 with 2 caveats — 1. The house should be completed within 3 years from the end of the year during which the loan is taken and 2. This higher limit is applicable only for acquisition or construction but not for repairs, renewals or reconstruction, for which the old limit of ₹ 30,000 continues to be applicable.

There is no limit on the interest on loans taken for business, commercial or let-out properties.

The interest rates are interesting. Different organisations use different perspectives while announcing their rates. You are advised to take professional help to choose your lender.

Both the concessions, deduction for repayment of capital u/s 80C and of interest u/s 24 are allowed only when the income from house property becomes chargeable to tax. In other words, the construction should be complete, the flat should be ready for occupation and the municipal annual value is known. However, if the interest payable is for a period prior to the year in which the property was acquired or constructed, it shall be deducted in 5 equal annual installments commencing from the year of purchase or construction. The ceilings are applicable to the aggregate of interest payable and the annual installments distributed over 5 years taken together. Similar facility is not available for repayment of capital.

If the construction or acquisition is completed any time in a FY, the interest paid during the entire FY is deemed to be the normal interest though a part of the FY is pre-construction period.

There is no restriction on the source of the funds borrowed to claim the exemption of interest. It is only the tax deduction u/s 80C that requires the loan to be taken from specified sources.

Housing loan is cheap and the tax concessions make it cheaper. Therefore take as large a loan as possible for as long a period as possible, even if you have enough funds on hand.

Many NRIs treat purchase of a house as an investment offering hedge against inflation. When the market price of the property keeps pace with inflation you make payment against the original price with money that becomes cheaper and cheaper. Therefore, they buy a house and keep it under lock and key. In India, it is quite dangerous to give a house on rent. It is quite difficult to evict a non-cooperative tenant even if he stops paying rent. The judiciary is virtually non-existent.

Do not buy a house just because of the tax benefits. There are better methods to save the tax. Similarly, do not buy a house as an investment. You will be putting too many eggs in one basket. Buy it, only if you need it for your personal use. Giving it on rent is fraught with risks.

RBI has made it mandatory for banks not to charge any penalty if borrowers pay back home loans taken on floating interest rates before the end of their repayment schedule. If you are in a fixed interest rate regime, you might face a penalty, which, in some cases may run up to 2% of the outstanding balance.

Where a mortgage was created by the previous owner during his/her lifetime and the same is subsisting on the date of his / her death, the successor obtains only the mortgagor's interest in the property and by discharging the mortgage debt, he / she acquires the mortgagee's interest in the property and thus, the amount paid to clear off the mortgage is the cost of acquisition of the mortgagee's interest in the property which is deductible as the cost of acquisition u/s 48 of the Act. But, if the property is mortgaged by the assessee himself / herself, then the amount paid for discharge of the debt is not part of cost of acquisition – *V. S. M. R. Jagdishchandran v CIT [1997] 93 Taxman 389 (SC)* and *RM. Arunachalam v CIT [1997] 227 ITR 222 (SC).*

The expenses incurred towards society charges should be deducted from the rent for determining the taxable income from properties.

Funds Borrowed Abroad for Purchase of Property in India

Sec. 25 specifically prohibits deductibility under the head 'Income from house property' of any annual charge or interest chargeable which is payable outside India on which tax has not been paid or deducted in India. What if the assessee treats this as his 'Business income?' ROIs are prohibited by FEMA from indulging in business of real property. What if the interest is paid out of the repatriable interest earned on NRE, FCNR accounts? Sec. 14A introduced by FA01 states that the total income can be computed without allowing any deduction in respect of expenditure incurred in relation to income which does not form part of the total income.

This is in line with the intent of the tax legislation. The rent has its nexus in India and therefore it is taxable in India. The interest paid outside India is forex, not taxed in India.

As far as the deduction on repayment of the loans is concerned, it is available only if the loan is taken from specific approved sources and these do not include loans taken abroad.

House held Jointly with a Resident
Yes, an NRI can be owner of a house jointly with a Resident. But there are some precautions to be taken —
1. If he has paid his share of acquisition through forex, he should make direct payments to the builder. Sending drafts in the name of a friend or the joint holder may hamper repatriability when the house is eventually sold.

2. The share of each holder should be well defined and ascertainable for computing the amount of income from housing property, either notional or otherwise. The contribution of the funds should also preferably in the proportion of the defined share.

3. Housing loans, if any, should be taken either strictly in individual names or jointly in the same ratio. This helps in arriving at the amount of tax concessions on housing finance.

4. No loans are easily given on houses in joint names because, in the case of default, a part of a house cannot be confiscated. It is possible that you yourself do not need a loan. In that case, you can stand as a co-obligant or a guarantor to the loan taken by the joint owner.

Resident Holding Property Outside India

Sec. 4 of FEMA prohibits a Resident to acquire, hold, own, possess or transfer any immovable property situated outside India without special or general permission of the RBI unless he —

(a) is a national of a foreign state,

(b) has acquired it on or before 8.7.47 and continues to hold it with RBI permission, and

(c) has acquired it by way of gift or inheritance from a person who had a legal right to hold it, or by way of purchase out of forex held in RFC account.

These restrictions surely conflicts with the Liberalised Remittance Scheme which allows any Resident in India to remit up to US$ 2,00,000 abroad per FY for some current and capital transactions, which include purchase of property abroad.

Do not Purchase House in Wife's Name
Refer Chapter *Gift Tax has Come Back.*

TDS on Sale of Property
This subject is covered in Chapter — *Tedious TDS*

15

Special Provisions

NRIs enjoy the benefit of 'Special Provisions' u/ss 115C to 115-I, dealing with tax on incomes from certain Foreign Exchange Assets (FEA) which the assessee has acquired, purchased or subscribed to in convertible foreign exchange. These are :

1. Shares in an Indian company but not units of MFs.
2. Debentures (convertible as well as non-convertible) issued by an Indian company which is not a private company as defined in the Companies Act 1956.
3. Deposits with an Indian company which is not a private company as defined in the Companies Act 1956.
4. Securities of the Central Government as defined in Sec. 2(2) of the Public Debt Act 1944.

Any income which is derived from FEA is connoted as *investment income*. The definition of FEA does not include bank deposits! But mostly, these can be brought under the purview of the provisions through the above mentioned point-3, 'deposits with an Indian company'. All the banks (i) of which shares are listed in the stock market (e.g., SBI, HDFC Bank, ICICI Bank), (ii) which continue to be Indian companies (e.g., United Western Bank Ltd.) and (iii) nationalised banks which were originally incorporated as Indian companies before nationalisation are eligible for the concessions of special provisions.

None of the foreign banks, or co-operative banks are eligible for this facility, a point which dawns only when it is too late.

Salient Features

■ The NRI is given the option in respect of investment income to be governed either by the special or the general provisions of the ITA. This option can be exercised by expressing his desire through his return of income. He is free to decide for each FY as to whether he wants to opt for the special provisions or not.

■ If the individual opts for the special provisions, his total investment income, without taking any cognizance of the income threshold or deductions under Chapter VI-A, is taxed as a separate block at a flat rate of 20% and @10% on LTCG, unless exempt.

- In case the assessee has other taxable income in addition to investment income, the other income will be taxed at the rates as per the general provisions, where the income threshold and Chapter-VIA are operative.

- U/s 115G it is not necessary to furnish a return of income if the total income consists only of investment income or income by way of LTCG or both and TDS has been correctly applied and there is no additional tax liability. In practice, it is better to file returns to establish continuity.

- In order to avoid delays in remitting the sale proceeds of FEA, Sec. 204(*iia*) authorises an AD to deduct tax if it is not a short-term gain and remit the balance to the NRI or credit it to his NRE account, without the requirement of any NOC from the Department.

- U/s 115F, LTCG arising out of transfer of FEA is not charged to tax if the net consideration is reinvested in FEA within 6 months from the date of transfer. If part of the consideration is invested, proportionate deduction would be allowed. There is a lock-in of 3 years on the new asset acquired. If this new asset is transferred within that period, the exempted capital gains would be brought to tax as LTCG of the year in which the new asset is transferred.

Continuation of Special Provisions
When an NRI becomes a Resident, the concession of the Special Provisions continue to apply till the assets are eventually transferred.

To Be or Not to Be
The special provisions have lost almost all their sheen since, in the case of shares, the dividend as well as tax on LTCG are exempt and short-term gains are taxed @15%. No one will opt for this Special Provision where the rate is 20%.

To find out the level of income at which these provisions become meaningful, let us assume an NRI's entire income of ₹ 17.00 lakh is investment income from FEA.

If he opts for normal rates, his tax liability is ₹ 3.40 lakh and if he opts for Special Provisions his tax liability is also ₹ 3.40 lakh. This means that the Special Provisions become meaningful only when the investment income crosses the level of ₹ 17 lakh.

Wait a minute. This is not true. If the assessee opts for normal rates, he can use the deductions under Chapter VI-A; not so for Special Provisions. The break-even income level works out at ₹ 20.00 lakh, above which, the Special Provisions become useful. These also become useful when he has both investment and non-investment incomes and his non-investment income is over ₹ 10 lakh, taking him to 30% tax zone. At this level, if he does not opt for Special Provisions, he will have to pay 30% tax even on his investment income.

Obviously, the creed of those who can use Special Provisions has almost vanished. It is difficult to understand why such provisions which have outlived their utility are not deleted from the legislation.

Good News

A. Sinha & Rao Ranvijay Singh (AAR 762 of 2007 dt. 3.3.08) held, — NRO deposits shall be treated as FEA and interest thereon shall be treated as investment income u/s 115C(c) which is liable to be taxed @ 20.6%. The only conditions applicable are that the funds in the account should be made out of convertible foreign exchange and further that the account should be in a banking company which is not a private company as per Companies Act.

Some of the very enterprising ADs take advantage of 'Special Provisions' to bring down the TDS rate at 20.6% (Refer Chapter *Tedious TDS*) provided the account balance represents deposits made only in forex.

16
Loans & Overdrafts

Any businessman knows for a fact that loans and overdrafts are excellent leveraging devices for boosting his bottom line. Most of the NRIs prefer to park their funds in India to obtain higher returns and opt for instruments having loan facility even if they have no need for it at the current juncture.

General Conditions
Use of credit card in India by an ROI shall not be deemed as borrowing or lending in rupees.

The rate of interest and margin on all loans may be decided by the ADs, subject to the latest RBI directives.

The funds borrowed either by a Resident or an ROI can be used for his personal requirements and / or own business but not for —

(i) Business related with the prohibited transactions such as chit fund, agriculture or plantation, TDRs, etc.

(ii) Any investment, whether by way of capital or otherwise, in any company, partnership firm, proprietorship concern, any entity whether incorporated or not, or for relending. Such investment includes purchase of immovable property or shares, debentures, bonds, etc., issued by companies in India, including margin trading or derivatives.

Loans can be granted against the security of NRE, FCNR and NRO term deposits but not SB. The banks should not mark any type of lien, direct or indirect, against SB deposits. The term of the loan shall not exceed the balance maturity period of the deposit. The facility of premature withdrawal of NRE / FCNR deposits shall not be available where loans against such deposits are availed of. This requirement should be specially brought to the notice of the deposit holder while sanctioning the loan.

ADs may permit overdraft in the account of the account holder.

Loans to Depositor & 3ʳᵈ Party against NRE / FCNR
There was a ceiling of ₹ 100 lakh on Rupee of Forex loans against security of NRE or FCNR deposits. This ceiling has been dropped w.e.f. 12.10.12. Premature withdrawal of such deposits shall not be permitted. This requirement may specifically be brought to the notice of the deposit holder. The existing loans which are not in conformity with these instructions shall continue for their existing term and shall not be rolled over / renewed.

Rupee loans may be granted by ADs provided —
* There is no direct or indirect forex consideration paid to the NRI depositor for agreeing to pledge his deposits.

* There is no transaction between the guarantor and the borrower involving forex until the guarantee is invoked or the loan is settled. If the guarantor is forced to discharge his guarantee, the NRI may enforce his claim against the Resident borrower. If the liability is discharged by payment out of rupee balances, the amount recovered becomes non-repatriable.

* A Resident, being a principal debtor can make payment to any ROI who has met his liability. The amount remitted or credited shall not exceed the rupee equivalent of the amount paid by the ROI guarantor against the invoked guarantee.

Forex loans in or outside India can be granted by ADs provided the document is executed by the deposit holder himself and not by his PoA or LoA holder.

If the repayment is made by using the NRO account, the interest has to be charged at the full commercial rate in force.

FEMR (Deposit) permits a branch outside India of an AD to give a forex loan against the security of NRE or FCNR deposit.

Loans to NRIs against Shares/Properties, Non-repatriable
An AD can grant a loan in India in rupees to NRIs on non-repatriable basis against the security of shares or other securities or immovable property in India.

Temporary Overdrawing

ADs may allow overdrawing in NRE SB account, up to ₹ 50,000. Such overdrawing together with the interest should be cleared within 2 weeks, out of inward remittances through normal banking channels or by transfer of funds from other NRE accounts.

Forex Borrowing by Residents from NRI Relatives

AP (DIR) Circular 24 dt. 27.9.03 grants general permission to borrow up to US$ 2,50,000 or its equivalent on a repatriable basis by an individual Resident from his close NRI relative subject to—

   * The loan shall be free of interest.

   * The minimum maturity period of the loan shall be 1 year.

   * The amount of loan is received by inward remittance in free forex through normal banking channels or by debit to the NRE account of the NRI.

AP (DIR Series 2011-12) Circular 95 dt. 21.3.12 allows the borrower to repay the installments, interest and other charges directly to NRE account of the lender concerned.

Rupee Loans by Residents to NRI Close Relatives

A Resident individual may give a loan to a close NRI relative by way of crossed cheque or electronic transfer, subject to —

(a) It is free of interest and the minimum maturity is 1 year.

(b) It should be within the overall limit under the Liberalised Remittance Scheme of US$ 1,25,000 per FY (Refer Chapter *Forex Availability — Residents*).

(c) It should be credited to the NRO account of the NRI.

(d) The loan amount shall not be remitted outside India. It should be utilised for the borrower's personal requirements or his own business in India.

Where an authorised dealer in India has granted loan to an NRI, a Resident close relative is permitted to repay the loan taken by NRI by crediting the borrower's loan account through the bank account of such a relative.

Borrowing in Rupees by Residents, Non-repatriable
A Resident individual, partnership or proprietorship firm, may borrow in rupees on repatriable or non-repatriable basis from an NRI subject to—
* The term of the loan shall not exceed 3 years.

* The rate of interest should not exceed 2% over the bank rate.

Loans to NRI Employees
Indian companies are allowed to give term loans in rupees to their NRI/PIO staff for personal purposes, including purchase of housing property in India. The loan shall be granted in accordance with the Lender's Staff Welfare or Housing Loan Scheme. The amount shall be credited to the employee's NRO account. This facility is also available to employees of branches outside India for forex loans.

SEBI Circular CFD/DIL/3/2013, dt. 17.1.13 states that some listed entities have been framing their own employees benefit schemes wherein Trusts have been set up to deal in their own securities in the secondary market. It is apprehended that some entities may frame such schemes for manipulating the price of the securities. This is a fraudulent and unfair trade practice. Now, listed entities are prohibited from framing any employee benefit schemes involving acquisition of own securities from the secondary market.

Loans for ESOP
ADs are allowed to grant Rupee term loans to their NRI / PIO employees for acquiring its shares under its ESOP subject to —
(a) The loan should not exceed 90% of the purchase price of the shares or ₹ 20 lakh whichever is lower. Incidentally, these limits are also applicable to loans to Resident employees.

(b) The amount shall be paid directly by the bank to the company and should not be credited to the borrowers' accounts in India.

Loans to Foreign National Employees
ADMA Circular 36 dt. 11.9.97 has imposed a ceiling of ₹ 5 lakh on loans granted to foreign nationals, not permanently resident in India, for personal purposes such as purchase of household articles, etc. The same ceiling is applicable to liaison offices of the

companies. The terms and conditions should be the same as those applicable to its staff Resident in India.

Housing Finance

An AD or an approved housing finance institution may provide housing loan to an NRI with Indian passport (and not to PIOs) for acquiring a residential house in India. The loan is subject to —
* Term of the loan should not exceed 15 years.

* The quantum of loans, margin money and the period of repayment shall be at par with those applicable to Resident borrowers.

* The loan shall be fully secured by equitable mortgage of the property proposed to be acquired, and if necessary, also by a lien on the borrower's other assets in India. A Resident close relative may also be taken as a co-obligant or guarantor.

* Repayment by close relative in respect of loan in rupees availed by NRI was restricted to housing loans only. AP (DIR) Circular 19 dt. 16.9.11 has granted general permission to Residents to repay loans availed by their NRI close relatives for any purpose.

* The amount should not be credited to borrower's NRE account.

* Where the property is rented out, the entire rental income, even if it is more than the prescribed instalments should be adjusted towards repayment of the loan.

* Rate of interest shall conform with RBI and NHB directives.

* The flat shall be used by the NRI for self-occupation on return to India and not for any other purpose.

Where the land is owned jointly by an NRI borrower with a Resident close relative, the relative should be taken as a co-obligant or guarantor. In such cases the payment of margin money and repayment of the loan installments should be made by the NRI. The loans can also be given to Residents with NRI as a co-obligant.

An NRI requires prior approval of RBI for mortgaging an immovable property to a party abroad.

AP (DIR) Circular 95 dt. 26.4.03 has extended the loan facility for repairs, renovation and improvement of residential accommodation owned in India by NRIs as well as PIOs.

Change in the Residential Status of the Borrower

An AD may (or may not) allow continuance of loan or overdraft of a Resident who subsequently becomes an ROI. In such cases, payment of interest and repayment of loan may be made by inward remittance or out of legitimate resources in India of the borrower.

If a rupee loan was granted by a Resident to another Resident and the lender subsequently becomes an NRI, the repayment of the loan by the Resident borrower should be made by credit to the NRO account of the lender.

Company Deposits

Circular AP (DIR) 89 dt. 24.4.04 prohibits deposits by NRIs with persons other than ADs out of forex.

However, an Indian proprietorship concern / firm, or a company (including a credit-rated NBFC registered with RBI) can accept deposits from NRIs on non-repatriation basis subject to —

* In the case of a company, the deposit may be accepted either under private arrangement or a public deposit scheme.

* The term of the deposit shall not exceed 3 years.

* For NBFCs the rate of interest shall be in conformity with RBI guidelines. In other cases it shall not exceed the rate prescribed under the Companies (Acceptance of Deposit) Rules, 1975.

* The amount received shall be only by debit to NRO account and should not arise from inward remittances or transfers from NRE.

* The interest earned on such deposits, being current income, is repatriable subject to tax compliance.

* The borrower shall not utilise the amount for relending (not applicable to NBFC) or for any of the prohibited activities for NRIs.

17

Tedious TDS

During the process of liberalisation and globalisation, India has given the NRIs a plethora of investment opportunities, on repatriable and non-repatriable basis. However, the authors of legislation entrusted with implementing the vision have not done their home work properly. This has resulted in an NRI walking on the red carpet laid for him with 'WELCOME' signs being entrapped.

Take the case of an NRI intending to purchase a residential property. He is told that — If the consideration is paid out of forex remitted through normal banking channels or the funds held in NRE, repatriation of the amount equivalent in forex paid for the acquisition is permissible when he sells the property for maximum two such properties. Even the properties purchased out of NRO funds (non-repatriable) can be remitted under the US$ one million facility. (Refer Chapter, *Forex Remittances — NRIs*). *Excellent*!

When he actually buys it, he finds that u/s 195(1), he has to apply TDS on the capital gains incurred by the seller if the consideration is ₹ 50 lakh or over. How does he know what is the capital gain of the seller? Well, simple! He applies TDS on the entire sale consideration. This is harsh.

Another way is by way of the seller paying the tax on the capital gains incurred by him even before the due dates for paying the tax. Thereafter, the buyer makes an application to the AO to indicate the amount of TDS by his general or special order and on receiving such order applies the TDS indicated in the order. This is nicely explained in *Syed Aslam Hashmi* v *ITO [2012] 26taxmann.com6*.

The NRI faces a bigger difficulty if and when he sells this house in due course. It is he who has to apply TDS. U/s 203A, every person deducting or collecting tax is required to obtain Tax Deduction and Collection Account Number (TAN). This is different from PAN.

Fortunately the recent FA15 has mitigated this difficulty largely. At present, to reduce the compliance burden on such one-time transactions, for reporting of tax deducted from payment over a specified threshold made for acquisition of immovable property (other than rural agricultural land) from a Resident seller by a Resident buyer, u/s 194-IA, the deductor is allowed to quote his PAN in place of TAN. This facility has now been extended to NRIs. He can give details of his PAN in place of TAN.

What if the NRI does not have a PAN since he was not taxable in India? Even if he was taxable, it is not mandatory for an NRI to own a PAN. Well, he will have to get one.

Then again, the NRI seller has several options to save this tax on capital gains such as buying another house or investing in REC/ NHAI Bonds. Can the ITO accept his intentions? The answer is in the negative. He can apply for a refund through filing of his tax returns for the year.

Moreover, the benefit of setting off the basic threshold against the capital gains and filing Form-15G or 15H for non-deduction of TDS are not available to NRIs. The only way of avoiding TDS for an NRI as provided u/s 195(2) is to request the ITO (Form-13) for issuing a certificate to the person who is responsible for applying TDS (Form-15AA) allowing them not to apply TDS or apply it at lesser rate.

The moot question is — Why should any AO issue any order unless he likes the face of the buyer or the seller?

TDS RATES

Though, for ease of understanding, we have not mentioned the applicability of cess @ 3% on TDS, note that it is always applicable for NRIs but not for Residents. Yet another injustice.

What is the sanctity of having different rates for different incomes? (See Table-1). It behooves the Department to have a standard uniform rate, convenient for itself as well as the taxpayers. The TDS is not the final tax payable. Advance tax is a close relative

Table-1 : TDS Rates

Income Avenue	%
Investment income	20
LTCG from unlisted shares & income under Special Provisions	10
Other LTCG, unless exempt	20
STCG from listed shares & Equity-based Units of MFs	15
Interest on forex loans by Government or an Indian concern	20
Royalties & Fees for Technical Services	25
Winnings from lotteries, crossword, puzzle, horse race, etc.	30
On the whole of the other income	30

of TDS. Moreover, the balance tax, if any, is paid along with filing of his tax returns.

TDS Thresholds

TDS is not required to be applied if the payments do not exceed prescribed threshold limits — Refer Table-2. Readers are requested to take cognizance of these thresholds during our subsequent discussion.

Since an RNOR is basically a Resident, the base rates and thresholds as applicable to Residents is applicable to him. Particular attention is drawn to interest received from bank deposits where the base rate is 10% and the threshold is ₹ 10,000 for Residents and the rate is 30% without any threshold for NRIs.

Table-2 : TDS Thresholds-₹

Section	Nature of Payment	Threshold ₹
194B	Winnings from lottery or crossword puzzles	10,000
194BB	Winnings from horse races	5,000
194C	Payment to contractors	
	— for single transaction	30,000
	— for aggregate transactions	75,000
194D	Insurance commission	20,000
194H	Commission or Brokerage	5,000
194-I	Rent	1,80,000
194J	Fees for professional or technical services	30,000

Because of technological advancements and availability of KYC of the depositor, it is now possible for a bank to add the interest paid to the depositor by all its branches put together. Therefore, the recent FA15 requires the TDS to be applicable at bank level and not branch level. Moreover, since Recurring Deposits are same as Time Deposits, these also have been brought under the ambit of application of TDS. We are afraid that in the near future this provision will become applicable at the level of all the banks.

Non-Resident Entertainer
U/s 194E, TDS rate is 20% for payments made to a non-resident:
(a) sportsman (including an athlete), who is not a citizen of India, or

(b) sports association or institution, or

(c) entertainers (such as a theatre, radio or television artists and musicians) who are not citizen of India.

The term, 'entertainer' is not defined anywhere and this might lead to ambiguity and consequent litigations related with its scope and applicability.

Sec. 194A : Interest other than Interest on Securities
Interest paid by a bank, including a co-operative bank or a post office suffers TDS @10% if the interest exceeds ₹ 10,000. This limit was applicable per branch of the bank. In all other cases the limit continues to be ₹ 5,000.

Sec.194A(3v) offers a general exemption from applying TDS on interest by all co-operative societies to its members. The co-operative banks availed of this exemption by making their depositors as members of different categories. Now, Sec. 194A has been amended to clarify that this exemption provided to co-operative societies will not apply to the payment of interest on time deposits (or recurring deposits) by the co-operative banks.

Brokerage to Distributors
Explanation-I to Sec. 194H defines 'commission or brokerage' to include any payment received or receivable, directly or indirectly,

by a person acting on behalf of another person for services rendered (not being professional services) or for any services in the course of buying or selling of goods or in relation to any transaction relating to any asset, valuable article or thing, not being securities.

CBDT Circular 786 dt. 7.2.2000 declares that commission and brokerage payable to a non-resident agent for securing export business is not taxable in India.

In the case of MFs, some countries including USA and England do not approve of investment in MFs, FDs and some other investment products in India. However, the taxability of such income depends upon DTAA. For instance, under Article 22 of DTAA between India and UAE, the payment of brokerage is in the nature of other income and the same will not be taxable in India.

Royalties & Fees for Technical Services
The TDS is 10%, the same as the tax payable (See Chapter *Income Tax-Royalty or Fees for Technical Services*).

Salary Paid Outside India
Now comes a bombshell. Expatriate employees' salary for working in India is chargeable to tax in India, whether a part or the whole of the salary and allowances are received in or outside India. This issue was raised in *CIT* v. *Eli Lilly & Co. (India) P Ltd.*, which was decided by the Supreme Court on 25.3.09. It held, "TDS had to be applied on the salary and allowances paid abroad, even if the Indian Company was unaware of the payments made abroad by the foreign employer of the expat. It is the duty of the Indian company to apply TDS even on salary and allowances paid abroad by the foreign company, particularly when no work stood performed for the foreign company and the total remuneration stood paid only on account of services rendered in India during the period in question."

Jewellery
FA12 has amended Sec. 206(c) to provide that the seller of bullion and jewellery shall, at the time of receipt of such amount in cash, collect tax @1% of sale consideration from every buyer of bullion

and jewellery, if it exceeds ₹ 2,00,000. Payment by any other means does not attract this provision.

Buy-back of Unlisted Shares
Refer Chapter, *Shares and Securities.*

DTAA
Refer Chapter, *Double Taxation Avoidance Agreement.*

Certificate Received Late
Many a time, assessees have to forfeit such credit on account of TDS certificates not received in time from the issuer. FA02 has amended Sec. 155 to provide that in such cases if the relevant certificate is produced before the ITO within 2 years of filing the related return, credit for TDS would be accorded in that year.

Procedure for Refund of Tax
In the case of NRIs there are many circumstances where income does not either accrue or it accrues but the excess amount has been paid as TDS. This may happen where the contract is cancelled in part or full or change of law or because of a mistake. This warrants refund to the resident responsible for applying TDS but he could not do so because the refund is payable to the person who has earned the income and not to the deductor.

Circular 7/2007 dt. 23.10.07 has solved this difficulty by allowing this amount to be refunded directly to the deductor.

The amount paid into the Government account in such cases to that extent, is no longer 'tax'. In view of this, no interest u/s 244A is admissible on such refunds. Similarly, no expenses related with amount representing TDS refunded is allowable.

Such a refund should be granted only after obtaining an undertaking that no certificate u/s 203 has been issued to the NRI. If it has been issued, the person claiming the refund should either retrieve it from the NRI or should indemnify the Department from any possible loss on account of a separate claim of refund for the same amount by the NRI. The refund should be granted only if the deductee has not filed return of income and the time for filing it has expired.

The limitation for making a claim of refund shall be 2 years from the end of the FY in which TDS is applied. However, all pending cases may also be considered.

Forex Income : Conversion into Rupees

As per Rule 115, the rate of exchange for the calculation of the value in rupees of any forex income shall be the telegraphic transfer buying rate of such currency as on the specified date.

For following incomes, specified date means the last day of the month immediately preceding the month in which —

(a) Salary is due, or is paid in advance or in arrears.

(b) Interest on securities is due.

(c) Profits and gains from the business of operation of ships which is deemed to accrue or arise in India.

(d) Dividend is declared, distributed or paid by the company.

(e) Capital gains where the capital asset is transferred.

For following incomes, specified date means the last day of the previous year unless such income is received in, or brought into India by the assessee or on his behalf before the specified date in accordance with the provisions of FERA (now FEMA) —

(a) Income from house property.

(b) Profits and gains of business or profession (other than from operation of ships).

(c) Income from other sources (other than dividends and interest on securities).

In the case of capital gains arising from the transfer of shares in, or debentures of, an Indian company, the rate of exchange shall be —

(a) For converting the cost of acquisition : Average of TTBR and TTSR of the forex initially utilised for purchase of the asset.

(b) For converting expenditure incurred in connection with its transfer : Average of the TTBR and TTSR.

(c) For converting full value of consideration received or accruing on its transfer : Average of the TTBR and TTSR.

(d) For reconverting capital gains computed in the forex initially utilised for its purchase into rupees : TTBR of such currency as on its date of its transfer.

However, where TDS is required to be applied on such incomes, the specified date would be the date on which the tax was required to be deducted and the exchange rate would be the TTBR of such currency on this date.

Telegraphic Transfer Buying Rate (TTBR) and Telegraphic Transfer Selling Rate (TTSR) are the SBI rates for buying and selling forex made available through a telegraphic transfer.

Uniform Rate of Exchange
In the case of capital assets acquired in foreign exchange, where the amount received in forex has to be converted into INR for determining the value of the acquisition and the consideration received for transfer of such a capital asset, it is the uniform rate of exchange which should be adopted for the purpose. It has been held by the Karnataka High Court, in the case of *Jaya Kumari and Dilhar Kumari v CIT [1991] 189ITR99*, that the exchange value prescribed in Rule 115 must necessarily be followed in computing the capital gains or loss, as the case may be. If the revenue takes the value of pound sterling as on 1-1-1954 (now 1-4-1981) as per Sec. 48 for the purpose of determining the acquisition value of the capital asset and the exchange rate of pound sterling as on the date of salè, it would be acting outside the scope of the Rules.

No TDS on Software
Notification 21/2012 SO 1323(e) dt. 13.6.12 declares that w.e.f. 1.7.12 no TDS shall be made u/s 194J on payment by a resident transferor for acquisition of software where —

(i) the software is acquired in a subsequent transfer and the transferor has transferred the software without any modification,

(ii) tax has been deducted —
    (a)under Section 194J on payment for any previous transfer of such software; or
    (b)U/s 195 on payment for any previous transfer of such software from a non-resident, and

(iii) the transferee obtains a declaration from the transferor that the tax has been deducted either under clause (*iia or b*) along with the PAN of the transferor.

Rupee Denominated LT Infrastructure Bonds

Sec. 194LC provides that if an Indian company borrows money in foreign currency from a source outside India, either under a loan agreement or by way of issue of long-term infrastructure bonds as approved by the Central Government, then the interest payment to a non-resident person would be subject to a concessional TDS @ 5%. The current provisions do not envisage the concessional TDS being applicable for Indian Rupee borrowings.

The section has been amended to provide that where a non-resident (not being a company) or a foreign company has deposited any forex in a designated account through which such sum, converted in rupees, is utilised to subscribe to long-term infrastructure bonds then, such borrowing shall be deemed to have been made in forex.

194LD — Extension of Concessional Tax Period

Sec. 194LD provides for application of TDS at the lower level of 5% in the case of interest payable before the 1.6.15 to FIIs and QFIs on their investments in Government securities and rupee denominated corporate bonds provided that the rate of interest does not exceed the rate notified by the Central Government in this regard. This limitation date for external commercial borrowings has been extended by 2 years at 30. 6.17.

Interest Paid by PE to its HO Abroad

It has now been clarified that a PE in India of a Non-resident is deemed to be a person separate and independent of the Non-resident person of which it is a PE. The provisions relating to computation of total income and determination, collection, and recovery of tax would apply to it. Therefore, the PE in India shall be obligated to apply TDS on any interest payable to either its HO or any other branch or PE, etc., outside India. Non-deduction of tax would result in disallowance of interest claimed as expenditure by the PE and may also attract levy of interest and penalty.

18
Before Leaving and After Returning

Any person, after becoming an NRI is required to inform the following institutions about change in his residential status —
  (a) banks where he has savings or term deposits,
  (b) companies where he has shareholding in physical form,
  (c) DPs where he has demat accounts, and
  (d) MFs whose units he holds.

The banks will redesignate his running accounts as NRO. Some banks close all such accounts and open new ones, causing the account holder untold inconveniences such as requirement to change his KYCs, ECSs, etc. The companies and DPs will inform RBI to enable it monitor the limit on shareholding of all NRIs put together and the MFs will monitor the TDS and repatriability of the funds.

In practice, most of the NRIs do not inform. Fortunately, many of them do not face any problems because the regulatory mechanism of the regulators is not yet in place. Obviously, a few are apprehended and we hope you are not one of them. Realise that nothing is gained by breaking this rule.

It is also necessary to file the tax returns with status as an NRI. If the Indian income is below the taxable threshold, there is no need to file the returns, and if these are to be filed, an NRI need not have a PAN card. It is prudent to file the returns to maintain continuity and possess the card which you may need sometime.

Even after becoming an NRI, one is free to deal with all the investments and assets held prior to becoming an NRI any which way he desires. The only restriction is that, in theory, the original corpus is non-repatriable whereas in practice, it can be remitted under the one-million per FY facility. Income arising out of these assets is repatriable subject to tax compliance.

It is advisable to give a Power of Attorney (PoA) to a trustworthy Resident for ease of operations of bank accounts, investments and other financial transactions. All ADs have their own Letter of Authority (LoA) for the limited purpose of effecting local disbursements and withdrawals for household expenses. It is not necessary to inform the change in status to the accounts offices of PPF and Post Office Schemes.

RETURNING NRI

A person who returns to India permanently, is required to take within a reasonable period, the following actions —

1. Inform the banks, MFs, DPs, etc. about the change in his status. Then these entities will redesignate these as Resident accounts.

2. The NRE and FCNR accounts can be closed either immediately or allowed to run up to their maturity. Such deposits are treated as Resident deposits from the date of return. The originally contracted rates of interest will continue to be applicable until the maturity of the accounts. The FCNR remains tax-free if and only if the returning NRI becomes an RNOR but the NRE becomes taxable from the day of his return, irrespective of the status. Premature withdrawals attract penal provisions.

3. There is also an option of transferring part or full balance to the credit of NRE and FCNR accounts to RFC account within a reasonable period from the date of the arrival in India. There is no penalty for such transfers.

If an NRI is on a short visit to India, the account may continue to be treated as non-resident account even during his stay in India.

If the required actions are not taken in a reasonable time, one would be violating FEMA. He would also lose the benefit of *Special Provisions* as discussed in a previous chapter. What is *reasonable time* is not indicated in the Act and there are many who do not inform for years together on the grounds that they might decide to go abroad once again. Acceptance of such an intention by the AO would depend upon the rent received by him.

Keeping Assets Abroad

FEMA Sec. 6(4) permits an NRI returning to India permanently to continue to hold, own, transfer or invest in foreign currency, foreign security or any immovable property situated outside India, if such assets were acquired, held or owned by him when he was an ROI or inherited these from an ROI. The income and sale proceeds of assets held abroad need not be repatriated.

Similarly, Sec. 6(5) permits an ROI to hold, own, transfer or invest in Indian currency, security or any immovable property situated in India if such currency, security or property was acquired, held or owned by such person when he himself was a Resident or inherited these from a Resident.

This general permission will not apply in respect of any asset received after becoming a Resident by way of gift or inheritance from abroad. Similarly, the benefit is not available on earnings from employment secured subsequent to the return. If the ex-NRI wishes to retain such assets abroad or liquidate them and deposit the money in an RFC account, he has to apply for permission to RBI.

19

Forex Remittances — NRIs

Indian rupee has virtually become fully convertible. NRIs need no more hesitate to grab good investment opportunities in their motherland without any fear of not being able to repatriate the funds abroad, if and when needed. As a matter of fact, the convertibility has reached such a level that they can remit even their non-repatriable funds without much of a difficulty. These are the funds they owned before leaving India or inherited assets thereafter or invested forex on non-repatriable basis.

The procedure for tax compliance as discussed in Chapter *General Provisions* has to be followed for all the types of remittances.

Remittance of Current Income

Sec. 2(*j*) defines 'current account transaction' to mean a transaction other than a capital account transaction and without prejudice to the generality of the foregoing such transaction includes —

(i) payments due in connection with foreign trade, other current business services and short-term banking and credit facilities in the ordinary course of business,

(ii) payments due as interest on loans and as net income from investments,

(iii) remittances for living expenses of parents, spouse and children residing abroad, and

(iv) expenses in connection with foreign travel, education and medical care of parents, spouse and children.

Remittance of current income like rent, dividend, pension, interest, etc. of NRIs is freely allowed. It can also be debited to their NRO accounts if they have such an account. The option of crediting the current income to NRE account is available provided the AD bank is satisfied that the credit represents current income and the procedure for tax compliance has been followed correctly.

Remittance up to US$ 1 million

An NRI is allowed to remit up to US$ one million per FY out of his NRO balances or sale proceeds of assets (inclusive of those acquired by way of inheritance or settlement).

NRI may remit sale proceeds of immovable property acquired by him by way of —

(a) purchase out of rupee funds (or as a Resident), or
(b) inheritance or legacy or gift, or
(c) settlement made by either of his parents or a close relative and the settlement taking effect on the death of the settler, or
(d) settlement without the settler retaining life interest in which case, this may be reckoned as transfer by way of gift.

The remittance can be effected only when it is sought for *bona fide purposes* to the satisfaction of the AD.

The facility is also available to a citizen of foreign state, not being a citizen of Nepal or Bhutan or a PIO for all purposes who —

(a) has retired from an employment in India, or
(b) has inherited the assets from a resident in India, or
(c) is a widow (but not a widower) of an Indian citizen who was a resident in India.

Moreover, this facility is also available for funds acquired under a deed of settlement made by either of his parents or a close relative and the settlement taking effect on the death of the settler, on production of the original deed of settlement.

It is necessary to produce documentary evidence in support of the acquisition, inheritance or legacy of assets by the remitter. Additionally, proof of tax compliance is also necessary.

This US$ 1 million facility is over and above the repatriation of the sale proceeds of immovable property purchased through forex (Refer Chapter *Immovable Property*).

In case the remittance is to be made in more than one installment, all installments should be remitted through the same AD.

Now comes good news! The NRI was allowed to remit the forex abroad but was not allowed to deposit it into his NRE account. If he needed to do so, he had to remit it to his bank abroad and remit it back into his NRE account. AP (DIR) Circular 117 dt. 7.5.12 has now permitted the transfer of such funds from his NRO account to NRE account within the overall ceiling of US$ one million per FY.

The tax, if any, must be paid out of the sale proceeds. The rest of the amount can be remitted abroad or credited to NRE account.

The remittance facility in respect of sale proceeds of immovable property is not available to citizens of Pakistan, Bangladesh, Sri Lanka, China, Afghanistan, Iran, Nepal and Bhutan. The facility of remittance of sale proceeds of other financial assets is not available to citizens of Pakistan, Bangladesh, Nepal and Bhutan.

For arriving at annual ceiling of remittance, sale proceeds of shares and immovable property owned or held by the citizen of foreign state on repatriation basis in accordance with the FEMR — Acquisition and Transfer of Immovable Property in India and FEMR — Transfer of Indian Security by an ROI shall not be included.

To Be or Not to Be
NRIs were smarting under a feeling of injustice arising out of the fact that they own large assets in India but their utility to them was zero. Now, not only the income arising from these assets but also the base capital can be remitted to be utilised any which way.

India is a great parking place for investible funds of NRIs. The money multiplies faster here. This opportunity should not be lost just because it has now become possible to convert rupees in forex and remit it abroad. The limit of US$ 1 million can be used every FY. Therefore, NRIs should indulge only in need-based remittances.

Other Issues

1. A foreigner who has come to India for study or training and has completed it, may remit the balance in his account, representing funds derived out of remittances received from abroad or forex proceeds of FE sold to an AD or stipend or scholarship received.

2. Foreign nationals on temporary visit are allowed to take back the unspent amount of forex against Encashment Certificate or Bank Certificate in Form-ECF or Form-BCI respectively. Both the ECF and BCI are valid only for 3 months for reconversion of rupees into forex in all the cases, temporary visits or otherwise. Take care.

3. Rupee loans can be availed by foreign nationals or liaison offices of foreign companies only for personal purposes such as purchase of household articles up to a maximum of ` 5 lakh on the total borrowings of the depositor and his dependents from all the banks.

4. The RBI has, in a press release dt. 2.5.03 clarified that foreign nationals, including PIOs, while in India, are free to pay charges towards booking airline and train tickets, hotels, hospitals, etc. either in Indian rupees or in equivalent foreign exchange.

5. Notification FEMA 5/2000-RB dt. 3.5.2000 allows diplomatic missions, diplomatic personnel and non-diplomatic staff, who are the nationals of the concerned foreign countries and hold official passport of foreign embassies to hold deposits maintained in foreign currency accounts, subject to the conditions stipulated therein.

6. Notification GSR 90(E) dt. 18.9.07 permits ADs in India to effect remittance of assets of Indian companies under liquidation subject to compliance with the order issued by a court, Official Liquidator or the liquidator in the case of voluntary winding up.

Payment in Rupees

The following transactions are permitted by the RBI —

1. Requests for cash by foreign visitors or NRIs may be acceded up to US$ 3,000 or its equivalent.

2. Any person, to receive any payment in rupees —
   (a) By order or on behalf of a ROI during his stay in India out of rupee funds provided to him by sale of forex to an AD or a money changer in India.

   (b) Against a foreign bank cheque, draft, travellers cheque or foreign currency notes. The forex so received shall be sold to an AD or a money changer within 7 days of its receipt.

   (c) By a postal or money order issued by a post office outside India.

3. A Resident, to make any payment in rupees —
   (a) Towards meeting expenses of a ROI who is on a visit to India on account of boarding, lodging and related services or travel to and from and within India.

   (b) To an ROI, by means of a crossed cheque or a draft for purchase of gold or silver in any form imported by such person in accordance with the Foreign Trade (Development and Regulations) Act, 1992 or under any other law, rules or regulations for the time being in force.

   (c) To bear the medical expenses of a visiting NRI/PIO who is a close relative.

4. A company in India, to make payment in rupees to its whole time director who is an ROI and is on a visit to India for the company's work and is entitled to payment of sitting fees or commission or remuneration, and travel expenses to and from and within India, provided the requirements of any law, rules, regulations, directions for making such payments are duly complied with.

20

Forex Availability — Residents

RBI permits more than sufficient forex for specific needs of all Residents, inclusive of those who have permanently returned to India. Therefore, it is advisable not to have RFC, RFCD and EEFC accounts or leave forex abroad only for maintaining the repatriability.

General Conditions
* Remittances of forex to Nepal, Bhutan, Mauritius, Pakistan or Bangladesh, Cook Islands, Egypt, Guatemala, Indonesia, Myanmar, Nauru, Nigeria, Philippines and Ukraine are prohibited. Investments in Nepal are permitted only in Indian Rupees and in Bhutan in Indian Rupees as well as in freely convertible currencies. All dues receivable on investments made in freely convertible currencies, as well as their sale and winding up proceeds are required to be repatriated to India in freely convertible currencies only. The automatic route facility is not available for investment in Pakistan.

* If the rupee equivalent exceeds ₹ 50,000, either for any one or more drawals reckoned together for a single journey, the entire payment has to be made only by a crossed cheque or banker's cheque or pay order or demand draft or debit / credit / prepaid cards.

* Foreign visitors and NRIs are allowed to convert up to US$ 5,000 in rupees.

* It is not mandatory for ADs to endorse the amount of forex sold for travel abroad on the passport of the traveller, unless the traveller himself desires to have the details recorded. For a private visit, it should invariably be endorsed. In the case of a child travelling on a parent's passport, the endorsement is made on the joint passport.

* Residents may take or send up to two commemorative coins outside India, other than those covered by the Antique and Art Treasure Act, 1972. FEMR (Possession and Retention of Foreign

Currency) allows a Resident to possess foreign coins without limit.

* Traveller's cheques should be signed by the traveller in the presence of an authorised official.

* FEMR (Realisation, Repatriation and Surrender of Foreign Exchange) requires a Resident to whom forex is due or accrued from other sources and where the amount exceeds US$ 2,000 to take all the reasonable steps to realise and repatriate it to India and in no case take any action, to ensure that —
  (i) receipt by him of the whole or part of that forex is delayed, or

  (ii) forex ceases in whole or in part to be receivable by him.

  The Resident shall repatriate it to India and —
  (a) Sell it to an AD.

  (b) Retain or hold it in RFCD.

  (c) Use it for discharge of a debt or liability denominated in forex to the extent and in the manner specified by the RBI.

* In case the forex purchased for a specific purpose is not utilised for that purpose, it can be utilised for any other eligible purpose.

* A Resident individual should surrender received, realised, unspent, unused forex within 180 days from his date of return. This liberalised uniform time limit of 180 days is applicable only to Resident individuals and that too in areas other than export of goods and services. However, he can retain with him forex up to US$ 2,000 (plus foreign coins without any limit) or deposit it in RFCD. Exchange so brought back can be utilised by the individual for subsequent visit abroad. Where a person comes to surrender forex after the limit period is over, the AD should not refuse to purchase it merely because the prescribed period has expired.

* A Resident who has gone abroad for studies or who is on a visit to a foreign country may open, hold and maintain an account with a bank outside India during his stay there. However, on his return to India, the balance in the account should be repatriated.

* ADs may issue a guarantee on behalf of their customers for import of services, provided —
  (a) The guarantee amount does not exceed US$ 500,000.
  (b) AD is satisfied about the bona fides of the transaction.
  (c) AD ensures submission of documentary evidence for import of services in the normal course, and
  (d) The guarantee is to secure a direct contractual liability arising out of a contract between a Resident and a Non-resident.

* All applications for forex exceeding prescribed limits should be referred to — The Regional Office of the Exchange Control Department under whose jurisdiction the applicant is functioning or residing. AP (DIR) Circular 31 dt. 18.10.02 states that a Nodal Officer has been appointed at each Regional Office of RBI to dispose of applications on the same day itself and forward by fax or e-mail. The circular lists the name, telephone and fax number and e-mail address of the Nodal Officer at each Regional Office.

* There are certain transactions which are included in Schedule II to the Rules, where prior approval of the Government of India is required for remittance of such Current Account Transactions. Such items include cultural tours, advertisements in foreign print media, hiring charges of transponders, membership of P&I Club, etc. However, Rule 4 does not apply where the payment is made out of funds held in RFC or EEFC Account of the remitter.

* Where permits or approvals are issued by RBI or GOI, forex may be sold within the period of validity stated on the permit or approval and the sale be endorsed on the reverse of it.

* Out of the overall forex being sold to a traveller or a student going abroad, forex notes and coins may be sold up to the following limits in $s or its equivalent —
  (a) US$ 5,000 : Iraq or Libya.

  (b) Full exchange : Islamic Republic of Iran, Russian Federation and other Republics of Commonwealth of Independent States.

  (c) Other countries : US$ 3,000.

Balance can be in the form of travellers cheque or banker's draft.

Current Account Transactions Liberalised

RBI Circular 76 dt. 24.2.04 has removed or diluted the requirement of RBI's prior approval relating to current account transactions on remittances by residents in following cases —

* Payment for securing health insurance from a company abroad.

* Earnings of artistes e.g., wrestler, dancer, entertainer, etc.

* Commission to agents abroad for sale of residential or commercial plots in India, exceeding 5% of the inward remittances. ADs now may freely allow such remittances up to US$ 25,000 or 5% of the inward remittance, per transaction, whichever is higher.

* Short term credit to overseas offices of Indian companies.

* Where export earnings of the advertiser were less than ₹ 10 lakh during each of the preceding 2 years.

* Where the agreement for technical collaboration had not been registered with RBI. Henceforth, ADs may allow remittances for royalty and payment of lump sum fee, provided the royalty does not exceed 5% on local sales and 8% on exports and lump sum payment does not exceed US$ 2 million.

* Use of trademark or franchise in India. However, RBI's prior approval will continue to be required for remittance towards purchase of trademark or franchise.

* Hiring charges of transponders. Henceforth, the proposal for hiring of transponders by TV Channels and internet service providers will require prior approval of the Ministry of Information & Broadcasting.

Resident Holding Property Abroad

Under Sec. 6(4) of FEMA, a Resident may hold, own, transfer or invest in foreign currency, foreign security or immovable property situated outside India if such assets were acquired, held or owned by him when he was an ROI or inherited these from an ROI.

Circular AP (DIR) 90 dt. 9.1.14 has clarified that such assets cover

* Forex accounts opened and maintained by such a person.

* Income earned through (i) employment or business or vocation outside India taken up or commenced or (ii) from investments made or (iii) from gift or inheritance received.

* Forex including any income arising therefrom, and conversion or replacement or accrual to the same, held outside India by a Resident acquired by way of inheritance from an ROI.

Such a Resident may freely utilise all his eligible assets abroad as well as income therefrom or sale proceeds thereof received after his return to India for making any payments or any fresh investments abroad, provided the cost of such investments and/or any subsequent payments received therefrom are met exclusively out of funds forming part of eligible assets.

Private & Business Visits

ADs may release forex on a self-declaration basis, not exceeding US$ 10,000 or its equivalent in one FY for one or more visits, including tourism (or any other purpose) to any country (except Nepal and Bhutan). This can be released in addition to forex released for any other eligible purposes subject to respective limits.

Visits for attending o an international conference, seminar, specialised training, study tour, apprentice training, etc., are treated as business visits. For such visits exchange may be released by the AD on the basis of self-declaration of the applicant up to US$ 25,000 per trip irrespective of the duration of stay of the individual. The exchange can be released in two or more installment per visit.

Miscellaneous Purposes

Limits have been raised to a whopping US$ 1,00,000 each, without insisting on any supporting documents for —

(a) Employment abroad, including processing and assessment fees for overseas job applications,.

(b) Emigration and emigration consultancy fees — US$ 1,00,000 or the amount prescribed by the country of emigration, whichever is less. The forex released is only to meet the incidental expenses in the country of emigration. No forex can be remitted for earning points or credits.

(c) Maintenance of close relatives abroad.

(d) Education including tie up arrangements with universities abroad, per academic year — US$ 1,00,000 or the amount as per the estimates from the educational institution abroad, whichever is higher.

(e) Medical Treatment abroad.

Exchange can be released without insisting on any estimate from the hospital or doctor either in India or abroad. For amount exceeding this limit, an estimate from the doctor in India or hospital/doctor abroad, is required.

Moreover, a Resident individual can remit up to US$ 25,000 for maintenance expenses of a patient going abroad for medical treatment or check-up abroad or for accompanying as attendant to a patient going abroad for medical treatment or check-up

A person who has fallen sick after proceeding abroad is also entitled for the same.

In addition to these, exchange to the extent needed may be released by the ADs for the following purposes —

* Remittance by tour operators or travel agents to overseas agents, principals, hotels, etc.

* Fee for participation in global conferences and specialised training.

* Remittance for participation in international events and competitions (towards training, sponsorship and prize money).

* Film shooting.

* Disbursement of crew wages.

* Remittance towards fees for examinations held in India and abroad and additional score sheets for GRE, TOEFL, etc.

* Skills / credential assessment fees for intending migrants.

* Visa fees.

* Processing fees for registration of documents as required by the Portuguese / other Governments.

* Registration / subscription / membership fees to International Organisations.

* Other permissible current account transactions without any limits subject to the AD verifying the bona fides of the transaction.

* Securing health insurance from an insurer abroad.

LIBERALISED REMITTANCE SCHEME (LRS)

This Scheme was introduced by AP (DIR) Circular #90 dt. 6.3.12 and Circular #97 dt. 28.3.12.

Resident individuals including minors (but not corporates, partnership firms, HUF, Trusts, etc.), can remit up to a prescribed limit for any permitted capital and/or current account transactions or a combination of both. AP (DIR) Circular 138 has fixed the limit at US$ 1,25,000 w.e.f. 3.6.14.

The facility under LRS is *in addition* to those already available for private travel, business travel, studies, medical treatment, etc., and also for acquisition of qualification shares.

AP (DIR) Circular # 5 dt. 17.7.14 has clarified that the Scheme can also be used for acquisition of immovable property outside India.

Under LRS,
* Remittance entitlements can be consolidated in respect of family members subject to individual family members except for gifts and donations. These cannot be made separately and are subsumed under the LRS limit.

* Investments can be made in MFs, Venture Funds, unrated debt securities, promissory notes, immovable property, shares of both

listed and unlisted overseas company, debt instruments or any other asset outside India such as objects of art subject to the Foreign Trade Policy.

* Rupee gift or loan to a NRI/PIO close relative within the LRS limit can be given by credit to the NRO account of the donee. For details, see Chapter *Loans and Overdrafts.*

* The Scheme can be used for outward remittance in the form of a DD either in the resident individual's own name or in the name of beneficiary with whom he intends putting through the permissible transactions at the time of private visit abroad, against self declaration of the remitter in the format prescribed.

* Gifts by individuals and donations by corporates up to US$ 5,000 per FY per remitter or donor other than Resident individuals. Such gifts and donations by Resident individuals are subsumed under the LRS.

* Remittance of funds for acquisition of ESOPs and ESOPs linked to ADR / GDR. LRS has been extended to ESOPs offered by a foreign company to a Resident employee or a Director of an Indian office, etc. (Refer Chapter *Employees' Stock Option --* Residents & Foreign Shares).

* Resident individual may acquire a foreign security, if it represents qualification shares for becoming a director of a company outside India. The number of shares acquired shall be the minimum required for holding the post of director and in any case shall not exceed 1% of the paid-up capital of the company.

* Resident individual must apply to RBI for permission to acquire shares in a foreign entity offered as consideration for professional services rendered by him to the foreign entity. Now, general permission has been granted for acquiring shares of a foreign entity in part/full consideration of professional services rendered to the foreign company and also in lieu of Director's remuneration.

* A.P. DIR 106 dt. 23.5.13 permits w.e.f. 5.8.13 Resident individuals to set up Joint Ventures or Wholly Owned Subsidiaries outside India for bona fides business activities under this scheme.

Remittance facility under the Scheme is not available for —
(a) Margins or margin calls to overseas exchange counterparty.

(b) Purchase of FCCBs issued by Indian companies in the overseas secondary market.

(c) Trading in forex abroad.

(d) Remittances directly or indirectly to Nepal, Bhutan, Mauritius, Pakistan and to countries identified as non co-operative countries and territories.

(e) Remittances directly or indirectly to those individuals and entities identified as posing significant risk of committing acts of terrorism as advised separately by RBI to the banks.

Miscellaneous

Circular AP (DIR) 37 dt. 19.10.11 clarifies that the investor can retain and reinvest the income earned on investments made under the Scheme. He is not required to repatriate the funds or income generated out of investments made. Remittance is on a gross basis and not on net of repatriation from abroad. This means that once a remittance has reached US$ 1,25,000, no further remittance is possible during the FY even if the proceeds of the investments have been brought back into India.

The individual will have to designate a branch of an AD through which all the remittances under the Scheme will be made. He should have maintained the account for at least one year prior to the remittance. For a new customer, ADs should carry out due diligence on the opening, operation and maintenance of the account.

Banks should not extend any kind of credit facilities, not even against security of the deposits to facilitate remittances under the LRS.

It is mandatory to have PAN for remittances under the Scheme.

Individuals can also open, maintain and hold foreign currency accounts with a bank outside India for making remittances under the Scheme. Such accounts may be used for putting through all transactions connected with or arising from remittances eligible under LRS. Note that an offshore banking unit in India is not treated as an overseas branch of a bank in India.

Dividends as well as STCG received from abroad are chargeable to tax in India in the hands of the investor at the normal rates of tax, based on their slab rate. LTCG in the case of foreign companies is charged to tax @ 20% after claiming the benefits of indexation. The investor has the right to claim the benefit of DTAA.

FOREIGN SECURITIES & RESIDENTS

General permission has been granted to a Resident for purchase or acquisition of securities —
(a) Out of funds held in RFC account.

(b) Bonus or Rights shares on existing holding of foreign currency shares.

(c) Gift from a person Resident Outside India.

(d) Under Cashless ESOP of a company incorporated outside India, provided it does not involve any remittance from India.

(e) Inheritance from a person whether resident in or outside India.

(f) When not permanently resident in India, out of his foreign currency resources outside India.

(g) Purchase of shares of a JV / WOS abroad of the Indian promoter company by the employees or directors of Indian promoter company which is engaged in the field of software where the consideration for purchase does not exceed US$ 10,000 or its equivalent per employee in a block of 5 calendar years.

(h) Purchase of foreign securities under ADR / GDR linked stock option schemes by resident employees of Indian companies in the knowledge based sectors, including working directors provided purchase consideration does not exceed US$ 50,000 or its equivalent in'a block of 5 calendar years.

A Resident individual holding qualification or rights shares may sell these, without prior approval of RBI, provided the sale proceeds are repatriated to India through normal banking channels and documentary evidence thereof is submitted to the AD.

Gifts of Securities

As per AP (DIR) Circular 14 dt. 15.9.11, a Resident who proposes to gift to an ROI any security including shares or convertible debentures requires RBI's prior approval. The limit on value of security to be gifted together with any security already gifted by the transferor, has been raised from US$ 25,000 during a calendar year to US$ 50,000 per financial year.

Pledge/Sale of Foreign Securities

The shares acquired by Residents in accordance with the provisions of FEMA are allowed to be pledged for obtaining credit facilities in India from an AD Category-I bank or a Public Financial Institution.

The Resident may sell such shares provided the proceeds thereof are repatriated not later than 90 days from the date of sale.

MISCELLANEOUS PROVISIONS

Small Value Remittances

ADs may release forex not exceeding US$ 25,000 for all miscellaneous non-trade current account transactions on the basis of a simplified application-cum-declaration version of Form-A2 in place of the normal Form-A2. The payment should be made by a cheque drawn on the applicant's bank account or by a DD.

Donations by Corporates

Further, AP (DIR) 25 dt. 1.3.02 allows Indian corporates with proven track record to contribute funds from their forex earnings up to 1% of the forex earnings during the previous 3 FYs or US$ 5 million, whichever is less for —

(a) Creation of chairs in reputed educational institutes;

(b) Donations to funds (not being an investment fund) promoted by educational institutes; or

(c) Donation to a technical institution or body or association in the field of activity of the donor company.

Post Office
GSR 405(E) dt. 3.5.2000, of RBI permits anyone to buy from any post office, any forex in the form of postal orders or money orders.

Export and Import of Indian currency
This is covered in Chapter, *Baggage Rules*.

Tax Clearance Certificate No More Required
Ministry of Finance & Company Affairs declared that from 9.1.03 onwards, any person who is not domiciled in India or who is domiciled in India at the time of his departure but intends to leave India as an emigrant or intends to proceed to another country on a work permit for taking up any employment or other occupation in that country will not be required to obtain a tax clearance certificate from income tax authorities. However, in some specific cases, the authorities will specifically notify the emigration authorities that such persons should not be allowed to leave India without obtaining a tax clearance certificate. Excellent action! This has nullified the rampant corruption that existed while issuing such clearance.

21

Baggage Rules

Each and every person coming to India from abroad, whether a resident or tourist, an Indian or foreigner, must have a fairly broad idea of the Baggage Rules in India to avoid subsequent heartaches.

General Provisions
* No import license or Customs Clearance Permit (CCP) is required for the clearance of goods as bona fide baggage.

* There is no provision in the baggage rules to endorse the value of the baggage in passports. Passenger who desires to possess some sort of written proof may request for endorsement at the back of the return ticket.

* The various ceilings on allowances are per individual and cannot be pooled with that of another, even between husband and wife.

* A passenger may request the customs for issue of an import/ export certificate for articles of high value such as video cameras, cassette recorders, jewellery, etc., at the time of his arrival or departure from India, to facilitate its re-import or re-export subsequently, without affecting the free allowance available. Normally, such goods are packed and therefore, it is inconvenient to take these out for inspection of the officer. In such cases, the certificates can be issued in advance in custom houses, international airports and sea ports. Such advance certificates are valid for one year.

* Carrying narcotic drugs is strictly prohibited and the punishment can be even a death sentence.

* Import of consumer goods in commercial quantity is not treated as part of bona fide baggage.

* Goods brought through a carrier or courier are not 'gifts' or 'personal baggage' of the carrier. These will be classified as

imported goods requiring a valid import licence. The rates are governed under the Courier Imports (Clearance) Regulations, 1998 (Circular 56/95-Cus dt. 30.5.95).

* Used bona fide personal and household articles of a deceased person are exempt from any duty. A certificate from the Indian Mission declaring that the goods did belong to the deceased person should be produced by the carrier of the goods to customs — MoF Notification 103 (F. 56/7/Cus VI) dt. 19.7.69. In such a case, the value should be ignored, especially when the person is the widow of the deceased person — *Padma K. Fokul Fandhi* v *Collector of Customs, Mumbai* 1995 (78) ELT 265 (Tribunal).

* Passenger may request detention of dutiable or prohibited articles for being returned to him while leaving India. The request can be made either for payment of duty or for re-export or subsequent production of documents. The request for detention cannot be entertained after the goods have been confiscated and/or penalty imposed. However, if the passenger has made a true declaration and it is subsequently realised that the same cannot be cleared for home consumption, he can opt for detention.

If the passenger does not come for clearance of the goods within the period given in the receipt, the authorities can dispose of the goods, deduct customs duty and incidentals and refund the balance.

CLASSES OF ARTICLES

Articles specified in Annexure-I are prohibited. Only one unit of the first 14 items specified in Annexure-II can be imported whereas items in Annexure-III can be imported in any quantity, subject to the overall limit applicable to the passenger. Quantities exceeding the limit are subject to a concessional duty (Refer *Valuation of Goods & Custom Duty*).

Items which attract general allowance for duty-free imports are given in Table-1. Items for personal use are available in Table-2 whereas household items are available in Table-3.

Annexure-I
1. Fire arms.
2. Cartridges of fire arms exceeding 50.
3. Cigarettes exceeding 100 (reduced from 200 by the recent FA14) or cigars exceeding 25 (reduced from 50) or tobacco exceeding 250 grams.
4. Alcoholic liquor or wines in excess of two litres.
5. Gold or silver, in any form, other than ornaments.

Annexure-II
1. Colour Television or Monochrome Television.
2. Digital Video Disc Player.
3. Video Home Theatre System.
4. Dish Washer.
5. Music System.
6. Air Conditioner.
7. Domestic Refrigerators of capacity above 300 litres.
8. Deep Freezer.
9. Microwave Oven.
10. Video Camera with or without combination of one or more of
    (a) Television Receiver; (b) Sound recording or reproducing apparatus; (c) Video reproducing apparatus.
11. Word Processing Machine.
12. Fax Machine.
13. Portable Photocopying Machine.
14. Vessel.
15. Aircraft.
16. Cinematographic films of 35 mm and above.
17. Gold or Silver, in any form, other than ornaments.

Annexure-III
1. Video Cassette Recorder or Video Cassette Player or Video Television Receiver or Video Cassette Disk Player.
2. Washing Machine.
3. Electrical or Liquefied Petroleum Gas Cooking Range.
4. Personal Computer (Desktop).
5. Laptop Computer (Notebook).
6. Domestic Refrigerators of capacity up to 300 litres.

Table-1 : General Duty Free Allowance Items

Airconditioner	Exposure meter	Processed food
Bedding	Films	Radio
Bicycle	Fishing rod	Rain coat
Binocular	Flash units	Razor & blades
Blanket	Food processor	Record player
Blender	Frying pan	Refrigerator
Calculator	Games	Room heater
Car coat	Garments	Rotisserie
Car stereo	Glassware	Service trolley
Carpet sweeper	Gloves	Sewing machine
Cassette player	Golf set	Shoes & socks
Cassette recorder	Hair clipper	Slide projector
Cassette tape	Hair dryer	Smoking pipe
Cheese tins	Hand bag	Sports equipment
Chewing gum	Handkerchief	Stationery
Chocolates	Wall pictures	Still camera
Cigarette	Head-gear	Tape recorder
Cigarette lighter	Headphone	Telephone set
Clock	Health equipment	Textiles
Coffee maker	Heating tray	Time piece
Confectionery	Iron	Toaster
Cooking stove	Iron board	Toiletries
Cosmetics	Juice extractor	Toys
Costume jewellery	Kitchen utensils	Tuner
Crockery	Knitting machine	TV Set
Curios	Lacquer-ware	Two-in-one
Cutlery	Meat grinder	Umbrella
Decoration pieces	Medicines	Under garments
Deep freezer	Mixer	Vacuum cleaner
Deck amplifier	Mosquito destroyer	Vase
Dictaphone	Movie camera	Video camera
Digital audio disc	Movie projector	Video player
Digital clock	Music system	Video tape
Dinner set	Musical Instrument	Voltage regulator
Dish washer	Nail cutters	Wall paper
Door bell	Ordinary typewriter	Washing machine
Dry fruits	PC	Water cooler
Electric fan	Perfume	Water heater
Electric iron	Phonograph records	Water/air purifier
Electric toaster	Photographic outfits	Weighing scale
Electric micro oven	Playing cards	Wig
Electronic typewriter	Polish	Wrist watch
Embroidery	Pressure cooker	

Table-2 : Personal Effects

Bedding	Handkerchiefs	Pants	Sarees
Blankets	Hair dryer	Petticoats	Salwars
Bedsheets	Hair curler/styler	Perfumes	Shoe polish
Sleeping bag	Hearing aids	Toilet articles	Shoe brush
Boiler suits	Headgear	Cosmetics	Spectacles
Blouses	Chair for Invalid	Suits	Tops
Dresses	Jeans	Shirts	Towels
Dentures	Lungis	Shoes	Underwear
Frocks	Neckties	Socks	Umbrella
Gloves	Nighties	Shaving kit	Walking stick

Table-3 : Household Effects

Blender	Kitchenware	Toaster	TV
Crockery	Linens	Utensils	Music System
Cutlery	Liquidizer	Air Conditioner	Camera
Iron	Oven	PC	Typewriter
Egg beater	Pressure cooker	Refrigerator	Tapes
Glassware	Rotisserie	Deep Freezer	Films
Juicer	Tablewares	VCR/VCP	Vehicles

As per Circular 72/98-Cus. dt. 24.9.98 personal effects would also include the following —

(a) Personal jewellery.
(b) One camera with film rolls not exceeding twenty.
(c) One video camera/camcorder with accessories and with video cassettes not exceeding twelve.
(d) One pair of binoculars.
(e) One portable colour television (not exceeding 15 cm in size).
(f) One music system including compact disc player.
(g) One portable typewriter.
(h) One perambulator.
(i) One tent and other camping equipment.
(j) One computer (laptop/note book).
(k) One electronic diary.
(l) One portable wireless receiving set (transistor radio)
(m) Professional equipments, instruments and apparatus of appliances including professional audio/video equipments.
(n) Sports equipments — one fishing outfit, one sporting firearm with 50 cartridges, one non-powdered bicycle, one canoe less

than 51 metres long, one pair of skids, two tennis rackets, one golf set consisting of 14 pieces with a dozen golf balls.

(o) One cell phone.

(p) Cinematographic films, exposed but not developed.

DUTY-FREE ITEMS

All over the world, no duty is levied on used personal effects, (excluding jewellery), required for satisfying daily necessities. Though there is no limit, the number of items should be reasonable. One wrist watch, irrespective of its value, is personal effects.

Residing in India (Rule-3)

A Resident tourist is a person with an Indian passport or a foreigner normally residing in India, who has gone abroad on a short trip. The recent FA14 has increased the duty-free allowance for such a tourist returning after a trip abroad of more than 3 days from ₹ 35,000 to ₹ 45,000. The allowance for children up to 10 years of age unchanged at ₹ 15,000. For a trip of 3 days or less the allowance remains unchanged at ₹ 12,000 for those over 10 years and ₹ 3,000 for children up to 10 years of age.

China, Nepal, Bhutan or Myanmar (Rule-4)

For those returning after a stay of more than 3 days from China, Nepal, Bhutan or Myanmar (Burma) other than by land route, the ceiling is ₹ 6,000. For passengers up to 10 years of age, the allowance is of ₹ 1,500. For 3 days or less, there is no concession.

Professionals (Rule-5)

Indian professional returning from abroad after training, education, contractual employment, etc., with a stay of —

(a) 3 to 6 months : Used household articles — ₹ 12,000 and Professional equipment ₹ 20,000.

(b) 6 months to 365 days : Used household articles — ₹ 12,000 and Professional equipment ₹ 40,000.

(c) Minimum 365 days during the preceding 2 years on termination of his work and who has not availed this concession in the preceding 3 years is allowed duty-free import of household articles and personal effects which have been in the possession and used abroad of himself or his family for at least 6 months and not mentioned in Annexure-I, Annexure-II and Annexure-III — ₹ 75,000. This concession is not available to those who were merely on training abroad, unless the passenger is a government official deputed on training abroad.

This concession cannot be availed in conjunction with TR concessions specified by Rule-8. These allowances are in addition to those offered by Rule-3 or Rule-4 or Rule-6.

'Professional equipment' consists of portable equipment, instrument, apparatus and appliance as are required in the profession by a carpenter, plumber, welder, mason, and the like and shall not include items of common use such as cameras, cassette recorder, dictaphone, personal computer, typewriter, and other similar articles.

Jewellery (Rule-6)
Notification 25/2013-Customs (NT), w.e.f. 1.3.13 has raised the limit to import, free of duty, jewellery up to ₹ 50,000 (from ₹ 10,000) for males and ₹ 1,00,000 (from ₹ 20,000) for females. This rule is also applicable to a person transferring residence.

Even an infant can enjoy this full concession provided the jewellery is for bona fide use of the infant. The value of jewellery is determined at the prevailing international rates. Import of old jewellery for conversion into new one and subsequent re-export is not permitted.

There is no value limit on the export of gold jewellery through baggage, if it constitutes the bona fide baggage of the passenger (F. 495/19/93-Cus VI, dt. 6.10.94). Note that incentives for export of jewellery through legal commercial channels are more attractive.

Commercial export of gold jewellery through the courier mode is permitted subject to observance of prescribed procedures.

Foreign Tourists (Rule-7)
Foreign Tourist is a person not normally Resident in India who

enters India for a stay of not more than 6 months, in the course of any 12 months, for legitimate non-immigrant purposes, such as touring, recreation, sports, health, family reasons, study, pilgrimage or business.

Such a tourist, either of Indian origin or otherwise is allowed used personal effects and travel souvenirs if these are for his personal consumption. Balance should be re-exported when he leaves India.

Whereas the tourists of Indian origin can avail the general allowances available to passengers who are Indian Resident or a foreigner residing in India as per Rule-3, the tourists of foreign origin can bring articles up to ₹ 8,000 for making gifts.

There is no free allowance for tourists of Nepalese or Bhutanese origin coming from their respective countries.

A tourist of (i) Pakistani origin coming from Pakistan other than by land routes and (ii) of any origin coming from Pakistan by land route, can bring articles up to ₹ 6,000 for making gifts.

The land routes are —

Amritsar	(1) Amritsar Railway Station (2) Attari Roads (3) Attari Railway Station (4) Khalra.
Baroda	(5) Assara Naka (6) Khavda Naka (7) Lakhpat (8) Santalpur Naka (9) Suigam Naka.
Delhi	(10) Delhi Railway Station.
Ferozepur	(11) Hussainiwala.
Jodhpur	(12) Barmer Railway Station (13) Munabao Railway Station.
Baramullah	(14) Adoosa.
Poonch	(15) Chakan-da-bagh.

Under Public Notice 34-ITC(PN)/78 dt. 16.5.78, an NRI or a PIO, major or minor, who is normally Resident abroad is entitled to import articles of personal and household effects up to ₹ 5,000, subject to certain conditions. Baggage of family members may be pooled or treated separately. This allowance should be allowed irrespective of educational qualification or profession of the tourist. For example, goldsmith can bring with him his plumbing tools.

Transfer of Residence (Rule-8)

A person on *Transfer of Residence* (TR) to India is a person whose minimum stay abroad is of 2 years immediately preceding the date of his arrival on TR. The total stay in India on short visits during these 2 preceding years should not exceed 6 months and he should not have availed this concession in the preceding 3 years. The concessions can be availed only once in 3 years. This condition cannot be relaxed.

In case there is a shortfall of up to 2 months in the stay abroad and if his early return is on account of terminal leave or vacation or any other special circumstances, it can be condoned by Assistant Commissioner of Customs. The Commissioner has the power to extend this period up to 6 months in deserving cases.

Persons who had availed TR were required to stay in India for minimum one year after their return; not any more.

Indian diplomats, if called back to India in public interest before the stay of 2 years, are also eligible for the concessions provided a certificate to that effect from the ministry of external affairs is produced and the items have been in use and possession of the diplomat for more than 6 months.

Articles allowed free of duty are — used personal and household articles, other than those listed in Annexure-I or Annexure-II but not Annexure III. This is in addition to the allowances offered by Rule-3 and Rule-4 and Rule-6.

TR is not available to each member of the family if they are having a common establishment and staying together. Not more than one unit of each item can be imported by a family.

The passengers, including foreign nationals, will have to pay duty on brand new items for personal use or gifts. Any article will be presumed to be in use if it has been in possession of the passenger for one year. Physical appearance that an article looks new is no ground for denying TR benefit. Purchase bill is to be taken as sufficient evidence. TR benefit must be allowed unless the revenue has sufficient evidence to prove otherwise — *Jiwa Singh* v. *Union of India and Another 1990 (45) ELT 229 (Del.)*.

Even if the goods are offending and liable to confiscation, exemption of TR cannot be denied — *Naresh Lokumal Serai* v. *Commissioner of Customs (Export) Raigad 2006 (203) ELT 0580 Tri-Bom.*

TR for Foreigner Specialist

A foreigner with special technical knowledge or experience, finding that he cannot take the benefit of TR for one reason or another, (e.g., his resident permit of visa is for less than one year) may be allowed with prior approval of RBI, to get his goods released on giving a suitable bond. Other conditions of TR would prevail. The bond can be cancelled if and when he gets the visa extended.

The Indo-Pak Baggage Rules

The Baggage Rules, 1994, are applicable also to Indians and Pakistanis arriving from Pakistan ever since the Indo-Pak Baggage Rules have been rescinded. For export of baggage of passengers proceeding to Pakistan, export trade control concessions contained in Handbook of Import-Export Procedure are applicable. All the provisions regarding the Baggage Rules, 1998 will be applicable to passengers arriving from Pakistan.

TR of Persons from Nepal or Bhutan

There is no passport and visa restrictions between India and Nepal or Bhutan. Therefore, it is difficult to enforce provisions of TR. Nevertheless, persons employed in the Indian Embassy or the Indian Co-operation Mission, can obtain certificates about their bona fide transfer. In other individual cases the concessions are given on the basis of certificate given by the Indian Embassy in Nepal.

Unaccompanied Baggage (Rule-9)

The provisions of all these Rules are also extended to unaccompanied baggage, of goods in possession of the passengers when he was abroad except where they have been specifically excluded. The concessions, to the extent of shortfall availed on the accompanied baggage can be claimed on unaccompanied baggage.

It should be shipped by the passenger within one month of his arrival or dispatched by air within a fortnight of his arrival. The time limit can be extended by assistant commissioner of customs in deserving cases. The unaccompanied baggage can arrive in India up to 2 months prior to the arrival. This limit can also be extended up to one year for reasons to be recorded by the assistant commissioner. For articles shipped beyond these limits, the benefit of duty free import will not be available to the passenger.

Such baggage can also be received by a friend or relatives of the passenger.

NRIs passing through India in transit may also pay the freight in rupees only if it was obtained by sale of forex by the traveller.

The freight rates are normally half the usual cargo rates with a minimum charge for 10 kgs. Freight on accompanied baggage can be accepted in rupees if the fare of the traveller to India was collected in rupees either in India or abroad.

Public Notice 29/86 states that no demurrage is chargeable for storage of baggage since it is baggage and not cargo. This also applies to cases where the goods were detained at the instance of the customs — *R. K. Pariyar* v. *International Airport Authority of India, 1993 (63) ELT 411 (Del).*

Crew Members (Rule-10)
A crew member of a foreign-going vessel is treated on par with Resident passengers for his baggage at the final pay off on termination of his engagement and Rule-3 to Rule-9 would be applicable. In addition, he would also be eligible to the concessions related with import of gold and silver, since a retired employee ceases to be a member of the crew.

The crew members are not allowed to bring costly gadgets like air conditioners, music system, refrigerators, etc., on payment of baggage duty without an import licence, except where such items have been specifically permitted under the Exim Policy in force or under public notice or order issued by the DGFT.

Normally, he signs contracts lasting for small durations and therefore, these Rules can be used repeatedly. Any individual coming to India for a short stay who typically makes more frequent visits, and also an airline crew, may bring petty items like chocolates, cosmetics, cheese, and other petty gift items up to ₹ 1,500 (raised from ₹ 600 by Notification 25/2013-Customs (NT) w.e.f. 1.3.13) per visit for his personal or family use.

A foreign-going vessel includes a vessel —

(a) of a foreign government taking part in a naval exercise;

(b) or aircraft proceeding to a place outside India for any purpose whatsoever; and

(c) engaged in fishing or any other operation outside the territorial waters of India.

PROHIBITED OR RESTRICTED ITEMS

Following items are prohibited from being carried either in checked-in or hand baggage —

◆ Briefcase with built-in alarms or lithium batteries and/or pyrotechnic materials.

◆ Compressed gases, toxic, refrigerated liquids, like camping gas devices.

◆ Corrosive products, acids, mercury, alkali and wet batteries.

◆ Flammable liquids, coal gas, paints and thinners.

◆ Asbestos materials.

◆ Oxidising agents such a chloride of lime and peroxide.

◆ Flammable solids, matches and material which ignite easily substances capable of spontaneous combustion or which on contact with water emit flammable gases.

◆ Poisonous and infectious substances.

◆ Radioactive substances.

Hand bag cannot carry — Gels, Alcohol, Liquids, Creams, Lotions, Sharp articles, etc.

Fire Arms

Import of fire arms is strictly prohibited. Import of Cartridges in excess of 50 is also prohibited. However, in the case of persons transferring their residence to India for a minimum period of one year, one fire arm of permissible bore can be allowed to be imported on payment of applicable duty subject to —

(a) It was in his possession and used abroad for at least one year.

(b) It shall not be sold, loaned, transferred or parted with, for consideration or otherwise, during his lifetime.

(c) He should have a valid arms licence from the local authorities.

Thanks to the terrorists, it is very difficult to get any permission.

Renowned shooters and rifle clubs can import arms and ammunition, of permissible bore for their own use and even for gift purpose, on the recommendation of the Department of Youth Affairs and Sports. An application has to be made using Form given in Appendix-8 of the Handout of Procedures to DGFT.

One Laptop Computer Imported as Baggage Exempt

Notification 11/2004 dt. 8.1.04 has exempted from the duty one laptop computer (notebook) when imported into India by a passenger of the age of 18 years or above (other than a member of the crew).

Replacement of Defective Items

Notification 49/96 Cus dt. 23.7.96 exempts articles and components parts thereof when imported for replacement of defective items.

Pets, Wild Animals & Antiques

Export of most species of wild life, exotic birds, wild orchids and articles made from flora and fauna such as ivory, musk, reptile skins, furs, tiger skins, shahtoosh, etc., is prohibited.

Circular 94/2002-Cus dt. 23.12.02 permits import of up to two dogs and cats per passenger at one time, subject to the production of the required health certificate from the country of origin and examination of the pets by the concerned Quarantine Officer. In such cases, the passengers may not be asked to produce the import licences or import sanitary permits. In all other cases, Circular 9/2002-Cus dt. 30.1.02 applies according to which, bona fide pet animals may be brought into the country only against an import sanitary permit issued by the Department of Animal Husbandry & Dairying or against an import licence issued by the DGFT.

Export of Antique items is prohibited. Artifacts/items over 100 years old are considered antiques.

GIFTS

Any person may buy from any post office any forex in the form of postal orders or money orders. Import of goods which are otherwise freely importable is also permitted without requiring a CCP. In other cases the permit is issued on an application by the Licensing Authority on merits of each case.

A gift to an entity in India can be made subject to —

1. It is made for donee's personal use.

2. It is made by post or otherwise.

3. It does not contain vegetable seeds exceeding one pound in weight, bees, tea, books, literature which is prohibited, canalised items, alcoholic beverages, and consumer electronic items (except hearing aids, life saving equipments, apparatus and appliances and parts thereof).

4. Consumer goods made to charitable, religious or educational institutions and others specified by central government.

5. CIF value of the gift parcel does not exceed ₹ 5,000, vide Notification 87/99 Cus dt. 6.7.99. Postal charges or the air freight shall not be taken into account for determining the value limit.

6. Under para 11.4 of Import Export Policy 1997-2002, goods of value not exceeding ₹ 15,000 in a licensing year may be exported as a gift. Items in the negative list of exports require a license except in the case of edible items.

Postal Imports

Remittances against bills received for imports by post parcel may be made by ADs, provided such goods are normally despatched by post parcel. The parcel receipts must be produced as evidence of despatch through the post and an undertaking must be furnished in Postal Appraisal Form or Customs Assessment Certificate as evidence of import within 3 months from the date of remittance, even if the parcel has already been received in India. Where goods are not of a kind normally imported by post parcel or where the AD is not satisfied about the bona fides of the applicant, the case should be referred to the RBI for prior approval with full particulars together with relative parcel receipt and Postal Appraisal Form or Customs Assessment Certificate.

ADs may make remittances towards import of books by post parcel by booksellers or publishers against bills received for collection, irrespective of the amount involved, against endorsement on the import licence wherever applicable in the normal course. They may also make remittances even if import licences covering the imports have been issued subsequent to the date of import subject to endorsement on such licences.

IMPORT & EXPORT OF CURRENCY

Persons bringing in forex in the form of foreign currency, bank notes and travellers' cheques are required to declare them to the customs authorities in Currency Declaration Form, if the aggregate value thereof exceeds US$ 10,000 or its equivalent and / or the value of foreign currency notes exceeds US$ 5,000 or its equivalent. This facility is per individual, including children, major or minor.

ADs and their exchange bureaux are required to issue Encashment Certificates (EC) in Form-ECF in all cases of purchase of forex from the public, irrespective of whether the Currency Declaration Form (CDF) has been submitted or not by the tenderer of the forex and whether the tenderer requests for the certificate or not. In the absence of encashment certificate, unspent local currency held by non-resident visitors will not be allowed to be converted into forex.

Tourists, while leaving India, are allowed to take with them forex not exceeding an amount brought in by them at the time of their arrival in India. As no declaration is required to be made for bringing in currency notes up to equivalent of US$ 5,000, generally they can take with them at the time of their departure currency notes not exceeding this limit.

AP (DIR) Circular 39 dt. 6.9.13 has raised the limit from ₹ 7,500 to ₹ 10,000 in respect of the Indian currency notes that a Resident going outside India or coming into India. AP (DIR) Circular 146 dt. 19.6.14 has further raised this limit to ₹ 25,000

Since Indian notes and coins (other than ₹ 500 or ₹ 1,000 notes) are acceptable currency in Nepal and Bhutan, travellers can carry Indian currency without any limit but in denomination not above ₹ 100. There is no necessity of carrying forex.

Note that there is no forex exchange counter after immigration.

WEIGHT & SIZE OF BAGGAGE

This is based on weight or number of bags, depending upon the airline. Each passenger is normally allowed to carry as free baggage allowance 40 kgs in first class, 30 kgs in executive class and 20 kgs in economy class. However, a lady's hand bag, reasonable reading material, purse, overcoat, wrap, blanket, umbrella, walking stick, a small camera, binoculars, infant's carrying basket, infant's *en-route* food for consumption, any prosthetic device for passenger's use such as crutches, collapsible wheel chair, etc., are allowed free.

Each passenger is allowed to checked-in bags, each one not exceeding linear dimension (length + breadth + height) of 158 cms and weighing not more than 32 kgs. Passengers in any class with infants (paying 10% of adult fare, not entitled to a separate seat) are allowed one extra piece of checked-in bag up to 10 kgs with total linear dimension not exceeding 115 cms, plus other items as they are allowed under the weight system.

First class and Executive class passengers are allowed to carry two hand bags in the cabin, the total weight of which should not exceed 12 kgs. The economy class passenger can carry only one bag of not more than 8 kgs. The individual dimensions of each piece should not exceed 55 cms × 40 cms × 20 cms. One stroller per child within the allowance is permitted.

A passenger can book additional seat at normal fare to carry hand baggages, the total weight of which is under 75 kgs per seat.

If the bag exceeds the prescribed limits in weight or dimensions, the excess baggage rate is charged which is normally @1% of the normal first class one way fare per kilogram. This slightly varies depending upon the airline and the destination.

Travellers on flights originating from Jammu, Srinagar and Leh are not allowed to carry any hand baggage.

Loss, Delay or Damage of Baggage

The airlines reimburse the loss arising out of loss, delay or damage to the baggage but the rates differ depending upon the air line. Air India pays US$ 20 per kilo for checked baggage and US$ 400 per passenger for unchecked baggage, unless a higher value is declared in advance. No liability is undertaken for goods which are fragile or perishable. For travel wholly between one US point to another, the US law requires the airlines to pay at least US$ 1,250 per passenger.

If a passenger wishes to cover the risk comprehensively, he may go in for insurance of unbreakable articles at a nominal premium of approximately 1% of the insured value declared. Insurance companies make payment on depreciated value of the goods. The passenger is also entitled for compensation if his goods are damaged provided they were properly packed. The payment towards settling the claim may take between 3 weeks and 3 months.

Until the baggage is traced, the airlines meets the essential expenses of the passenger. The amount depends on the profile of the passenger including the class in which he was travelling and the distance from his residence.

Detained Baggage

A passenger may not be in a position to clear a part of his baggage for many reasons, mainly, his inability to pay the duty. He can ask the customs to detain his baggage either for re-export when he leaves India or for payment of the duty or production of related documents subsequently. If he does not come within the time limit specified in the detention receipt, the Customs can dispose the goods. To be able to refund the balance after deducting the duty and the penalty, if any, it collects enough data from the passenger to be able to do so.

When a contraband article is seized, a panchanama should be made at spot. Sometimes, it may not be possible to do so because of lack of facilities. Panchanama has to be witnessed by persons who are locally available for giving evidence later, if required. Merely because some employees were called as they happened to be available, it is no ground to view their evidence with suspicion — Sec. 108 para 13 of the Custom Act, 1962.

Take Care

Some touts and unauthorised persons operate, particularly in the unaccompanied baggage centre of Air Cargo Complexes. It may be quite possible that some of the assessing officers are hand in gloves with them. How else can you explain the presence of these shady characters in the complex? If you keep your list ready, you have nothing to worry. However, the procedures are quite complicated and it is better to employ a recognised clearing agent.

Whenever a dispute arises in respect of bona fide nature of the baggage sought to be cleared under TR, the matter can be brought to the notice of the additional deputy collector of customs for appropriate decision.

VALUATION OF GOODS & CUSTOM DUTY

In view of the difficulty encountered in fixing the value of used items, the government has fixed tariff value of a number of items usually imported by the passengers as baggage. In other cases, the value is fixed on the basis of purchase bills, depreciation (mostly in the case of cars) and other available data. Normally, the value as declared by the passenger is accepted unless proved otherwise. The burden of proof lies on the Department. The rate of exchange as in force on the date on which a bill of entry is presented will be taken for ascertaining allowances and duty.

If there is any unutilised portion of duty-free allowance, a set off of that portion is allowed before charging the duty. No such set off is allowed on unaccompanied baggage.

Articles which exceed the duty-free allowance can be cleared on payment of duty @ 35% ad valorem. Fire arms, cartridges, cigarettes, cigars or tobacco in excess of the quantity allowed is charged customs duty @ 100% ad valorem. Educational cess @ 3% take the applicable rates to 36.05% and 103% respectively.

Goods imported through postal parcels, packers and letters on which total duty payable is not more than ₹ 100 are exempt from customs duty. Similarly, bona fide gifts imported by post or as air freight up to ₹ 10,000 (exclusive of postal or freight charges) are exempt.

The rate of custom duty on VTR or VCR in combination of TV or otherwise, VCP and TV sets, B&W or coloured is 10%.

The rates of duty cited above are liable to frequent changes and therefore you will do well by checking the latest rates applicable.

Misdeclaration or non-declaration attract penal actions. Goods up to ₹ 500 in excess of the declared quantity may be allowed clearance on payment of duty. Excess beyond this limit up to ₹ 2,000 may be allowed on payment of duty and fine. Goods beyond this limit up to ₹ 5,000 may attract penalty besides confiscation whereas goods in excess of ₹ 5,000 may attract, besides other actions, prosecution.

Special Concession

As per Notification 13/2004-Cus dt. 8.1.04 w.e.f. 9.1.04, total exemption on items listed in Annexure-II and concessional duty @15% ad valorem for those in Annexure-III is charged to —

(a) any person returning to India after having stayed abroad for at least 365 days during the 2 years immediately preceding the date of arrival in India. Refer Rule 5 for whom duty-free allowance is ₹ 75,000. The person should declare in writing that the goods have been in his possession abroad or the goods are purchased from a duty-free shop located in the arrival hall.

(b) any person on a bona fide Transfer of Residence (TR) to India as part of his bona fide baggage. Refer Rule-8 for whom duty-free allowance is ₹ 5,00,000. The person should give an additional declaration affirming that no other member of the family has availed of or would avail of this benefit.

Notification 48/2007-Cus dt. 12.11.07 permits Government of India officials proceeding abroad on official postings to carry along with their personal baggage, food items (free or restricted or prohibited) strictly for their personal consumption.

CLEARANCE CHANNELS — GREEN & RED

The green channel is for those not having any dutiable or restricted goods whereas the red is for others. If the goods pass the conditions applicable to the green channel, only 10% of the packages will be opened for examination by the customs. Full examination will be resorted to only in cases of doubts arising out of such percentage examination. Passengers are normally cleared on an oral declaration. It is prudent to have a list of the articles giving their description and value along with all purchase receipts for articles brought as baggage.

For mishandled baggage the passenger should obtain a landing certificate from the airlines and get it countersigned by customs indicating specifically the unutilised portion of the free allowance. This would enable the passenger to avail the unutilised portion of the duty-free allowance if and when the baggage is found.

It is obligatory for disembarking passengers to declare details of plants, seeds, other planting materials, meat and meat products, dairy products, live or ornamental fish, poultry and poultry products. It is also obligatory to declare goods in excess of the free allowance, prohibited or restricted goods, including narcotic drugs, wildlife and its products, arms, explosives, and also commercial goods at the Red Channel Counter. Attempt to import these goods through non-declaration can lead to penal consequences, including arrest.

REGISTRATION FOR FOREIGN NATIONALS

If you are entering India on a Student, Employment, Research, Medical, Medical attendant or missionary visa, which is valid for over 180 days, you are required to register with the Foreigners Registration Officer under whose jurisdiction you propose to stay, within 14 days of arrival in India, irrespective of your actual period of stay.

Foreigners visiting India on any other category of VISA that is valid for over 180 days are not required to register themselves if their actual stay does not exceed 180 days on each visit. If such a foreigner happens to find that his stay would go beyond 180 days, he should get himself registered before he crosses the limit.

PIO card holders should also register for the first stay exceeding 180 days.

Foreign nationals who are exempt from registration are —
(a) those having VISA for 180 days or less;
(b) children under 16 years of age, irrespective of the type of VISA;
(c) those holding OCI card.

Irrespective of the type of VISA, Pakistani nationals are required to register within 24 hours and Afganistan nationals within 14 days of their arrival in India.

For updated information and in case of any difficulty or complaint, you can contact the Customs Officer (PRO).

MOTOR VEHICLES

Cars are excluded from definition of baggage. Import of passenger cars, Jeeps, multi-utility vehicles and motor cycles, etc., both new and second hand, can be imported against an import licence and on payment of customs duty. However, the following persons do not require licence —

(a) Individuals coming to India for permanent settlement after 2 years of continuous stay abroad provided the car has been in his possession for a minimum of 1 year abroad. Short visits to India are to be ignored as provided for in the baggage rules. Consequently, such individuals cannot import brand new cars.

(b) Legal heirs or successors of a deceased relative residing abroad.

(c) A physically handicapped person if the vehicle is specially designed for him. Only one vehicle is allowed and it shall not be sold within 2 years.

A second hand or used vehicle means a vehicle that has been sold, leased or loaned prior to its importation into India. It shall not be older than 3 years from the date of manufacture and shall have a minimum road-worthiness for 5 years.

In all the cases, the new as well as the old vehicles shall have —
(a) A speedometer indicating the speed in kilometres per hour.

(b) Right hand steering and controls. Manufacturers can import left hand drive vehicles only for testing and research.

(c) Photometry of the head lamps to suit keep-left traffic.

Motor cars, motor cycles and scooters, new or old, are chargeable to customs duty on the basis of their list price prevailing in the country of their manufacture on the date on which the bill of entry is presented. Trade discount and depreciation are to be adjusted. Depreciation for used cars is taken from the date of registration to the date of shipment or the date of departure of the owner from abroad, whichever is earlier. Freight, insurance and landing charges are to be added to the price to arrive at the final assessable value.

Import of new vehicles is permitted only through Customs ports at Nhava Sheva, Kolkata, Chennai, Delhi Air Cargo and at ICD Tughlakabad.

Import of new vehicles is permitted only through Customs ports at Nhava Sheva, Kolkata, Chennai, Delhi Air Cargo and at ICD Tughlakabad.

Depreciation Rates

Per quarter in	%
1st year	4.0
2nd year	3.0
3rd year	2.5
4th year & onwards*	2.0
*subject to overall limit of 70%	

This structure of depreciation is applicable to all the used items imported as baggage. The depreciation for each year is to be computed on the Written Down Value method. However, where the straight line method is used to save time it is accepted even when it is beneficial for the passenger.

FA12 has increased the basic customs duty from 60% to 75% on completely built units of large cars, MUVs, SUVs permitted for import without type approval of value exceeding US $ 40,000 and engine capacity exceeding 3000 cc for petrol and 2500 cc for diesel.

Car Registration Licensing and Insurance

You must register and license your vehicle unless you are visiting India for less than 3 months. This is required even if you have been exempted from import duty. You will have to submit a Customs Declaration Form and an undertaking for the re-export of the vehicle. You must take your vehicle for registration to the Regional Transport Office as soon as possible and obtain a license. An international driving license is valid in India.

You will be required to show to the RTO that you are adequately insured covering all the risks, including third party liabilities before you register your vehicle.

22

PAN is PAIN

As per Sec. 139A (5a&b), from 1.1.05 it is mandatory to quote PAN on challans for any payments due to the Department. Moreover, Sec. 139A(5c) read with Rule 114B makes it compulsory to quote PAN in all documents pertaining to some financial transactions, mainly purchase and sale of shares and MF schemes. Because of the distance, NRIs find it very difficult to obtain a PAN mainly due to lack of understanding of the exact requirements. This is an attempt to clarify the position in detail.

Though NRIs are not mandatorily required to possess a PAN, it is advisable for all those who have or likely to have in near future taxable income in India.

How to Obtain PAN

UTI Investor Services Ltd. (UTIITSL) and National Securities Depository Ltd. (NSDL) are authorised to issue PAN cards. The fee for preparation and delivery of a tamper proof card is Rs. 67 plus courier charges, if any, to be paid at IT PAN Service Centre or the TIN Facilitation Centre. Details of service charges and delivery time are available on their respective websites.

Addresses

UTIITSL —

The Vice President
IT PAN Processing Centre
UTI Investor Services Ltd.
Plot No. 3, Sector - 11
CBD, Belapur
Navi Mumbai-400 614
e-mail.- utiisl-gsd@mail.utiisl.co.in
Tel 022-27561690
Fax 022-27561706

NSDL —

The Vice President
Income Tax PAN Services Unit, NSDL
4th Floor, Trade World, A Wing
Kamala Mills Compound
S. B. Marg, Lower Parel
Mumbai-400 013
e-mail.- tininfo@nsdl.co.in
Tel 022-2499 4650
Fax 022-2495 0664

Coupon number or Acknowledgement number, as the case may be, should be mentioned in all communications.

Application Form-49A can be downloaded from the website of the Department or UTIISL or NSDL (www.incometaxindia.gov.in, www.utiisl.co.in or tin.nsdl.com) or photocopied (on A4 size 70 GSM paper) or obtained from any other source. The Form is also available at IT PAN Service centers and TIN Facilitation centers.

If an application is submitted through Internet and payment made through a 'nominated' credit card, the PAN is allotted on priority (TATKAL) and communicated through e-mail.

It is illegal to obtain or possess more than one PAN [Sec. 139A(7)].

Filling the Application Form
Form must be filled and signed using black ink only. Note that —

* Individual applicants will have to affix 2 recent coloured photographs (Stamp Size : 3.5 cms × 2.5 cms). Three signatures are required — 1. At the left side of the photograph across the photograph. 2. Box provided below the photograph, and 3. On page two in the box at end of the form.

* Full Name is required in the order of Surname, First name and middle name. However, provision is available in the form for you to select the style in which your name is to appear in PAN card. For instance, if your name is Sunil Raghav Shah, you can ask for S. R. Shah to be printed on the card. Only father's name is required to be filled in the Form, even by female applicants, irrespective of their marital status.

* Assessing Officer (AO) code pertaining to International Taxation Directorate are available on the website of service providers. However, in case of doubts the first international taxation Assessing Officer of Delhi may be used as default AO code.

* NRIs not having any Indian residential address may provide a foreign address. Such applicants should indicate the address at which the PAN card should be sent in column-6 and also invariably mention their email-id in column-7.

* Codes 99 and 999999 should be entered for State and PIN fields respectively by those who do not have any Indian address.

However, actual foreign ZIP/PIN code should be mentioned in any of the 5 address fields (preferably last) along with the name of the country.

* The previous requirement of mentioning the name of a Representative Assessee in India has been dropped.

Proofs of Identity & Address

S.O. 2394(E) dt. 17.10.11 has stipulated that copy of any one of the following documents is sufficient for the purpose —

(a) Passport or visa.

(b) PIO/OCI card.

(c) NRE account statement.

(d) Other national or citizenship identification number.

(e) Bank account statement (not more than 2 months old) in country of residence.

(f) Certificate of residence in India or Residential permit issued by the State Police Authority.

(g) Registration certificate of the Foreigner's Registration Office showing Indian address.

(h) Appointment letter or contract from Indian company or certificate (in original) of Indian service providers and finally,

(i) Taxpayer Identification Number duly attested by 'Apostille' (in respect of countries which are signatories to the Hague Apostille Convention of 1961) or by Indian embassy or High Commission or Consulate in the country where the applicant is located.

(j) From 3.2.14 onwards, every applicant will have to submit self-attested copies of proof of identity, address and date of birth documents and also produce original documents for verification.

In case the PAN applicant is a minor, any of above documents of any of the parents or guardian shall serve as proof of Address. In case PAN application is made on behalf of a HUF, any of above documents of the Karta will serve as proof of Address.

Non-individuals having no office in India should submit a copy of registration certificate of their country duly attested by Indian Embassy in the country where applicant is located.

DEPOSITORY PARTICIPANT

It is also necessary to have a PAN while opening an account with a DP for share transactions in demat format.

NRIs/PIOs who are not able to obtain PAN for one reason or the other but are holding securities in physical form and desire to sell the same, may be permitted to open a 'limited purpose account' without PAN subject to —

◆ These accounts will be 'suspended for credit' which means, only credits arising out of corporate benefits and demat of physical certificates will be permitted.

◆ These accounts cannot be used for getting credit from IPOs, any off-market or secondary market transactions, etc.

◆ These accounts can remain operational only for a limited period of 6 months to regularise the account. The DPs shall freeze non-regularised accounts thereafter.

◆ The account holders can sell the securities lying in these accounts only through a registered broker on the stock exchange.

◆ Where there is difference in the maiden name and current name of the investor (predominantly in the case of married women), DPs can collect the PAN card proof as submitted by the account holder. However, this would be subject to the DPs verifying the veracity of the claim of such investors by collecting sufficient documentary evidence in support of the identity of the investor.

KYC NORMS FOR MUTUAL FUNDS

It is compulsory for all the MFs w.e.f. 3.3.08 to comply with KYC norms for all the applications including New Fund Offer applications of ₹ 50,000 or more. This requirement is applicable even to all the joint holders. This is grossly unjustified, inconvenient and unfriendly measure involving a national waste and benefits none. AMFI exists to protect the investors in MFs and we are surprised to find that this particular diktat has been issued by AMFI itself.

Application forms are separate for individuals and non-individuals. These can be downloaded from the website of AMFI/ MFs or obtained from any distributor.

If you have multiple folios within one Fund, you can instruct the MF to update the KYC against all the folios. A copy of the receipt allotted while submitting the KYC Form is required to be attached along with all new investment applications.

POWER OF ATTORNEY (POA)

Though the purchases can be made through direct remittances, it is obvious that an NRI requires to have a person in India to whom he has donated his PoA to dabble in shares on his behalf. Can he arrange for a PoA from abroad? Of course yes. Let us take the case of UK. All that he has to do is to —

(a) Get the PoA printed on a stamp paper of the required denomination as per UK Law and contact the Indian Embassy in UK.

(b) The person executing the power of attorney will sign in the presence of a notary who countersigns every page of the PoA.

(c) The PoA then needs to be sent to India and taken to the stamp office for getting it stamped for a denomination of ₹ 100.

(d) The person accepting the PoA will sign in the presence of the notary who attests his signature.

The authorities may feel that this is very easy. We do not.

To Sum

On reading my previous article one of my NRI readers, Mr. M. T. Antony observed, "Our stupid ministers and ridiculous bureaucracy outlandish, meaningless, counter-productive, self destructing bureaucracy continues unabated. Sorry to inject my personal philosophy. India is (next to China, USA and Japan) I am told, a super power. Why and for what reason India needs my hard earned money? If India needs it and if I am stupidly 'patriotic' can't they make it practical, easy for me to invest?"

We share his deep indignation and we are sure, almost all the NRIs are also reeling under same or similar reactions towards investment in India.

Dr. Manmohan Singh, during his address to Pravasi Bharatiya Divas symposium in 2006 had stated that it is the Indian diaspora which has rendered health to the Indian economy and has brought the capital account convertibility within its reach.

Unfortunately, the regulators appear to be repelling them.

ANNUAL INFORMATION RETURNS

U/s 285BA read with Rule 114E, the transactions of all persons, including NRIs undertaking any one of the following 7 specified financial transactions, equal to or over specified financial limits are required to be reported to the Department through Annual Information Return (AIR) —

		₹
1.	Cash deposits in a year in any bank SB account	10 lakh
2.	Payments in a year credit card	2 lakh
3.	Purchase of units of a Mutual Fund	2 lakh
4.	Acquisition of bonds or debentures	5 lakh
5.	Purchase of shares	1 lakh
6.	Purchase or sale of immovable property	30 lakh
7.	Purchase of RBI bonds	5 lakh

Take care.

23

Insurance and NRIs

Insurers may issue general as well as life policies denominated in forex through their offices in India or abroad to NRIs, provided the premiums are collected in forex from abroad or out of NRE accounts of the insured or his family members. For policies denominated in rupees, premium payments through NRO accounts can be accepted.

Circular AP (DIR) 72 dt. 17.1.03 allows policies to be issued in foreign currency to Residents of Indian nationality or origin who have returned to India after being NRIs, provided the premiums are paid out of forex remittances or from their RFC accounts.

Policies issued by overseas offices of Indian insurers may be transferred to Indian register, together with the related actuarial reserves, when the policy holder returns to India. Such forex policies shall be converted into rupee policies. However, if the policy is in force for 3 years or more, premiums may be also remitted through his resident assets. In such a case, the maturity proceeds or the amount of claim shall be repatriated to India within 7 days from the date of its receipt. If the premiums are continued to be paid in forex, the maturity proceeds or the amount of claim can be credited to his account abroad or the RFC account in India.

Settlement of Claims

NRIs can credit the proceeds of policies issued by insurance companies in India to their RFC or RFCD account on their becoming Residents. AP (DIR) Circular 6 dt. 20.7.04 permits Resident beneficiaries to be settled in forex and credit the proceeds to their RFCD. NRI beneficiaries may credit the same to NRE account.

Claims, maturity proceeds and surrender value of rupee life insurance policies issued to NRIs for which premiums have been collected in non-repatriable rupees may be paid only in rupees. The amount may be credited to NRO account if the beneficiary is

NRI and ordinary account if the beneficiary is a Resident.

The basic rule for settlement of claims on rupee life insurance policies in favour of an ROI claimant is that payments in forex will be permitted only in proportion to the amount of premiums paid in forex in relation to the total premiums payable.

If a beneficiary residing outside India desires remittance abroad, he should apply to RBI in Form-A2 together with Form-LIM(1), through their bankers for the approval.

Where the policies are assigned to an overseas bank, the credit in rupees of maturity proceeds, surrender value or death claim to the overseas assignee's account with an AD, require RBI's permission.

Where rupee policies are issued on life of a non-resident Indian national under the Married Women's Property Act, the beneficiaries will be the wife and/or children of the policy holder. He may appoint a bank in India or a relative as special trustee to receive the claims when due and distribute the same to the beneficiaries. Records of rupee life insurance policies cannot be transferred by the insurer from an office in India to an office outside India without prior approval of RBI.

RBI's prior approval is required for assignment of rupee life insurance policies held in Indian register by a Resident in favour of an NRI or by an NRI in favour of another NRI in a different country, except where the assignment is without consideration in favour of the policy holder's non-resident wife or dependent relatives. Applications to RBI should contain full details regarding beneficiaries and exact manner in which their shares will be disposed of by the special trustee.

Foreign Nationals not Permanently Resident in India
Policies denominated in forex or rupees may be issued to foreign nationals not permanently resident in India provided the premiums are paid out of forex or from their income earned in India or repatriable superannuation and pension funds in India. Claims, maturity proceeds or surrender value in respect of rupee policies

may be paid in rupees or allowed to be remitted abroad, if the claimant so desires. The restrictions on issue of rupee policies maturing within 7 years to foreign nationals not permanently resident in India have been withdrawn by AP (DIR) Circular 72 dt. 17.1.03.

In the case of foreign nationals in employment in India, the insurer may accept a certificate from an AD to the effect that the concerned foreign national was availing of recurring remittance facility.

Miscellaneous

◆ Premiums due on rupee policies issued to Indian nationals Resident in Myanmar may be accepted in rupees in India from friends, relatives of the policy holders subject to the condition that all payments under the policies will be made to the policyholders only in rupees after their arrival in India for permanent settlement. Cases of Chinese and Pakistani policyholders should be referred to RBI.

◆ Life insurance policies are regarded as securities.

◆ Notification FEMA 12, 2000-RB, dt. 3.5.2000 prohibits a Resident from taking any general or life insurance policy issued by an insurer outside India. However, AP (DIR) Circular 47 dt. 17.5.02 exempts units located in Special Economic Zones (SEZs) from the purview of this notification for general insurance policies. Accordingly, ADs are free to allow remittances towards premium for general insurance policies taken by units located in SEZs from insurers outside India provided the premiums are paid by the units in forex. Similar permission is granted for some marine and aviation insurance.

◆ AP (DIR) Circular 76 dt. 4.2.04 states that approval from Ministry of Finance (Insurance Division) for securing insurance on health from a company abroad is no more required and ADs may freely allow such remittances.

◆ Under AP (DIR) Circular 72 dt. 17.1.03, insurers may pay commission in forex to their agents who are permanently resident outside India regardless of the fact that part of the business booked by them may be on the lives of Residents and related premiums are paid in rupees.

◆ Medical insurance policies in forex can be issued to Indian citizens who have gone abroad for employment and studies. Even when the premium can be paid in Indian rupees, some foreign insurers insist on payment in forex. Such payments are covered under the maintenance quota released by ADs under the delegated authority.

24

Gold Does not Glitter

The most important reason for India being a poor country is its richness in gold. It is estimated that Indian households hold over 20,000 tonnes (= US$ 1,100 billion!)of the yellow metal. And this is an unproductive asset. Everyone realises that even if a part of it is converted into productive capital, it will a great help in poverty eradication. India normally imports around 900 tonnes of gold every year. According to the World Gold Council, nearly 200 tonnes (= $ 11 billion) of gold entered India in 2014 through the illegal route. This leads to a loss in forex inflow of a similar amount and a loss in revenue by way of import duty of over US$ 1.1 billion.

Gold Import Scheme

To curb this menace, the government had promulgated Gold Import Scheme, granting general permission to those NRIs and PIOs who have stayed abroad for at least 6 months to bring as a part of their baggage gold up to 10 kilos and silver up to 100 kilos in any form, including ornaments or articles, provided the import duties are paid in forex, either abroad or here in India. Short visits up to 30 days shall be ignored unless the passenger has availed of the exemption under this scheme during this period. The prescribed quantity cannot be brought in installments within the prescribed period of 6 months.

Originally, the scheme was designed to discourage those indulging in hawala and smuggling. There was a yawning gap between the landed cost of gold or silver and its market price in India.

To begin with, the import duty was ₹ 250/10 gms on gold and ₹ 500/kg on silver. It was an instant success. This duty was raised almost each and every year under one pretext or another.

Now, have a look at the Table-1 which computes the maximum profit that can be earned per trip at the prevailing prices.

Table -1 NRI IMPORT SCHEME : PRECIOUS METALS

Prices as on : 30.4.15

Overseas Price		
Gold	$ 1,178.10 per Ounce	
Silver	$ 16.14 per Ounce	

IMPORT DUTY

GOLD - 10% ad valorem ₹ 2,402 per 10 gms
SILVER - 10% ad valorem ₹ 3,291 per kg

1 Ounce = 31.1034768 gms
1 $ =   63.42   rupees

	GOLD - 10 gms ₹	SILVER - 1 kg ₹
Price - Indian	26,623	36,550
- Overseas	24,021	32,909
MARGIN	2,602	3,641
DUTY	2,402	3,291
Profit	199	350

	₹	
Profit - On 10 kgs Gold	1,99,391	0.75%
Profit - On 100 kgs Silver	34,959	0.97%
Profit - Total per Trip	2,34,350	

Notes :
1. Octroi & Sales tax are leviable as per the tariffs, differing from state to state.
2. Excess Baggage Tariff of Airlines has been ignored.

The current import duty is 10% ad valorem and works out at around ₹ 2,402/10-gm on gold and ₹ 3,291/kg on silver. We started with ₹ 250 and ₹ 500 respectively.

Note that internationally gold is measured and sold in troy ounce = 31.1035 gms. Imperial ounce = 28.349 gms.

Yes, you earn a profit of around ₹ 2 lakh but you require a capital of around ₹ 3 crore. We do not think it is worth the effort.

There are some kinks. When you sell the precious metals in India and earn a profit, it would be considered as either a short-term gain or a long-term gain if you sell it after 3 years of its purchase by you or as business income since your intention while buying it was to sell. In any case, you may be entitled to claim expenses incurred 'wholly and exclusively' for the purpose of earning the profit or the capital gains. We claim that the cost of the airline ticket is definitely an expense incurred for this transaction. Whether or not it is incurred wholly and exclusively for buying and selling gold can be a matter of dispute between you and your ITO.

At this level the scheme has become unattractive. Consequently, the menace of smuggling has once again become rampant.

The passenger is allowed to bring the precious metals himself or import it within 15 days of his arrival. To avoid the hazards of carrying the gold personally, he can use customs bonded warehouses of SBI or Metal and Mineral Trading Corporation at Mumbai, Delhi, Thiruvananthapuram and special delivery centres. If he has paid the duty abroad and is found ineligible to import it after his arrival in India, refund would be given to him. He has to file a declaration on a prescribed form before the customs officer at the time of his arrival stating his intention of using the warehouses and pay the duty before clearance.

There is no condition that the source of earnings from which the metal has been purchased has to be verified. It is beyond the jurisdiction of customs officers to go into this aspect.

New Solutions of the Government

We were praying for reduction in the import duty of 10% on import of gold to a proper level for curbing smuggling. Instead, the recent FA15 has attacked the problem through a 3-pronged attack by —

1. **Gold Monetisation Scheme** : This new scheme will replace both the present Gold Deposit and Gold Metal Loan Schemes and handled by some banks and gold dealers. It will enable the depositors to earn interest in their metal accounts and the jewellers to obtain loans in their metal account. We hoped that the interest rate would be much higher than the one offered by SBI at 0.755-1% over tenures ranging from 3 to 5 years for the old schemes.

2. **Sovereign Gold Bond** : This will be an alternative to purchasing gold directly. The Bonds will carry a fixed rate of interest, and also be redeemable in cash at the face value of the gold, at the time of redemption.

3. **Indian Gold Coin** : It will carry the Ashok Chakra on its face. Such an Indian Gold Coin would help reduce the demand for coins minted outside India and also help to recycle the gold available in the country.

Yes, these steps are likely to offer an official and easy alternative to invest white money into gold. However, it has to be realised that the battle is against black money, havala and smuggling. The 10% import duty surely renders smuggling a better option, in spite of the various risks involved.

We strongly feel that the one and only way of curbing this menace is to give fillip to recycling of precious metal by providing a window where ornaments can be sold without getting fleeced. At present the buyer faces discount over 20% (!), and strangely, the authorities are oblivious of this menace.

Then again, will someone up there, look at the real estates which are purchased and kept locked up, for one reason or another? Can the government not take custody of all such flats and rent them out with a guarantee to the owner of reclaiming the premises for his own use, if and when he needs it? There is no reason on earth for the government to subsidise the financing cost of the white portion of the real estate cost since it serves as a convenient vehicle to invest his black money.

To Sum
We are surely back at square number one. Smuggling coupled with hawala has become once more extremely rewarding.

Smugglers have found ways to outsmart customs officials. All that they do is to declare bentex jewellery as gold, while going abroad. This jewellery is then dumped in the visiting country, and real gold jewellery is brought while returning to India. Some enter India from neighbouring countries like Nepal and Bangladesh.

Smuggling of gold, an illegal activity, is coupled with hawala transaction, another illegal activity. Forex for purchase of gold is picked up from NRIs who desire to send funds regularly to their relatives in India for their subsistence. Indian Rupees are paid to the relative in India at a premium over the forex exchange rate prevalent for normal banking channels. Needless to state that the Indian Rupees emerging from these routs give rise to a parallel black money market.

It is obvious that the increase in the import duty of precious metals is a retrograde step.

Tax Collected at Source
The current Sec. 206(C)(1D) require TDS @1% to be applied by the seller of bullion (excluding any coin or any other article weighing 10 gms or less) if the total sale value exceeds ₹ 2 lakh for bullion and ₹ 5 lakh for jewellery. FA13 has dropped the exemption of this stipulation applicable to coins and other articles.

Export of Gold Jewellery
There is no value limit on the export of gold jewellery by a passenger through baggage if it constitutes the bona fide baggage of the passenger. He may request the customs for issue of an export

25

Overseas Citizenship of India (OCI)

Good news for all PIOs. Recent FA15 has merged the PIO cards into OCI cards. The Government had introduced on 31.03.1999 PIO Cards for PIOs settled throughout the world. Now OCI cards have come into existence and have little better features.

OCI facility is available to any overseas Indian (other than a person who was a citizen of Pakistan or Bangladesh any time) as long as his home country allows dual citizenship under their local laws. On the other hand, the PIO card is not available to a person who was or is a citizen of Afghanistan, Bangladesh, Bhutan, China, Nepal, Pakistan or Sri Lanka at any time.

Such a foreign national should have been —
(a) Eligible to become citizen of India on 26.01.1950. Any person who or either of whose parents or any of whose grandparents was born in India as defined in the Government of India Act, 1935 (as originally enacted), and who was ordinarily residing in any country outside India was eligible to become citizen of India on 26.01.1950, or

(b) Was a citizen of India on or after 26.1.50, or

(c) Belonged to a territory that became part of India after 15.08.1947. Such territories are — (i) Sikkim from 26.04.1975 (ii) Pondicherry from 16.08.1962 (iii) Dadra & Nagar Haveli from 11.08.1961 and (iv) Goa, Daman and Diu from 20.12.1961.

His children and grand children, even if minors are also eligible.

A person who is already holding more than one nationality can also be an OCI as long as the local laws of at least one of the countries allow dual citizenship in some form or other.

An OCI card holder does not possess dual citizenship or nationality. He shall not be entitled to the following rights —
(a) Equality of opportunity in matters of public employment.

(b) Be a (i) President, (ii) Vice-President, (iii) Judge of the Supreme Court or High Court or (iv) a member of the House of the People, the Council of States, Legislative Assembly, Legislative Council.

(c) Be registered as a voter.

(d) For appointment to public services and posts in connection with the affairs of the Union or of any State.

As per Sec. 5(1g) of the Citizenship Act, 1955, a person who is registered as OCI for 5 years and is Residing in India for 1 year out of the above 5 years, is eligible to apply for Indian Citizenship to the Ministry of Home Affairs, Central Government. The same rule applies to minor children (even foreign-born) and spouses of foreign origin, married to Indians.

The benefits of OCI are —

◆ Multi-purpose, multiple entry, life-long visa for visiting India whereas for PIO card holder, it is for 15 years (for some old cases, 20 years).

◆ OCI does not require registration with local police authority.

◆ An NRI or a PIO is prohibited from acquiring agricultural or plantation properties. The press note dt. 2.12.05 by Ministry of Home Affairs states that one of the benefits of OCI is — Parity with NRIs in respect of all facilities to the latter in economic, financial and educational fields except in matters relating to the acquisition of agricultural/plantation properties. This implies that an NRI or a PIO does not have the right to purchase an agricultural land but an OCI card holder has the right. We feel that this is an aberration. How can a person with foreign nationality (PIO) have better rights than an Indian citizen (NRI)?

◆ Facilities as available to children of NRIs for obtaining admission to educational institutions in India, including medical colleges, engineering colleges, institutes of technology, institutes of management etc., under the general category.

Procedure

Every registered OCI will be issued a registration certificate which is printed like an Indian passport in different colour and an OCI visa sticker will be pasted in the person's foreign passport. Both these will have all necessary security features, including photograph.

An eligible person may apply to the Indian Mission or Post of the country of his nationality or of any other country if he is ordinarily residing there, along with the necessary proofs of his eligibility.

Application Form-XIX can be used directly on-line or downloaded from www.mha.nic.in and submitted through post. It can be jointly used by a family consisting of spouses and up to two minor children. Part -A of the Form can be filed on-line. A bar code and a reference number will be generated automatically as an acknowledgement. Part- B can be downloaded and printed on computer or written by hand in Block letters. Printed Part A and Part B of the application form have to be submitted in duplicate with all necessary enclosures. The concerned office will issue an acknowledgement number which can be used for enquiries in future.

If the applicant is not in the country of citizenship, the application can be submitted to the Indian Mission or Post of the country where he is ordinarily residing. If the applicant is in India, it can be submitted to the FRRO Delhi, Mumbai, Kolkata or Amritsar or to CHIO, Chennai or to the Under Secretary, OCI Cell, Citizenship Section, Foreigners Division, Ministry of Home Affairs (MHA), Jaisalmer House, 26, Mansingh Road, New Delhi-110011.Central processing of applications will occur in New Delhi. Ministry sends OCI cards to embassy/consulate.

An application where there is no reporting of criminal case against the applicant will be granted OCI within 30 days whereas in other cases it may take 120 days. An OCI certificate acquired on the basis of concealed information or misrepresentation, will be cancelled and such persons will be blacklisted for entry into India.

A registration certificate in the form of a booklet will be issued and a multiple entry, multipurpose OCI 'U' visa sticker will be pasted on the foreign passport of the applicant. For this purpose, the applicant has to send the original passport after receipt of the acceptance letter or verification of the application on-line.

In the case of loss of or damage to the certificate, an application has to be made to the same Indian Mission or Post which issued the certificate. A new OCI 'U' visa sticker will be issued. However, the applicant can continue to carry the old passport wherein OCI 'U' visa sticker was pasted along with new passport for visiting India without seeking a new visa, as the visa is valid for lifelong. Ditto for renewal of the foreign passport.

In the unlikely case of a person desiring to renounce OCI, he can use Form-XXII and send it to the Indian Mission or Post where OCI registration was granted.

Cost of PIO and OCI Cards
An OCI card cost is US$ 275 for US citizens and US$ 295 for others. If the application is rejected, the amount will be returned after deducting US$ 25 for US citizens and US$ 45 of others as processing fees. Fee for issue of duplicate OCI card is US$ 25 and PIO card is US$ 100.

Letter of Mr. Ashwin Kalbag
The following letter of Mr. Ashwin Kalbag published in *Economic Times* of 18.3.10 is a testimony of the fact that the OCI Card, leave alone the PIO Card, is useless. We have taken the liberty to drop and edit certain portions for conserving space —
"I ran into trouble in February 2010, at the Mumbai International airport. I had arrived with a newly issued US passport and an OCI card. As it turned out, I needed the class 'U' visa issued along with the OCI card, which was stamped in my expired US passport that I had not brought with me. I was made to pay US$ 40 for a 5-day temporary entry visa known as Temporary Landing Facility (TLF).

"The Bureau of Immigration (BOI) under the Ministry of Home Affairs (MHA) has a link 'Instructions (Foreigners)' on its website, http://www.immigrationindia.nic.in, clearly stating, 'On production of bona fide proof and on satisfaction of the FRRO/FRO cum District Superintendent of Police, a TLF may be granted for up to 15 days. Yet, I was granted only a 5-day TLF. The same link categorically states "foreigners carrying a valid PIO or OCI card along with their valid national passport are authorised to enter India without obtaining India visa separately.

"As an OCI card holder, I have a life-long visa to enter and exit India. I am purportedly free not to register with the FRRO even for stays lasting longer than 180 days. Yet, in a single swoop, in effect, my OCI card was rendered useless.

"It is impossible to obtain an OCI card without also being given a corresponding class 'U' visa. In that case producing the OCI card should be perfectly equivalent to producing the visa itself. OCI card grants a life-long visa. Unfortunately, when a passport expires, the OCI or PIO card needs to have the new passport linked to it, creating an entire bureaucracy around this process.

"It would perhaps be a better idea to model the OCI card after the US green card, as an Indian green card. The US green card is a standalone document that supersedes the permanent visa given at the time of its issuance. It may be produced at US immigrations without its concomitant visa.

"I went to several banks during my subsequent visit to Mumbai asking whether I could open an on-line trading account with which to trade Indian securities. Most banks had no knowledge of how to deal with OCI card holders!

"As recently as December 2009, the MHA implemented new regulations that affect visa holders' periods of authorised stay and registration in India, targeted at travellers with tourist visas, who have been in India for more than 90 days before travel abroad, or for more than 180 days within the past year. The regulation mandates a 2-month gap between successive visits to India.

"A lot of NRIs have long-term (5 or 10 year) tourist visas. They now have to apply for a re-entry permit from the appropriate CGI office in the US. The information on governmental websites is not specific enough to determine whether this affects PIO or OCI card holders. The US State Department's webpage http:// travel.state.gov/travel/cis_pa_tw/cis/cis_1139.html states — Citizens are advised to carefully review the latest regulations, which are included under the section titled 'Instructions (Foreigners)', and to be aware that implementation at ports of entry may be inconsistent.

"It took me 4 trips to the FRRO to get a visa extension covering my stay. If I were an NRI interested in doing business in India, this experience would give me a pause."

To Sum

We thank Mr. Ashwin Kalbag for warning the Indian diaspora about the various dangers associated with the use of OCI Card. It is really sad that the US State Department warns its citizens that 'implementation at ports of entry may be inconsistent'. This implies that the authorities at the ports are either not trained properly or are allowed to take different actions under the same situations depending upon whether they like the face of the card holder or not. And worst — The higher authorities do not appear to be interested in taking any corrective action for reasons best known to them. Is Dr. Manmohan Singh who initiated the idea of issuing OCI card aware of how his bright intentions are breached and ignored? We wonder . . .

26

Double Taxation Avoidance Agreement (DTAA)

In today's era of globalisation, movement of personnel across countries is commonplace. An individual may work in India for some part of the year and the rest of the year in another country. In such cases, a question arises as to the taxability of the income of the individual, received overseas as well as in India. One country may want to tax the income on account of the residential status whereas the other country may want to tax, at least that part of the income on source basis.

DTAA between two countries supersedes their respective domestic tax laws. In other words, the assessee is entitled to higher benefit as is available under the DTAA and the domestic tax laws.

DTAA normally determines which country reserves the right to tax a particular stream of income. Sometimes, it may so happen that the DTAA may not give exclusive privilege to any one country to tax the income. For example, the resident country may have a right to tax some certain income whereas the source country also has a right to tax the same income. In such cases, double taxation is normally avoided by means of the resident country giving credit for the taxes paid in the source country.

There are two ways of granting DTAA reliefs —
1. Exemption : A particular income is taxed in only one of the two countries and is exempt in the other.
2. Tax Credit : An income is taxed in both the countries as per their respective tax laws read with the DTAA.

Example
Take the instance of the DTAA between India and the USA. An employee has worked till October 15th in India and the rest of the year in USA. Let us explore the way DTAA protects the employee from paying tax twice.

Article 16 of the DTAA deals with Dependent Personal Services, which is a jargon for salary income. The following is the relevant clause of the Article —

"Subject to the provisions of article 17 (Director's Fees), 18 (Income Earned by Entertainers and Athletes), 19 (Remuneration and Pensions in Respect of Government Service), 20 (Private Pensions, Annuities, Alimony and Child Support), 21 (Payments Received by Students and Apprentices) and 22 (Payments Received by Professors, Teachers and Research Scholars), salaries, wages, and other similar remuneration derived by a resident of a Contracting State in respect of an employment shall be taxable only in that State unless the employment is exercised in the other Contracting State. If the employment is so exercised, such remuneration as is derived therefrom may be taxed in other State."

So from the DTAA, we learn that the primary right of taxation is with India. The secondary right of taxation is with the USA. But since the income is being taxed twice, Article 25 of the agreement, dealing with granting relief from double taxation, states —

"Where a resident of India derives income which, in accordance with the provisions of this Convention, may be taxed in the United States, India shall allow as a deduction from the tax on the income of that resident an amount equal to the income-tax paid in the United States, whether directly or by deduction. Such deduction shall not, however, exceed that part of the income-tax (as computed before the deduction is given) which is attributable to the income which may be taxed in the United States."

This means that on the tax to be paid in India, the assessee is entitled to a deduction of the tax paid in the USA on the income earned there. Such deduction cannot exceed the tax (calculated as per the Indian tax laws) on the income earned in the USA.

The Residentship Rule
We have already discussed the fact that tax depends upon Residential status. What happens when a person is a Resident in both the countries as per their respective domestic laws? For example, a country may determine a person to be a Resident if he

stays in that country for more than 150 days. In such a case, it may be possible that he spends 182 days in India, and the rest in that country, thereby making him a Resident of both.

As per Article-4(1) of the UN Model Convention, dealing with Residentship rules which prescribes tie-breaking tests for persons who may qualify as Residents of both countries. Accordingly —

"1. For the purposes of this Convention, the term 'resident of a Contracting State' means any person who, under the laws of that State, is liable to tax therein by reason of his domicile, residence, citizenship, place of management, place of incorporation, or any other criterion of a similar nature . . .

"2. Where by reason of the provisions of paragraph 1, an individual is a resident of both Contracting States, then his status shall be determined as follows:

(a) he shall be deemed to be a resident of the State in which he has a permanent home available to him; if he has a permanent home available to him in both States, he shall be deemed to be a resident of the State with which his personal and economic relations are closer (centre of vital interests);

(b) if the State in which he has his centre of vital interests cannot be determined, or if he does not have a permanent home available to him in either State, he shall be deemed to be a resident of the State in which he has a habitual abode;

(c) if he has a habitual abode in both States or in none, he shall be deemed to be a resident of the State of which he is a national; and

(d) if he is a national of both States or of neither of them, the competent authorities of the Contracting States shall settle the question by Mutual Agreement Procedure (MAP) . . ."

DTAA confers the right of taxation either to the Resident or to the Source country (or distributes it between the two).

Procedure

Those availing of treaty benefits have to file returns of their income in India, even if those aren't liable to be taxed here. Prior to FY 10-11, those who didn't pay taxes in India, owing to the provisions under the double taxation avoidance agreement between India and the country of origin concerned, didn't have to file returns in India.

The taxpayer has to bifurcate his incomes to which provisions of a tax treaty apply. For instance, if he earns income from interest on bank deposits in India as well as abroad, he would have to state the interest earned on foreign income separately. He has to quote the Tax Identification Number (TIN) in case tax has been paid in a foreign country. If the TIN is not allotted by that country, he has to furnish his passport number. It is mandatory for a taxpayer with total annual income of more than ₹ 25 lakh to declare his domestic assets, including land, buildings, bank deposits, shares, insurance policies, loans, jewellery, bullion, drawings, paintings, yachts, boats, etc. As part of foreign asset reporting norms, an assessee also has to state his foreign bank account number and the details of the trusts in which he is a trustee.

The individual needs to submit a signed declaration, in a prescribed format to the ITO in India. He also needs to submit proof of his residence in the country abroad. This can either be a Tax Residency Certificate issued by the government of the country of residence or a copy of IT returns filed in that country. Further, such NRI investor would also be required to furnish Form 10F along with TRC, if such TRC does not contain information prescribed by the CBDT vide its Notification No. 57/2013 dt. 1.8.13. In countries like UAE where there is no income tax, a self declaration is sufficient.

The advantage to the investor is that when he files his returns in his country of residence, he can claim the benefit of the TDS and the advance tax already paid in India and only needs to pay the extra tax (if any) in that country. For example, if in that country the tax rate is 40% and he has paid TDS @15%, he only needs to pay the balance 25% tax in that country and not the entire 40%.

This is the general vein followed by all DTAAs. Some fine tuning may be required depending upon the exact provisions of DTAA between India and the host country. Such agreements are available on — www.incometaxindia.gov.in. Since such a fine tuning is a very complex exercise, you will do well by employing a consultant specialising in the field in your normal place of residence in India.

DTAA with Tax Havens

As per AAR, only liability to pay tax, both in India and the foreign country entitles a taxpayer to claim relief under the rules laid down in the DTAA. If a taxpayer pays tax or is liable to pay tax under the laws in force in one country alone, he cannot claim any relief from a non-existent burden of double taxation under the DTAA. The DTAA is for the benefit of taxpayers who are liable to pay tax twice on the same income. Therefore, no question of granting relief to the applicant from double taxation can arise.

In, *88ITR169 (SC)*, it was held that "doubly taxed income should be understood as income actually charged to tax". Since no tax is paid on income exempt u/s 10(38), there can be no presumption of tax having been paid u/s 112. Only the income on which tax has been paid abroad and which is again taxed in another country, is entitled to DTAA relief.

Taking into consideration these rulings, on incomes such as dividends, interest and capital gains, the rates specified in Finance Act in India have to be used.

Payments to NRIs in UAE

In respect of payments to be made to NRIs at the UAE, tax at source must be deducted at the following rates —

(a) Dividends : 5% of the gross amount of the dividends if the beneficial owner is a company which owns at least 10% of the shares of the company and 15% in all the other cases.

(b) Interest : 5% of the gross amount of the interest if such interest is paid on a loan granted by a bank carrying on a bona fide banking business or by a similar financial institution and 12½% of the gross amount of the interest in all other cases.

(c) Royalties : 10% of the gross amount.

Circular 734 dt. 24.1.96 proclaims that the above rates which are enshrined in the DTAA between India and UAE are to be strictly adhered to so as to avoid unnecessary harassment of taxpayers.

DTAA with USA

* In the case of taxation of income earned in the US, credit will be available in respect of taxes paid in the US. Such credit is available only in respect of federal taxes. No credit is available in respect of state tax and payment in respect of social security, insurance, etc.

* If a person is on a short term deputation of an Indian employer to the US and who has all other personal and economic connection attached to India, then he is regarded as a Resident in India even as per the treaty. India retains the right to global taxation in such a situation, as per treaty provisions.

* The scope of the DTAA covers only certain incomes and certain kinds of taxes. If there is a particular income or a tax in the domestic law which is not envisaged in the DTAA, then the DTAA would not apply. The Indian Fringe Benefit Tax is a case in point.

* It may be noted that US tax laws allow exemption on capital gains from sale of 'Main House'.

* The first thing to determine is the source and the residence country. This makes things simpler. In the case of Indians in the USA the source country is the USA which defines the source of the income. The residence country is of course India.

* There are several NRIs who get some pension from abroad. after returning to India permanently. Article 20 states that pensions would be taxable in the country of residence — that is India. However, Social Security Benefits or other public pensions are taxed only in America.

* Contributions of the foreign companies towards social security are mostly of two types. Generally, the contributions would accrue to the credit of the employees and would be payable only on superannuation. However, some countries have compulsory social security contributions which go as a premium for insuring the employment. The insurance company would make a lump sum payment or an annuity to the employee as and when there is any curtailment of earning capacity. Barring such special circumstances,

such contributions do not entail any benefit to the employees.

Mumbai bench of the ITAT in the case of *Gallotti Raoul* v *ACIT* 61ITD453 dealt with the taxability of compulsory contributions to be made to French Social Security Fund according to which every French national is under an obligation to affiliate with social security organisation and contribute a prefixed percentage of salary irrespective of the place of employment. It held that compulsory contributions to the extent to which the assessee has no domain over it, cannot be said to be an income in the hands of the employee. This is an instance of diversion of income by overriding title.

Such agreements between India and other countries, are available on — www.incometaxindia.gov.in.

ICICI Bank's NRO+

The bank has a special account designated as NRO FD Plus that is taxed at the lower rate of tax @15.45% governed by DTAA instead of the normal 30.9% governed by the ITA, if its customer gives a declaration along with the proof that he is from a region that has a DTAA with India. At present, the bank offers the facility to customers from the US, UK, Canada and Singapore.

The countries with whom India has DTAA are —

Armenia, Australia, Austria, Bangladesh, Belarus, Belgium, Brazil, Bulgaria, Canada, China, Cyprus, Czech Republic, Denmark, Egypt, Finland, France, Germany, Greece, Hashemite Kingdom of Jordan, Hungary, Iceland, Indonesia, Israel, Italy, Japan, Kazakstan, Kenya, Korea, Kuwait, Kyrgyz Republic, Libya, Malaysia, Malta, Mauritius, Mongolia, Morocco, Namibia, Nepal, Netherlands, New Zealand, Norway, Oman, Philippines, Poland, Portuguese Republic, Qatar, Romania, Russia, Singapore, Slovenia, South Africa, Spain, Sri Lanka, Sudan, Sweden, Swiss Confederation, Syria, Tanzania, Thailand, Trinidad and Tobago, Turkey, Turkmenistan, UAE, Egypt, Uganda, UK, Ukraine, USA, Uzbekistan, Vietnam and Zambia.

India has been entering into such agreements with many new countries so often that this list may not be exhaustive. DTAAs are available on www.incometaxindia.gov.in.

Case law

The judicial pronouncements made by ITAT Pune Bench 'B' in the case of *ACT* v *EPCOS AG Germany,* IT Appeal 398 (Pune) of 2007 is important and have a far-reaching effect.

The German company had two subsidiaries in India, namely, EIPL and EFPL. It provided support services to them in field of product marketing, sales and information technology from its centralised infrastructure in Germany. In the relevant previous year, assessee had disclosed receipts of the fees as well as interest on ECB loans. Assessee had accepted a tax liability on said receipts @10% on the basis of Article 12 of Indo-German tax treaty.

AO held that each and every activity of Indian subsidiaries was done under active supervision of assessee in India, and hence, assessee had a PE in India in form of its subsidiaries. He further held that even if the receipts in question were in nature of royalties those receipts were taxable on gross basis @20% u/s 44D, read with Sec. 115A.

The main pronouncements were —

1. A tax treaty is primarily a detailed instrument assigning taxing rights between two or more competing tax jurisdictions over a tax subject and unless a tax jurisdiction has a right to tax an income, it is irrelevant whether or not, under domestic tax legislation of that tax jurisdiction, income-in-question is taxable

2. In the case of cross-border tax situation between treaty partner States, logically first thing for a source tax jurisdiction is to establish right to tax under applicable tax treaty, and only if such a source tax jurisdiction indeed has right to tax, next thing is to be examined is taxability under domestic laws of that State.

3. The first step towards examining taxability of business profits in source country is to ascertain whether or not foreign enterprise has a Permanent Establishment (PE). And if it does have one, the quantum of business profits attributable to such a PE.

4. A PE means a fixed place of business through which business of foreign enterprise should be carried on. Merely because an Indian company conducts its business in India with help and

guidance it receives from a foreign company that gives help and guidance, it does not follow that the foreign company will be deemed to have a PE. In case an assessee receives 'royalties' and 'fees for technical services' but these receipts do not have an effective nexus with PE, and are not, therefore, attributable to PE, exclusion clause under Article 5(5), as also taxability under Article 7(1) and (2), is not triggered. Since no part of work of assessee was carried out in India in as much as there was no billing raised by assessee in connection with any services rendered in India and moreover Indian subsidiaries merely acted upon advice so given in e-mails and letters which were sent from outside India, action of subsidiaries could not alter situs of activities of assessee, and it could be said that assessee did not have a PE in India in form of Indian subsidiaries.

5. In view of above, it could be said that receipts in question were not attributable to PE in India and, therefore, there was no question of applicability of Sec. 44D, read with Sec. 115A.

FORM-8938 & FBAR

To contain tax evasion and avoidance by US citizens and residents, particularly Green Card holders, in respect of foreign assets, Form-8938 has been introduced starting with the tax year 2011.

This Form needs to be filed if the value of your foreign financial assets exceeds —

For a single assessee :

$50,000 at end of year or more than $75,000 during the year.

For Married joint assessee :

$100,000 at end of year or more than $150,000 during the year.

There are higher limits if you do not live in the United States.

Foreign Financial Assets include —

* Financial account maintained by a foreign financial institution.

* Stocks or securities issued by someone other than a US person.

* Financial instrument or contract where the issuer or counter party is someone other than a US person.

These encompass almost all the accounts that you may hold back in your home country such as Banks, Brokerage and securities, Commodity futures & options, MFs, DPs, Insurance policy with cash surrender value, Annuities with cash value, and most importantly, Pension Funds. Note that a state pension like the US social security is not included in the value.

Filing Form-8938 does not stop the requirement to file Form-TD F 90-22.1, otherwise known as the FBAR (Foreign Bank and Financial Accounts Reporting). This form still needs to be filed with the US Treasury by June 30 each year if you have certain financial accounts exceeding US$ 10,000 in value.

If you meet the following conditions, you must file an FBAR —

1. You are a US citizen or a Resident or an entity (like a company, partnership, trusts, estates) that was created under the laws of the 5b4 United States.

2. You have a financial interest or signature authority over the account by way of holding a legal title to the account. This means that you, either by yourself or jointly with others, control the disposition of assets held in the foreign accounts. This will apply even if the foreign account is owned by an agent or nominee on your behalf. In case of corporate, partnerships or trusts, they must own more than 50% of voting rights, capital or beneficial interest respectively.

3. The total of all your non-US bank and financial accounts exceeds US$ 10,000 even for a single day during the relevant calendar year. This is rather harsh. For instance, suppose you desire to buy a property in India. Surely, your Indian account will hold funds only for a few days before the money is paid to the seller of the property. But since the balance in the account would have exceeded US$ 10,000 for those few days, you must file FBAR.

The basic penalty for failing to file the Form is $10,000 going up to a maximum of $50,000 for continuing failure to file. Also if you fail to report income from the foreign financial assets the IRS will have up to 6 years to assess the tax rather than the normal 3 years.

Take care!

Indian banks cannot issue Form-1099 to their customers in the USA. However, on your request a certificate indicating the details of your deposit and interest earned during a calendar year (January-December) or a financial year (April-March) can be provided.

Where DTAA does not Exist (Sec. 91)

Sec. 91(1) provides for relief in respect of income tax on the income which is taxed in India as well as in the country with which there is no DTAA. Accordingly an Indian Resident is entitled to a deduction from the Indian income tax of a sum calculated on such doubly taxed income, at the Indian rate of tax or the rate of tax of said country, whichever is lower. In cases of the 92 countries with which India has a DTAA, a relief on doubly taxed income is available as per the respective DTAAs. The Act does not provide the manner for granting credit of taxes paid in any country outside India. Therefore, the recent FA15 has amended Sec. 295(2) to provide that CBDT makes rules to provide the procedure for granting the necessary reliefs.

Information related with Bank Accounts

In the USA all the banks and financial institutions report to the IRS (income tax authority of USA) all the interest or dividend income earned by any person.

IRS has the right to ask for such information only from Indian branches of banks incorporated in the USA. Normally, it cannot do so from the Indian banks, such as all the nationalised banks, UTI Bank, ICICI Bank, HDFC Bank, etc. However, in rare cases, if and when it asks, the answer will have to be provided by the banks.

Indian banks cannot issue Form-1099 to their customers in the USA. However, on your request a certificate indicating the details of your deposit and interest earned during a calendar year or a FY can be provided.

27

India has become a Tax Haven

Yes, India has become a tax haven.

You can arrange your affairs in such a fashion that irrespective of the size of your funds, you can earn much higher returns than those available anywhere else across the globe with high degree of safely and little tax.

If you are ready to take market related risks, go for Equity-based MF Schemes. The dividends are tax-free and so are the long-term capital gains. The short-term capital gains are charged to tax @15.45%.

For those who are risk averse, go for Debt-based FMPs of MFs with a term of over 3 years to earn the benefit of low tax on long-term capital gains. The after-tax returns are around 9%.

NRE deposits carry exchange risk. Under the new government, the economy is surely slated to improve fast and along with it, the rupee will go from strength to strength.

In any case, those who do not want to take the exchange risk, FCNR is a good bet.

To Sum
For sure, India has become a tax haven for an informed NRI.

There are different courses for different horses.

Bibliography

1. *Taxmann's Foreign Exchange Management Manual*, An Authorised Publication of Reserve Bank of India.

2. *Comparative Analysis of FEMA*, Jayant M. Thakur, Snow White Publications Pvt. Ltd.

3. *Foreign Exchange Management Law & Practice*, Rajiv Jain.

4. *Handbook for NRI*, Nabhi Publications.

5. *New Baggage Rules in India*, Nabhi Publications.

6. *Baggage Rules of India*, P. Veera Reddy & P. Mamatha, Commercial Law Publishers (India) Pvt Ltd.

7. FEMA Foreign Exchange Management Manual & Ready Reckoner, D. T. Khilnani, Snow White Publications Pvt. Ltd.

8. *Direct Taxes Law & Practice*, Dr. V. K. Singhania, Taxmann Publications Pvt Ltd.